Public Debt and Endogenous Growth

Contributions to Economics

http://www.springer.de/cgi-bin/search_book.pl?series=1262

Further volumes of this series can be found at our homepage.

Friedel Bolle/Michael Carlberg (Eds.)
Advances in Behavioral Economics
2001. ISBN 3-7908-1358-3

Volker Grossmann
Inequality, Economic Growth, and Technological Change
2001. ISBN 3-7908-1364-8

Thomas Riechmann
Learning in Economics
2001. ISBN 3-7908-1384-2

Miriam Beblo
Bargaining over Time Allocation
2001. ISBN 3-7908-1391-5

Peter Meusburger/Heike Jöns (Eds.)
Transformations in Hungary
2001. ISBN 3-7908-1412-1

Claus Brand
Money Stock Control and Inflation Targeting in Germany
2001. ISBN 3-7908-1393-1

Erik Lüth
Private Intergenerational Transfers and Population Aging
2001. ISBN 3-7908-1402-4

Nicole Pohl
Mobility in Space and Time
2001. ISBN 3-7908-1380-X

Pablo Coto-Millán (Ed.)
Essays on Microeconomics and Industrial Organisation
2002. ISBN 3-7908-1390-7

Mario A. Maggioni
Clustering Dynamics and the Locations of High-Tech-Firms
2002. ISBN 3-7908-1431-8

Ludwig Schätzl/Javier Revilla Diez (Eds.)
Technological Change and Regional Development in Europe
2002. ISBN 3-7908-1460-1

Alberto Quadrio Curzio/Marco Fortis (Eds.)
Complexity and Industrial Clusters
2002. ISBN 3-7908-1471-7

Friedel Bolle/Marco Lehmann-Waffenschmidt (Eds.)
Surveys in Experimental Economics
2002. ISBN 3-7908-1472-5

Pablo Coto-Millán
General Equilibrium and Welfare
2002. ISBN 7908-1491-1

Wojciech W. Charemza/Krystyna Strzala (Eds.)
East European Transition and EU Enlargement
2002. ISBN 3-7908-1501-2

Natalja von Westernhagen
Systemic Transformation, Trade and Economic Growth
2002. ISBN 3-7908-1521-7

Josef Falkinger
A Theory of Employment in Firms
2002. ISBN 3-7908-1520-9

Engelbert Plassmann
Econometric Modelling of European Money Demand
2003. ISBN 3-7908-1522-5

Reginald Loyen/Erik Buyst/Greta Devos (Eds.)
Struggeling for Leadership: Antwerp-Rotterdam Port Competition between 1870–2000
2003. ISBN 3-7908-1524-1

Pablo Coto-Millán
Utility and Production, 2nd Edition
2003. ISBN 3-7908-1423-7

Emilio Colombo/John Driffill (Eds.)
The Role of Financial Markets in the Transition Process
2003. ISBN 3-7908-0004-X

Guido S. Merzoni
Strategic Delegation in Firms and in the Trade Union
2003. ISBN 3-7908-1432-6

Jan B. Kuné
On Global Aging
2003. ISBN 3-7908-0030-9

Sugata Marjit, Rajat Acharyya
International Trade, Wage Inequality and the Developing Economy
2003. ISBN 3-7908-0031-7

Francesco C. Billari/Alexia Prskawetz (Eds.)
Agent-Based Computational Demography
2003. ISBN 3-7908-1550-0

Georg Bol/Gholamreza Nakhaeizadeh/
Svetlozar T. Rachev/Thomas Ridder/
Karl-Heinz Vollmer (Eds.)
Credit Risk
2003. ISBN 3-7908-0054-6

Christian Müller
Money Demand in Europe
2003. ISBN 3-7908-0064-3

Cristina Nardi Spiller
The Dynamics of the Price Structure and the Business Cycle
2003. ISBN 3-7908-0063-5

Michael Bräuninger

Public Debt and Endogenous Growth

With 89 Figures
and 10 Tables

Physica-Verlag
A Springer-Verlag Company

Series Editors
Werner A. Müller
Martina Bihn

Author

PD Dr. Michael Bräuninger
Institut für Theoretische Volkswirtschaftslehre
Universität der Bundeswehr Hamburg
Holstenhofweg 85
22043 Hamburg
Germany
michael.braeuninger@unibw-hamburg.de

ISSN 1431-1933
ISBN 3-7908-0056-2 Physica-Verlag Heidelberg New York

Cataloging-in-Publication Data applied for
A catalog record for this book is available from the Library of Congress.
Bibliographic information published by Die Deutsche Bibliothek
Die Deutsche Bibliothek lists this publication in the Deutsche Nationalbibliografie; detailed bibliographic data is available in the Internet at <http://dnb.ddb.de>.

Physica-Verlag Heidelberg New York
a member of BertelsmannSpringer Science+Business Media GmbH

http://www.springer.de

Softcover Design: Erich Kirchner, Heidelberg

SPIN 10924600 88/3130/DK-5 4 3 2 1 0 – Printed on acid-free and non-aging paper

Preface

This book considers public debt dynamics in various endogenous growth models, namely the *AK* model and explicit models of innovation and human capital accumulation. Furthermore, the closed economy, the small open economy and a two-country world are analysed. In the closed economy model, the focus is on budget deficit and public debt dynamics and their influence on capital growth and output growth. Then, in the open economy model, the effects on foreign debt growth are considered. In a two-country setting, public debt growth in one country affects growth in the other country. In each scenario the government either fixes the deficit ratio or the tax rate. For both strategies the steady state is derived and stability is analysed. Then, dynamics induced by various shocks and policy measures are explored. Many diagrams illustrate the dynamics.

I greatly benefited from comments by Michael Carlberg. In addition, Alkis Otto and Justus Haucap discussed with me many parts of the book. I wish to thank them all.

Hamburg, February 2003 *Michael Bräuninger*

Contents

1

Introduction

Public debt and economic growth are two issues of major concern in the debate about economic policy. Since the mid-1970s most OECD countries have experienced lasting budget deficits and, as a consequence, rising debt to GDP ratios. In the EU's largest economy, Germany, public debt exploded in the years following the reunification; and in Asia's largest economy, Japan, the ratio of debt to GDP doubled during the 1990s. Remarkably, in both countries, Germany and Japan, economic growth declined dramatically from the 1970s to the 1990s. All this contrasts to the US, where high deficits during the 1980s have turned into balanced budgets and even surpluses at the end 1990s, and growth rates have remained more or less stable.

This book will analyse the dynamics of public debt and economic growth. The analysis is based on endogenous growth models as developed in Romer (1986, 1987, 1990) and Lucas (1988). It proves useful to consider the different driving forces of endogenous growth in turn. In addition, is seems sensible to distinguish between the closed and the open economy. So the book consists of three major parts. Part I considers the closed economy. The production function is assumed to be of the AK type, which allows to capture the basic idea of endogenous growth models in a very simple way. The two chapters analyse the Solow model and the overlapping generations model. Part II again considers the closed economy. Here human capital accumulation and technical progress as forces of economic growth are explicitly modelled. Chapter 4 focuses on human capital accumulation in an augmented Solow model, and Chapter 5 considers technological progress in a Romer model. Part III is on endogenous growth in the open economy. Relying on AK production, Chapter 6 looks into the small open economy, whereas Chapter 7 deals with a world of two countries.

In the closed economy model, the focus will be on the dynamics of budget deficits and public debt and their influence on capital growth and output growth. The open economy then adds foreign debt growth. And in a two-country setting, public debt growth in country 1 affects growth in country 2. We will analyse the effects of an increase in the deficit ratio, a reduction of the tax rate or an increases in the purchase ratio. Moreover we will consider an increase in the saving ratio or in productivity. How do public debt growth and private capital growth develop over time?

With regard to the government budget constraint we assume that the government fixes the purchase ratio. Then, two different government strategies have to be distinguished: the government either fixes the budget deficit ratio or the tax rate. If the government fixes the deficit ratio, then according to the government budget constraint the tax rate will be endogenous. On the other hand, if the government fixes the tax rate, the deficit ratio will become endogenous. It will be shown that a fixed deficit ratio leads to a stable steady state with constant growth. In contrast, a fixed tax rate is not sustainable. Given a fixed tax rate, public debt growth increases over time, whereas capital growth and output growth decline continuously, become negative at some point of time and deteriorate further. This drives capital and output down to zero.

Now take a look at the structure of chapters. Each chapter starts with a brief introduction, where the fundamental literature is discussed. Then the two main sections consider the strategies of a fixed deficit ratio and a fixed tax rate. Within these sections, the first subsection presents the model and derives the steady state, then stability is analysed by means of growth diagrams and finally the dynamics induced by various shocks are examined.

Part I

The Closed Economy with AK Production

2

The Solow Model

2.1 Introduction

In this chapter we will analyse the dynamics of budget deficits, public debt and economic growth in a model with an AK production. This is a particularly simple way to capture the basic ideas of endogenous growth models, as they are developed in Romer (1986, 1987, 1990) and Lucas (1988). See Barro and Sala-i Martin (1995) and Aghion and Howitt (1998) for detailed expositions of different endogenous growth models.

The analysis of public debt in a neoclassical Solow growth model was first undertaken by Phelps and Shell (1969). They assume that the government makes transfers and fixes the budget deficit per head. It is shown that there are two long-run equilibria. One of them is stable, and the other is unstable. Carlberg (1984, 1985b, 1988, 1995) allows for public consumption and public investment and assumes that the government fixes the deficit ratio. In this situation there is a unique long-run equilibrium. What is more, there exists an optimal deficit ratio. In Carlberg (1983, 1988, 1995) it is assumed that the government fixes the tax rate. Necessary and sufficient conditions for the existence of a long-run equilibrium are derived. As a rule, there will be no long-run equilibrium. As an exception, if the saving ratio is very high and if the primary deficit ratio is extremely low, there will be two long-run equilibria. To sum up, a fixed tax rate generally cannot be sustained. In contrast, a fixed deficit ratio can be sustained.

Ihori (1988b) and Grill (1989) analyse the optimal deficit ratio. In models with public consumption and public investment, the government has an infinite horizon. Assuming a constant saving ratio, the optimal deficit ratio is derived.

Considering endogenous growth, Greiner (1996a) analyses public investment and public debt. The savings behaviour of households is characterized by utility maximization over an infinite horizon. The government fixes the tax rate. As a result, a deficit financed increase in the public consumption ratio reduces the growth rate. A deficit financed increase in the public investment ratio has an ambiguous effect on the growth rate.

The rest of the chapter is structured in three sections. The first section presents the model of a fixed deficit ratio, the second section analyses the fixed tax rate and in the third section it is assumed that the government optimizes the deficit ratio so as to maximize welfare over an infinite horizon. In each section, the first subsection presents the model. Further subsections are devoted to stability analysis and shock dynamics.

2.2 Fixing the Deficit Ratio

2.2.1 The Model

The investigation will be carried out within the following framework. There is a large number of identical firms. Each firm i produces a homogeneous commodity Y_i by means of capital K_i and labour N_i. The production function is of the Cobb-Douglas type $Y_i = AK_i^\alpha(EN_i)^\beta$, where $A > 0$ is a scale parameter, $\alpha > 0, \beta > 0, \alpha + \beta = 1$, and E is an exogenously given index of labour efficiency. Each firm maximizes profits $\Pi_i = Y_i - rK_i - wN_i$ under perfect competition. Here Π_i denotes profits of firm i, r the interest rate, and w the wage rate. As a consequence, each firm adjusts the input of capital so that the marginal product of capital equals the interest rate $\partial Y_i/\partial K_i = \alpha Y_i/K_i = r$. Correspondingly, the input of labour is adjusted to equate the marginal product of labour to the wage rate $\partial Y_i/\partial N_i = \beta Y_i/N_i = w$.

The aggregate production function is $Y = AK^\alpha(EN)^\beta$. It is assumed that labour efficiency is proportional to capital per worker $E = K/N$. For a more explicit model and the justification of this assumption see Barro and Sala-i-Martin (1995). As a consequence of the proportionality between labour efficiency and capital per worker, labour efficiency is endogenous for the economy.

Labour efficiency is growing if capital growth is above population growth. On the other hand, labour efficiency is falling if capital growth is below population growth.

Now insert $E = K/N$ into $Y = AK^{\alpha}(EN)^{\beta}$ to see that the aggregate production function simplifies to $Y = AK$. Hence aggregate output is proportional to aggregate capital. The markets for capital and labour are perfectly competitive. In each point of time, the amount of capital is given for the economy. Labour is supplied inelastically, and therefore labour supply N is also given exogenously. Due to competitive markets, the interest rate and the wage rate adjust to equate the supply and the demand of capital and labour. Hence the interest rate corresponds to the marginal product of capital $r = \partial Y/\partial K = \alpha A$, and the wage rate corresponds to the marginal product of labour $w = \partial Y/\partial N = \beta Y/N = \beta AK/N$. Output Y can be devoted to consumption, investment and government purchases $Y = C + I + G$.

Now let us consider the dynamics of public debt. The government raises loans and levies an income tax in order to finance government purchases and interest payments on public debt. It spends a fixed share of national income on goods and services $G = gY$ with purchase ratio $g = const.$ Besides this, the government borrows a fixed proportion of income $B = bY$ with deficit ratio $b = const.$ The budget deficit augments public debt $\dot{D} = B$. The government pays the interest rate r on public debt D, so interest on public debt amounts to rD. It also imposes a tax at the flat rate t on both factor income and debt income $T = t(Y + rD)$. Hence the government budget constraint can be written as $B + T = G + rD$. By using the behavioural functions, this identity can be reformulated in the following way $bY + t(Y + rD) = gY + rD$. Here, the purchase ratio and the deficit ratio are given, whereas the tax rate has to be adjusted.

Next we look at capital dynamics. Disposable income is the sum of factor income and debt income, net of tax respectively, $Y_d = Y + rD - T$. Households save a constant fraction of their disposable income $S = sY_d$ with saving ratio $s = const.$ To some extent, household savings are absorbed by public borrowing, and the rest is left for private investment $I = S - B$. Private investment augments private capital $\dot{K} = I$. By using the saving function one obtains

$\dot{K} = s(Y + rD - T) - B$. Further note $B + T = G + rD, B = bY$ and $G = gY$ to reach $\dot{K} = (1 + b - g)sY - bY$.

Summarizing the above, the model can be represented by a system of five equations:

$$Y = AK \tag{1}$$

$$r = \alpha A \tag{2}$$

$$\dot{K} = (1 + b - g)sY - bY \tag{3}$$

$$\dot{D} = bY \tag{4}$$

$$bY + t(Y + rD) = gY + rD \tag{5}$$

Here $\alpha, b, g, s, A, D,$ and K are exogenous, while $r, t, \dot{D}, \dot{K},$ and $Y$are endogenous.

The analysis is carried out in terms of growth rates. From the production function (1) it is immediately evident that output always grows at the same rate as capital. The growth rate of capital $\hat{K} = \dot{K}/K$ can be derived from (3) and (1), so we have:

$$\hat{Y} = \hat{K} = [(1 + b - g)s - b]\, A \tag{6}$$

As a result we may summarize:

Proposition 1. *Capital and output grow (or decline) at the same constant rate. Capital growth and output growth are determined by the saving ratio s, the deficit ratio b, the government purchase ratio g and the scale parameter A. An increase in the saving ratio or in the scale parameter leads to a rise in capital growth and output growth. An increase in the deficit ratio or in the government purchase ratio leads to a fall in capital growth and output growth.*

The obvious reason for a negative effect of the deficit ratio on the growth rate is that the budget deficit crowds out investment and thereby reduces capital formation. Further analysis of (6) gives rise to a critical deficit ratio:

$$b' = \frac{(1 - g)s}{1 - s} \tag{7}$$

If $b \gtrless b'$, then $\hat{Y} \gtrless 0$. This means that under a low deficit ratio the growth rate is positive. Under a high deficit ratio, on the other hand, the growth rate is negative. At exactly $b = b'$ zero growth occurs. In a numerical example with $g = 0.2$ and $s = 0.1$, the critical deficit ratio is $b' = 0.09$. Hence, the economy is growing if the deficit ratio stay below 9% and if the deficit ratio exceeds 9% the economy is shrinking. Instead assume $s = 0.15$. Then the critical deficit ratio is $b' = 0.14$.

Now let us assume the population to be growing, and let population growth be given by n. As it is obvious from (6) this does not affect output growth. What is needed for constant welfare is a constant income per head. And for a welfare improvement, growth in income per head is necessary. Output growth exceeds population growth ($\hat{Y} > n$) if the deficit ratio falls below a critical level:

$$b'' = \frac{(1-g)sA - n}{(1-s)A} \tag{8}$$

In a numerical example with $A = 0.25, g = 0.2, s = 0.1$ and $n = 0.01$ the critical deficit ratio is $b'' = 0.044$. Figure 2.1 visualizes the effect of the deficit ratio on output growth.

Next we analyse public debt. From (4) and (1) we derive the growth rate of public debt:

$$\hat{D} = \frac{bAK}{D} \tag{9}$$

As a result, public debt growth is determined by the deficit ratio, the scale parameter and the debt-capital ratio. Public debt growth is constant if the debt-capital ratio is constant. This is the case when public debt grows at the same rate as capital. Hence, in the steady state, public debt and capital have to grow at the same rate. Now equate (6) and (9) to obtain the debt-capital ratio in the steady state:

$$\frac{D}{K} = \frac{b}{[(1+b-g)s - b]} \tag{10}$$

The debt-capital ratio depends on the deficit ratio, on the government purchase ratio and on the saving ratio. If the deficit ratio is below the critical level b', the debt-capital ratio is positive. An increase in the deficit ratio or in

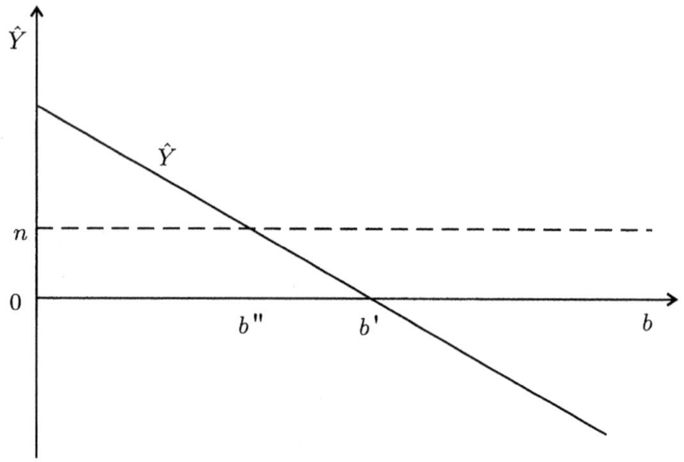

Figure 2.1.
Deficit Ratio and Output Growth

the government purchase ratio leads to a rise in the debt-capital ratio. An increase in the saving ratio leads to a fall in the debt-capital ratio. If the deficit ratio exceeds the critical level, the debt-capital ratio becomes negative. This suggests instability. Figure 2.2 shows how the debt-capital ratio depends on the deficit ratio.

Finally we consider the tax rate. Combine (10) and (2) to end up with the share of public interest in national income:

$$\frac{rD}{Y} = \frac{\alpha b}{(1+b-g)s-b} \tag{11}$$

By putting pieces together we are now able to calculate the tax rate. Divide (5) by Y, solve for t, and use (10) and (11) to obtain:

$$t = \frac{[(1+b-g)s-b]\,(g-b)+\alpha b}{(1+b-g)s-\beta b} \tag{12}$$

Table 2.1 presents a numerical example for the effects of the deficit ratio on the steady state. The assumed parameters are $\alpha = 0.3, A = 0.25, g = 0.2,$ and $s = 0.1$.

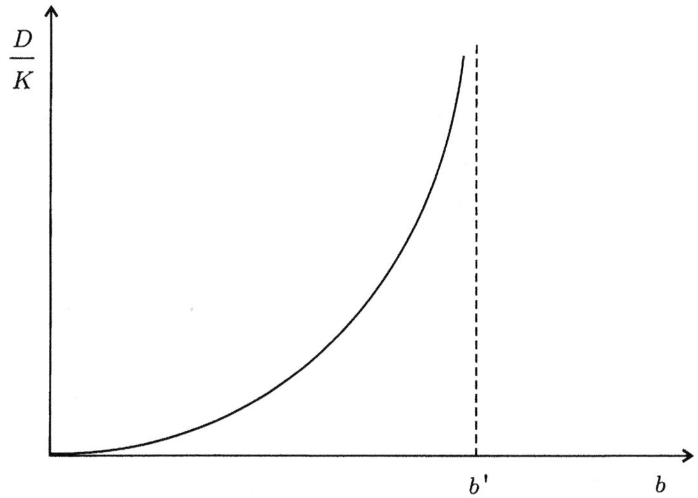

Figure 2.2.
Deficit Ratio and Debt-Capital Ratio

Table 2.1. The Long-Run Effects of the Budget Deficit

b	D/K	D/Y	t	$\hat{Y}$
0	0	0	0.2	0.020
0.01	0.141	0.563	0.223	0.018
0.02	0.323	1.290	0.252	0.016
0.03	0.566	2.264	0.291	0.013
0.04	0.909	3.636	0.34	0.011

2.2.2 Stability

In this section we will look at stability. Since output is proportional to capital, output always grows at the same rate as capital. Both growth rates are constant. The question remains as to whether public debt growth converges to capital growth. Hence we have to consider debt growth and capital growth:

$$\hat{D} = bAK/D \tag{13}$$

$$\hat{K} = [(1 + b - g)s - b]\, A \tag{14}$$

Debt growth depends inversely on the debt-capital ratio. In contrast, capital growth is independent of debt. Figure 2.3 shows the two growth rates in the case where capital growth is positive. At the intersection of the two lines, debt and capital grow at the same rate. Hence the economy is in the steady state. To the left of the steady state, debt growth exceeds capital growth, so the debt-capital ratio is rising. To the right of the steady state, capital growth exceeds debt growth, so the debt-capital ratio is falling. As a consequence, the steady state is stable.

Now let us consider the case where the deficit ratio exceeds the critical level b'. Then, capital growth is negative. In contrast, debt growth is always positive. Consequently, the two growth lines do not cross, and the debt-capital ratio goes to infinity, see Figure 2.4.

To summarize we may state:

Proposition 2. *If the deficit ratio stays below the critical level, the debt-capital ratio converges to the steady-state level. Hence in general a fixed deficit ratio can be sustained. However, if the deficit ratio exceeds the critical level, capital growth is negative and the debt-capital ratio explodes.*

2.2.3 Some Shocks

In the current section we shall trace out the processes of adjustment induced by four macroeconomic shocks in greater detail:

1) an increase in the deficit ratio ($b < b'$)

2) an increase in the deficit ratio ($b > b'$)

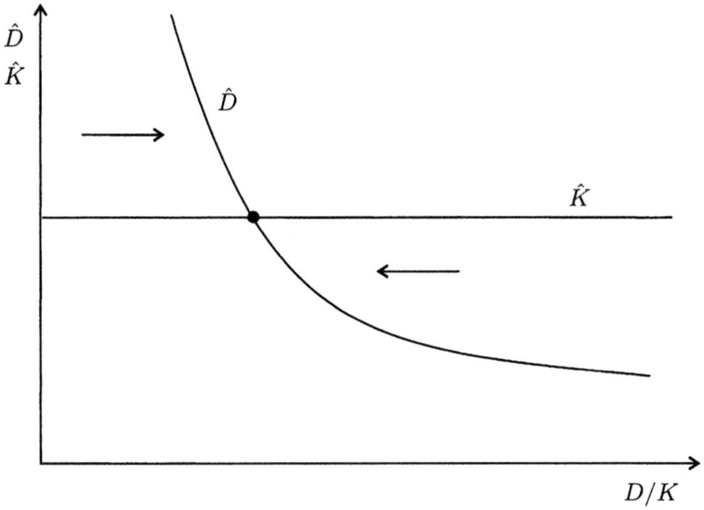

Figure 2.3.
Debt Growth and Capital Growth

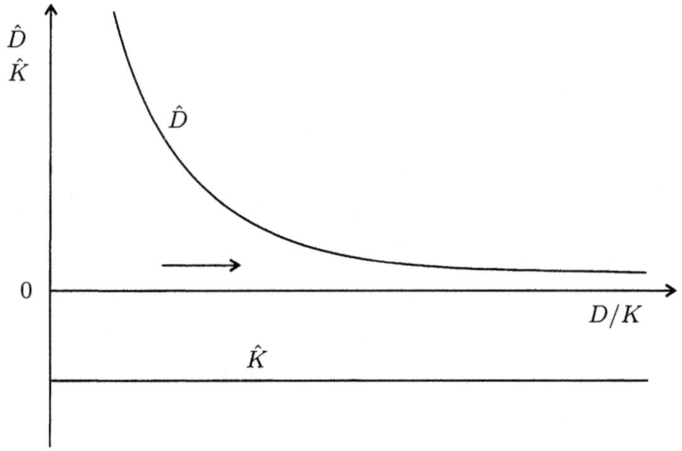

Figure 2.4.
Debt Growth and Capital Decay

3) an increase in the purchase ratio
4) an increase in the saving ratio.

1) An increase in the deficit ratio. First, we contemplate the case where the deficit ratio stays below the critical level. This situation is characterized by a stable steady state. Initially the economy rests in the steady state, as indicated by point 1 in Figure 2.5. The budget deficit and public debt grow at the same rate as capital and output. Against this background the government enhances the deficit ratio. As a consequence, in Figure 2.5, the $\hat{K}$ line moves downwards and the $\hat{D}$ line moves to the right. As indicated by points 2 and 3, debt growth increases and, at the same time, capital growth declines. The arrows illustrate how debt growth and capital growth develop over time.

Now we look at the process of adjustment in more detail. In the short run, capital and output do not respond. The rise in the deficit ratio leads to a rise in the budget deficit. Therefore, debt growth increases. The budget deficit crowds out investment. Therefore, capital growth and output growth decline. According to the budget constraint, the government is able to cut the tax rate, thereby lifting the level of consumption. Reduced output growth leads to a decline in tax revenue growth. Increased debt growth leads to higher public interest growth. This requires an increase in the tax rate. Higher taxes reduce consumption and higher public interest increases consumption. Overall consumption grows at the same rate as output.

Reduced output growth leads to reduced budget deficit growth. Therefore, in the medium run, debt growth declines. As time proceeds, the economy converges to a new steady state, marked as point 4 in Figure 2.5. In the new steady state, the budget deficit and public debt grow at the same rate as capital and output. The debt-capital ratio is constant. Compared to the steady state before shock, capital growth and debt growth are reduced. The debt-capital ratio is increased. Figures 2.6 and 2.7 show how debt growth, capital growth and the debt-capital ratio develop over time u. Figures 2.8 until 2.10 display the time paths of output, debt and consumption on a semilogarithmic scale.

Now look at a numerical example. Assume $A = 0.25$ and $g = 0.2$, $s = 0.1$. At the beginning, the deficit ratio is given as $b = 0.01$. The economy is in the steady state. The budget deficit and public debt as well as capital and output

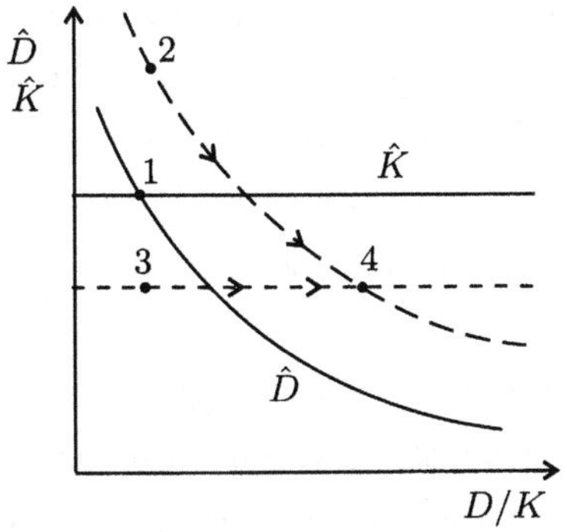

Figure 2.5.
Increase in Deficit Ratio

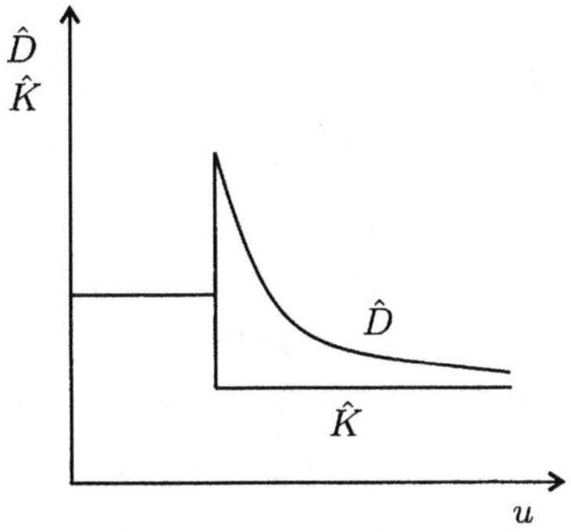

Figure 2.6.
Capital Growth and Debt Growth

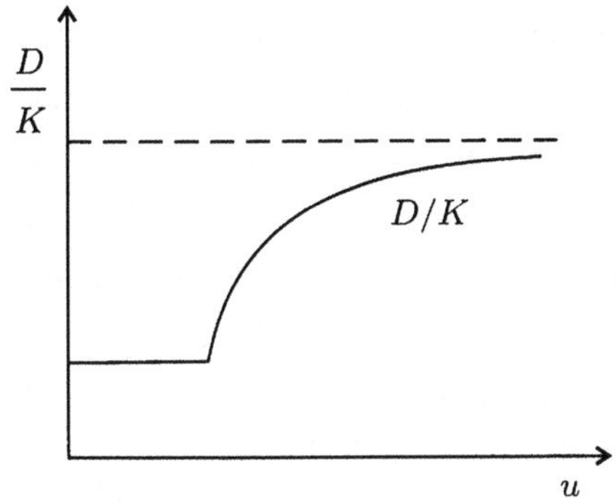

Figure 2.7.
Debt-Capital Ratio

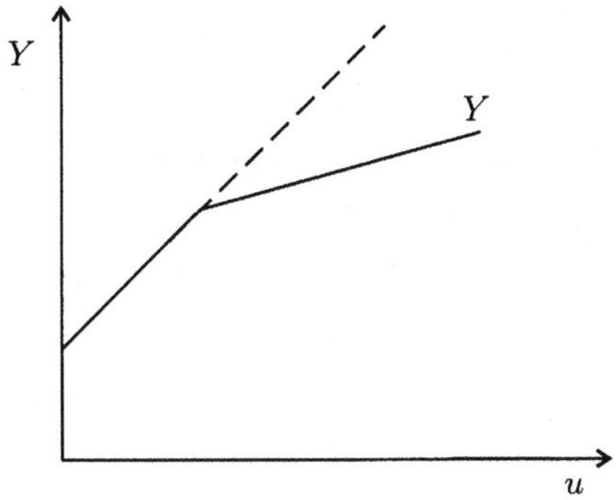

Figure 2.8.
Output

grow at a rate of 1.8%. Then the government increases the deficit ratio to $b = 0.02$. In the short run, capital growth and output growth decline to 1.6%. Debt growth increases to 3.6%. The budget deficit grows at the same rate as output. In the medium run, this leads to a decline in debt growth. In the long run, debt growth converges to output growth. In the new steady state, debt, capital and output grow at the rate of 1.6%.

Next have a look at the dynamics of consumption. In the original steady state, consumption grows at the rate of 1.8%. Then the government increases the deficit ratio. In the short run, this allows the government to cut the tax rate. Therefore, consumption improves. However, henceforth consumption grows at the rate of 1.6% only.

2) An increase in the deficit ratio, where the deficit ratio surpasses the critical level. Under these circumstances there is no steady state. At the start, let $b < b'$, so the economy grows at a constant rate. Public debt grows at the same rate as capital. Then the government lifts the deficit ratio above the critical level. In the short run, as a reaction, investment becomes negative. This means that capital growth becomes negative. As a consequence, output declines at a constant rate. However, public debt grows. Figure 2.11 illustrates the trajectories of capital growth and debt growth. Figure 2.12 shows the time paths of capital and debt on a semilogarithmic scale.

3) A hike in the purchase ratio, granted $b < b'$. In this situation there is a stable steady state. At the beginning, the economy is in the steady state. Public debt, capital and output grow at the same constant rate. Then the government pushes up the purchase ratio. In the growth diagram, the $\hat{K}$ line shifts downwards, see Figure 2.13. In the short run, on account of the budget constraint, the government has to raise the tax rate. This lowers savings and investment. Capital growth and output growth decline. Reduced output growth leads to reduced deficit growth. As a consequence, debt growth declines gradually. In the long run, the debt-capital ratio converges to a new steady state. In the new steady state, debt and capital grow at the same constant rate.

4) An increase in the saving ratio. At the start the economy rests in the steady state. Then the saving ratio soars. In the diagram, the $\hat{K}$ line moves upwards, cf. Figure 2.14. This leads to an increase in capital growth and output

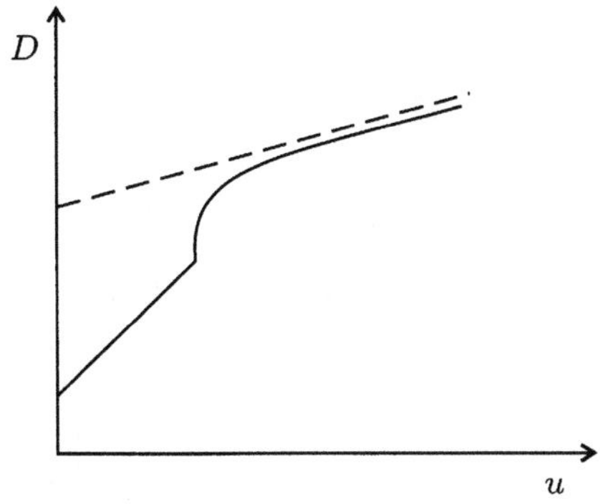

Figure 2.9.
Public Debt

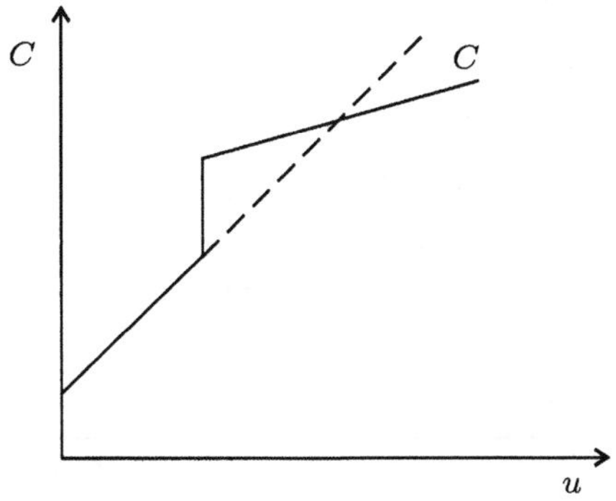

Figure 2.10.
Consumption

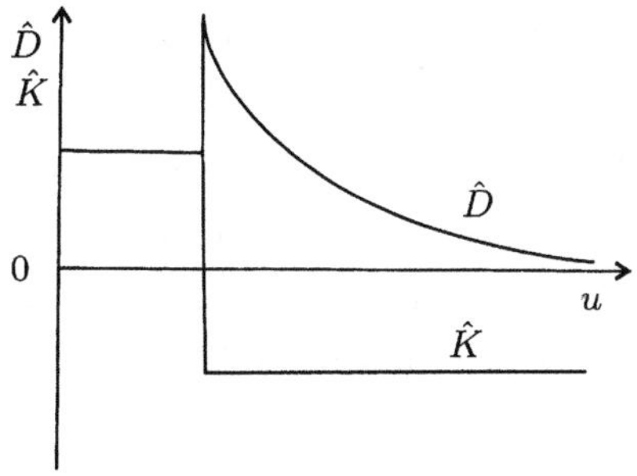

Figure 2.11.
Capital Growth and
Debt Growth ($b > b'$)

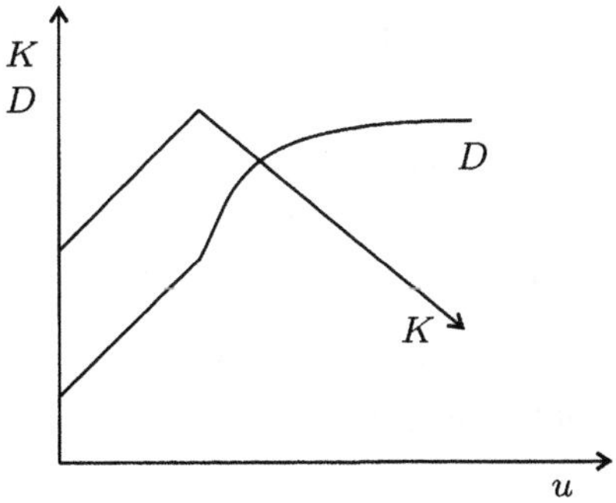

Figure 2.12.
Capital and Debt ($b > b'$)

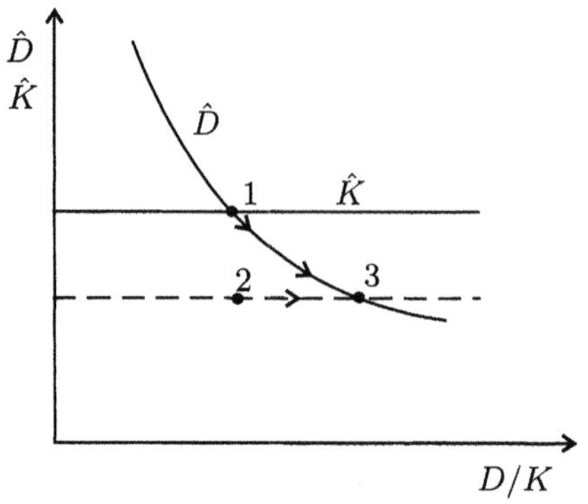

Figure 2.13.
Increase in Purchase Ratio

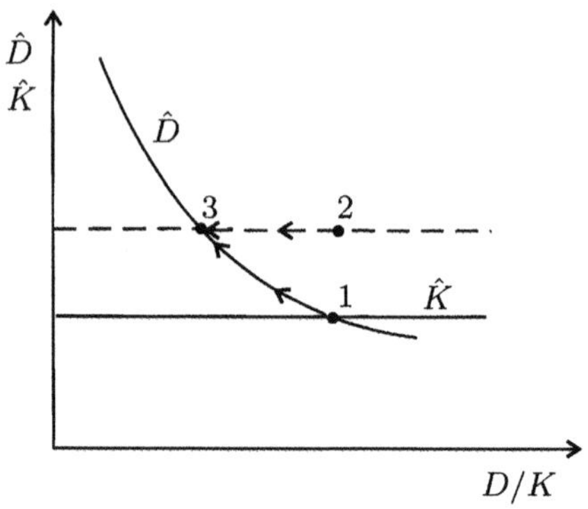

Figure 2.14.
Increase in Saving Ratio

growth. Asymptotically the economy tends towards a new steady state. The post-shock growth rates are above, and the debt-capital ratio is below the pre-shock level.

2.2.4 Summary

As a result, capital and output grow (or decline) at the same constant rate. Capital growth and output growth are determined by the deficit ratio. An increase in the deficit ratio leads to a decline in capital growth and output growth. In the steady state, public debt grows at the same rate as capital. There is a critical deficit ratio. If the deficit ratio is below the critical level, there will be a steady state that proves to be stable. If the deficit ratio is above the critical level, there will be no steady state. Capital growth is negative, but public debt growth is positive.

2.3 Fixing the Tax Rate

2.3.1 The Model

Firms produce a single commodity Y by means of capital K and labour N. The aggregate production function is $Y = AK^{\alpha}(EN)^{\beta}$, where $A > 0$ is a scale parameter, $\alpha > 0, \beta > 0, \alpha + \beta = 1$ and $E = K/N$. Hence the production function simplifies to $Y = AK$. Output Y can be devoted to consumption, investment and government purchases $Y = C + I + G$. Firms maximize profits $\Pi = Y - rK - wN$ under perfect competition. Here Π denotes profits, r the interest rate, and w the wage rate. The markets for capital and labour are perfectly competitive. Therefore, the interest rate corresponds to the private marginal product of capital $r = \partial Y / \partial K = \alpha A$, and the wage rate corresponds to the marginal product of labour $w = \partial Y / \partial N = \beta Y / N$.

Let us look at budget dynamics. The government spends a constant proportion of national income on goods and services $G = gY$ with purchase ratio $g = const.$ Additionally, the government imposes a proportionate tax on both factor income and debt income $T = t(Y + rD)$ with tax rate $t = const.$ Government purchases plus public interest minus tax earnings correspond to the budget deficit $B = G + rD - T$. The budget deficit in turn adds to public debt $\dot{D} = B$. From this we obtain $\dot{D} = gY + rD - t(Y + rD)$.

The next point refers to investment dynamics. Disposable income is the sum of the after-tax factor and debt income $Y_d = (1 - t)(Y + rD)$. Households save a constant proportion of disposable income $S = sY_d$ with saving ratio $s = const.$ One part of saving is absorbed by public borrowing, the other part is used for investment $I = S - B$. Investment in turn contributes to the accumulation of capital $\dot{K} = I$. From this it becomes apparent that $\dot{K} = s(Y + rD - T) - B$. Now use $T = t(Y + rD)$ and $\dot{D} = B$ to establish $\dot{D} + \dot{K} = s(1 - t)(Y + rD)$.

On this foundation, the model can be characterized by a system of four equations:

$$Y = AK \tag{1}$$

$$r = \alpha A \tag{2}$$

$$\dot{D} + \dot{K} = s(1 - t)(Y + rD) \tag{3}$$

$$\dot{D} = gY + rD - t(Y + rD) \tag{4}$$

Here α, g, s, t, A, D, and K are exogenous, whereas $r, \dot{D}$, $\dot{K}$, and Y are endogenous. This is in significant contrast to the strategy of fixing the deficit ratio, cf. Section 2.2. There the deficit ratio was exogenous while the tax rate was endogenous.

Now it is useful to analyse growth rates. Insert (1), (2) and (3) into (3) and divide by capital K to obtain the growth rate of capital. Then divide (3) by debt D to obtain the growth rate of public debt:

$$\hat{K} = [s(1-t) - (g-t)]\,A - (1-s)(1-t)\alpha A \frac{D}{K} \tag{5}$$

$$\hat{D} = (g-t)\frac{AK}{D} + (1-t)\alpha A \tag{6}$$

Both capital growth and public debt growth depend on the debt-capital ratio. Capital growth and public debt growth are constant if the debt-capital ratio is constant. In the steady state, public debt has to grow at the same rate as capital. The rest of this subsection will concentrate on the question of whether a steady state exists. For notational simplicity we define the primary deficit ratio $h = g - t$ and the debt-capital ratio $x = D/K$. Insert these definitions into (5) and (6) and equate the two growth rates to achieve:

$$hA/x + (1-t)\alpha A = [s(1-t) - h]A - (1-s)(1-t)\alpha A x \tag{7}$$

Then solve this quadratic equation for x:

$$x_{1,2} = -\frac{h + (\alpha - s)(1-t)}{2\alpha(1-s)(1-t)} \pm \sqrt{\frac{[h + (\alpha - s)(1-t)]^2}{[2\alpha(1-s)(1-t)]^2} - \frac{h}{\alpha(1-s)(1-t)}} \tag{8}$$

A steady state exists if and only if the debt-capital ratio x is both real and positive. To evaluate this condition take the reduced discriminant of (8) $U = [h + (\alpha - s)(1-t)]^2 - 4\alpha h(1-s)(1-t)$. The discriminant vanishes at:

$$h_{1,2} = (1-t)(\alpha + s - 2\alpha s) \mp (1-t)\sqrt{4\alpha s(1 + \alpha s - \alpha - s)} \tag{9}$$

A closer inspection of (9) reveals that h_1 and h_2 are both real and positive with $h_1 < h_2$. x in turn is real and positive if and only if:

$$s > \alpha \quad \text{and} \quad h \leq h_1$$

As a result we state:

Proposition 1. *A steady state does exist if and only if the saving ratio exceeds the capital elasticity and the primary deficit ratio stays below the critical level.*

Given that these conditions are satisfied, there are two steady states. If either the deficit ratio exceeds the critical level or the saving ratio is below the capital elasticity, there is no steady state.

Proof. Evidently equation (8) can be written as

$$x_{1,2} = \frac{-P \pm \sqrt{P^2 - Q}}{R}$$

where $P = h + (\alpha - s)(1 - t), Q = 4h\alpha(1 - s)(1 - t)$ and $R = 2\alpha(1 - s)(1 - t)$. Obviously Q and R are real and positive. P is an increasing function of h, and we observe $P = 0$ at $h = h' = (s - \alpha)(1 - t)$. With $s = \alpha$ we obtain $h' = 0$. For $s > \alpha$ we have $h' > 0$ and for $s < \alpha$ we have $h' < 0$. P^2 is a quadratic equation in h, which takes a minimum at $h = h'$. The solutions $x_{1,2}$ are real if $P^2 - Q > 0$. Since $P^2 - Q$ is a quadratic equation in h it has two solutions $h_{1,2}$ for $P^2 - Q = 0$. For $h < h_1$ and for $h > h_2$ we have $P^2 - Q > 0$. This gives rise to four cases.

1) $s < \alpha$: In this case P is negative, for any $h > 0$. Due to $P < 0$ both solutions are negative. To see this square both sides in $-P > \sqrt{P^2 - Q}$.
2) $s > \alpha$ and $h_1 < h < h_2$: We have $P > 0$ but $P^2 - Q < 0$. Hence both solutions are complex.
3) $s > \alpha$ and $h < h_1$: We have $P > 0$ and $P^2 - Q > 0$. Here both solutions are real and positive. To see this square both sides in $P > \sqrt{P^2 - Q}$.
4) $s > \alpha$ and $h > h_2$: We have $P > 0$ and $P^2 - Q > 0$. Hence both solutions are real. But due to $P < 0$, both solutions are negative. To see this square both sides in $-P > \sqrt{P^2 - Q}$. ■

Empirical evidence suggests that the saving ratio is well below the capital elasticity. Therefore even a small primary deficit cannot be sustained. However, there may be an exception to this rule. If the saving ratio is very large, then a very small primary deficit ratio is feasible. In summary, a fixed tax rate is normally not sustainable.

2.3.2 Stability

The dynamics of the model can be captured by the two growth equations for capital and public debt derived in the previous section. Insert the debt-capital ratio $x = D/K$ to obtain:

$$\hat{K} = [s(1-t) - (g-t)]\,A - (1-s)(1-t)\alpha Ax \tag{10}$$

$$\hat{D} = (g-t)A/x + (1-t)\alpha A \tag{11}$$

Figure 2.15 and 2.16 display the $\hat{K}$ line and the $\hat{D}$ line. The $\hat{K}$ line shows that capital growth depends on the debt-capital ratio. The $\hat{D}$ line shows that public debt growth depends on the debt-capital ratio. Figure 2.15 assumes the special case where the saving ratio is very high and the primary deficit ratio is extremely low. In this case there are two steady states x_1 and x_2. In these steady states, public debt and capital grow at the same rate. If the debt-capital ratio is below x_1, then debt grows faster than capital and therefore x increases. If the debt-capital ratio is between x_1 and x_2, then capital grows faster than debt and therefore x declines. If the debt capital-ratio is above x_2, then debt grows faster than capital and the debt-capital ratio explodes. As a result, we see that the steady state at x_1 is locally stable, i.e. it is stable if the initial debt-capital ratio is not too large $x \in [0, x_2]$. On the other hand the steady state at x_2 is unstable.

Figure 2.16 shows the growth lines for the normal case. In this case there is no steady state, i.e. the $\hat{K}$ line and the $\hat{D}$ line do not intersect. Debt growth always exceeds capital growth, so the debt-capital ratio grows. As a consequence, debt growth remains positive, while capital growth deteriorates become negative at some point of time, and deteriorate further. Capital declines to zero in finite time. Hence the economy will collapse. Summarizing we obtain:

Proposition 2. *If the conditions on the saving ratio and the primary deficit ratio are met, then one of the steady states is stable. In the normal case, there is no steady state, and the economy collapses.*

2.3.3 Some Shocks

Let the tax rate be smaller than the purchase ratio $t < g$. Two different scenarios have to be analysed. In the empirically relevant scenario, we have $s < \alpha$. As a consequence there is no steady state, cf. Section 2.3.1. In other words, if the saving ratio is low, a fixed tax rate is not sustainable. In the second scenario, we have $s > \alpha$. In this case a steady state exists if the

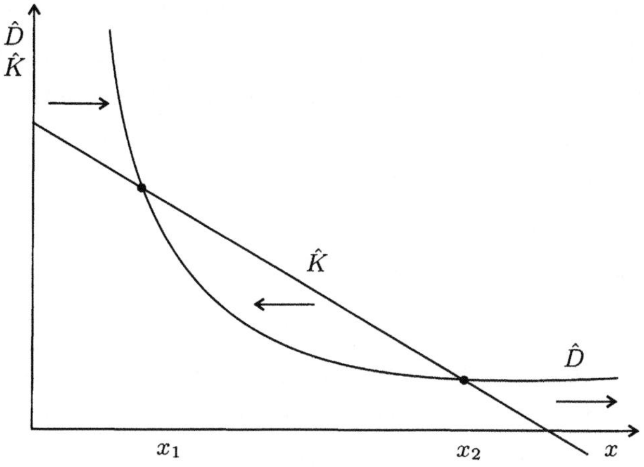

Figure 2.15.
Capital Growth and Debt Growth
Very High Saving Ratio and Very Low Deficit Ratio

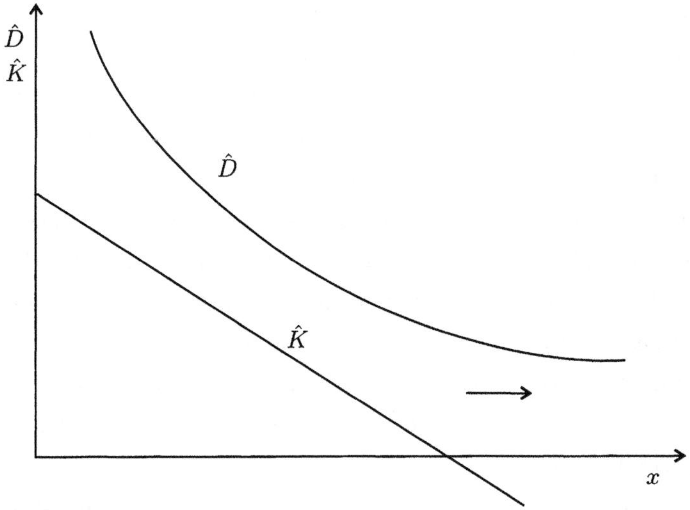

Figure 2.16.
Capital Growth and Debt Growth

primary deficit is not to large, which implies that the tax is above a critical level $t > t'$. Put in another way, if the saving ratio is high and if the tax rate surpasses the critical level, a fixed tax rate is sustainable. In the following we will analyse the processes of adjustment evoked by various fiscal policies:

1) a permanent tax cut $(s \leq \alpha, t < g)$

2) a transitory tax cut $(s \leq \alpha, t < g)$

3) a transitory tax cut $(s > \alpha, t > t')$.

1) Permanent tax cut $(s \leq \alpha, t < g)$. In this case there is no steady state. Initially, let the economy be in a steady state with $t = g$. There is no public debt $D = 0$ and so the budget is balanced. Capital and output grow at the same constant rate. In this situation the government reduces the tax rate. In the short run, output is not affected. The tax cut enhances consumption. Given the budget constraint, the government has to increase the deficit ratio, which depresses investment.

In the medium run, owing to the budget deficit, public debt starts to grow. Due to the decline in investment, capital growth and output growth are reduced. On account of growing public debt, interest payments on public debt increase. Since the tax rate remains constant, the government has to further increase the deficit ratio. Consumption depends on output and on debt income. While output growth declines, debt income growth increases. As a net effect, consumption growth declines.

In the long run, public debt growth becomes constant. On the other hand, capital growth declines continuously and becomes negative. And so do output growth and consumption growth. Obviously the economy enters a vicious circle where the government borrows in order to finance the interest payments on public debt. More and more borrowing is only possible by the sacrifice of capital. Hence the tax cut leads to a fatal crowding out. Ultimately the economy must collapse. This means that the fixed tax rate is not feasible in the long run. Figures 2.17 and 2.18 show the time paths of growth rates and Figures 2.19 to 2.21 portray the related time paths of some variables on a semilogarithmic scale.

2) Transitory tax cut $(s \leq \alpha, t < g)$. Again there is no steady state. Initially we assume $t = g$, a balanced budget $b = 0$ and no debt $D = 0$. Therefore, the economy rests in a steady state. Then the government lowers

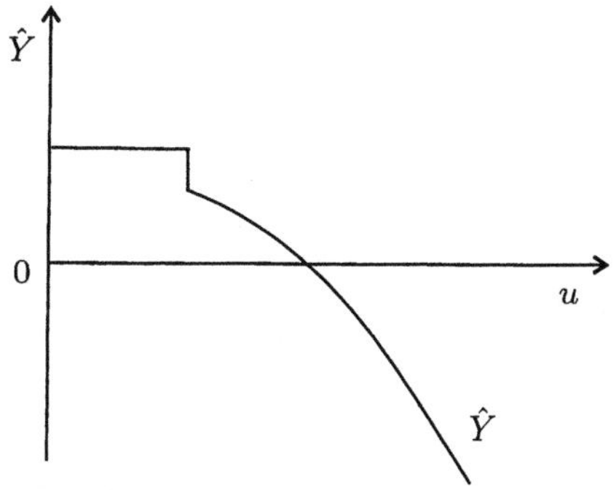

Figure 2.17.
Output Growth

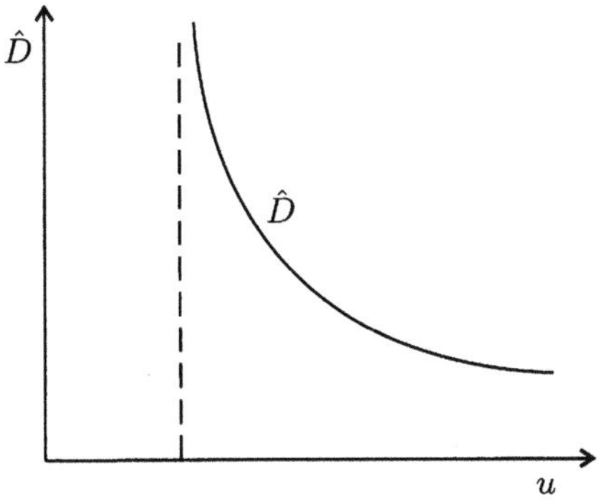

Figure 2.18.
Debt Growth

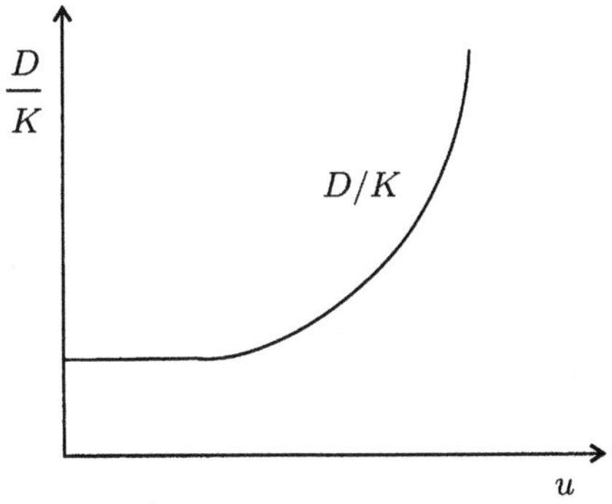

Figure 2.19.
Debt-Capital Ratio

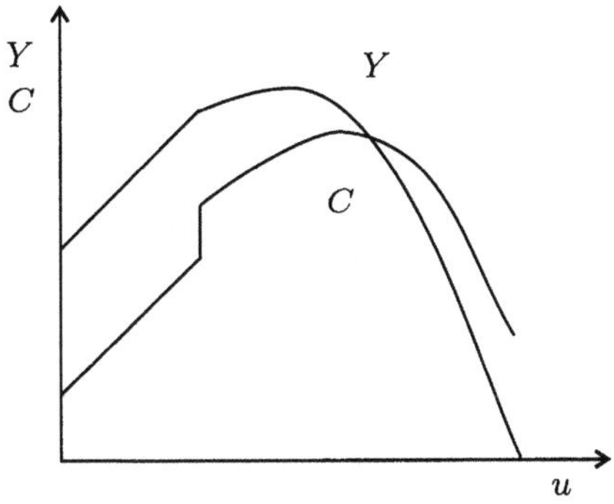

Figure 2.20.
Output and Consumption

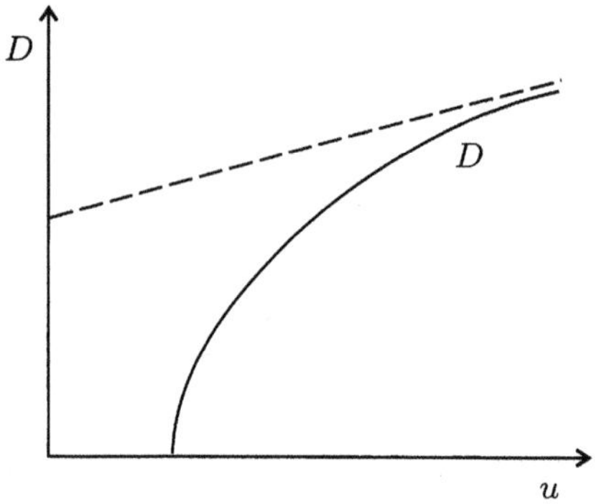

Figure 2.21.
Public Debt

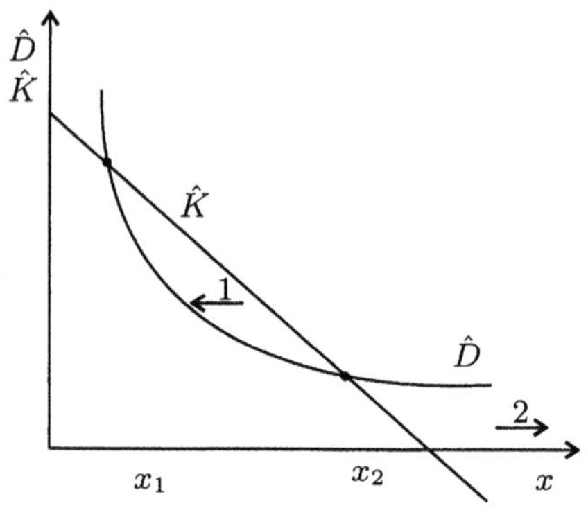

Figure 2.22.
Transitory Tax Cut

the tax rate, which gives rise to a budget deficit. Consequently public debt begins to grow. To bring the upward spiral to a halt, the government raises the tax rate back to its original level. Regardless of that, the budget remains in deficit, because of the interest payments the government has to make on debt already incurred. As a consequence, public debt grows. That is why capital growth declines. Ultimately the economy must break down, even though the tax cut is only transitory in nature.

3) Transitory tax cut ($s > \alpha, t \geq t'$). In this specific case there are two steady states. The economy is assumed to be in the stable steady state, with a low debt-capital ratio and high growth. Then the government reduces the tax rate below the critical level $t < t'$. Public debt growth is increased. Capital growth and output growth are reduced. The debt-capital ratio rises continuously. To avoid the decay of capital, the government increases the tax rate back to its original level. Two possible scenarios arise. In the first one, the government takes action in time. In the second, the government acts too late. Consider the first scenario. Here the government increases the tax rate back to its original level before the debt-capital ratio exceeds x_2, see Figure 2.22. In this case the growth rates of debt and capital return to their original steady-state level. In the second scenario, the government does not raise the tax rate until the debt-capital ratio has exceeded the critical level x_2. As a consequence, the debt-capital ratio further increases and capital growth further deteriorates.

2.3.4 Summary

Starting from a balanced budget, a tax cut leads to a budget deficit. Public debt emerges and begins to grow. In general, public debt growth converges to a constant level, while capital growth and output growth decline continuously, become negative at some point of time, and deteriorate further. Capital and output decline to zero in finite time. An exception occurs if the saving ratio is very high. In this case there are two steady states for extremely low primary deficit ratios. In these steady states, public debt and capital grow at the same constant rate. One of the steady states is stable, and the other is unstable. However, as the fundamental result, a fixed tax rate generally cannot be sustained.

2.4 The Optimal Deficit Ratio

2.4.1 The Model

So far we assumed that the government either fixes the budget deficit ratio or the tax rate. In this section we shall consider an alternative, where the government optimizes the budget deficit ratio to maximize welfare over an infinite horizon. Hence the government behaves as a social planner, and the model is analogous to the Ramsey (1928) model.

To start with we briefly review the structure of production. A large number of identical firms produce a single commodity Y by means of capital K and labour N. For the sake of simplicity, technology is of the Cobb-Douglas type. Hence each firm has a production function $Y_i = AK_i^{\alpha}(EN_i)^{\beta}$, with $A > 0, \alpha > 0, \beta > 0, \alpha + \beta = 1$, and $E = K/N$. Labour efficiency E is exogenous to the firm, but it is endogenous for the economy. As a consequence, the aggregate production function is $Y = AK$. There is full employment and perfect competition. Therefore, the wage rate equals the marginal product of labour $w = \beta Y/N$ and the interest rate equals the private marginal product of capital $r = \alpha Y/K = \alpha A$. Labour income is $wN = \beta Y$, and capital income is $rK = \alpha Y$.

Now consider the public sector. The government makes transfers to the private sector. The size of these transfers is fixed in relation to output $G = gY$

with $g = const$. Besides transfers, the government has expenditures to cover interest payments on public debt rD. Taxation of income finances a part of these expenditures, and public borrowing finances the other part. All types of income are taxed at a uniform rate so that tax revenue is $T = t(Y + rD)$, where t is the tax rate. Public borrowing B is fixed in relation to national income $B = bY$. The budget deficit in turn augments public debt $\dot{D} = B$. The government budget constraint is $bY + t(Y + rD) = gY + rD$. It is assumed that the government fixes the transfer ratio and optimizes the deficit ratio. The tax rate is then adjusted appropriately.

In contrast to previous sections, the government makes transfers and does not provide goods and services. Therefore, output can be used for consumption and investment $Y = C + I$. Investment in turn adds to the stock of capital $\dot{K} = I$. Factor income plus transfers and public interest minus tax load give the disposable income of households $Y_d = Y + G + rD - T$. Now use the government budget constraint $B + T = G + rD$ and $B = bY$ to reach $Y_d = (1 + b)Y$. Households save a certain proportion of disposable income $S = sY_d$ with $s = const$, which implies $S = s(1+b)Y$. Disposable income can either be consumed or saved $Y_d = C + S$. From this one can infer $C = (1 - s)(1 + b)Y$.

Now contemplate aggregate dynamics. Savings are used for the accumulation of assets. Assets are claims to private capital and the public debt $\dot{K} + \dot{D} = s(1 + b)Y$. Note the government budget constraint $B = G + rD - T$ and $\dot{D} = B$ to obtain the dynamics of capital $\dot{K} = Y - C$.

Having laid these foundations we are able to search for the optimal budget surplus. The government maximizes discounted utility within an infinite horizon:

$$W = \int_0^\infty e^{-\rho u} \log C \, du \tag{1}$$

subject to the constraint $\dot{K} = Y - C$. Here $logC$ stands for the utility function, ρ is the discount rate and u is time. Methods for the solution to this control problem are presented in Barro and Sala-i-Martin (1995). The solution is:

$$\dot{C} = \left[\frac{\partial Y}{\partial K} - \rho\right] C \tag{2}$$

The social marginal product of capital is $\partial Y/\partial K = A$. Therefore, the optimal path of consumption is $\dot{C} = (A - \rho)C$. However, notice that the externalities of capital accumulation are unobservable. Therefore, the government might underestimate the social marginal product of capital and may only notice the private marginal product $\partial Y/\partial K = \alpha A$. Of course, this is in some contradiction to the assumption of a fully informed social planner. In the following we posit that the government estimates the marginal product of capital as θA, where $\alpha \leq \theta \leq 1$. We will then treat $\theta = 1$ and $\theta = \alpha$ as special cases.

Summarizing the above, the model can be captured by a system of seven equations:

$$Y = AK \tag{3}$$

$$r = \alpha A \tag{4}$$

$$\dot{K} = Y - C \tag{5}$$

$$\dot{C} = (\theta A - \rho)C \tag{6}$$

$$C = (1 - s)(1 + b)Y \tag{7}$$

$$\dot{D} = bY \tag{8}$$

$$bY + t(Y + rD) = gY + rD \tag{9}$$

Here $\alpha, \theta, \rho, g, s, A, C, D,$ and K are exogenous, where $b, r, t, \dot{C}, \dot{D}, \dot{K}$, and Y are endogenous.

In the following we analyse growth rates. To start with, let us consider consumption growth. Equation (6) immediately delivers optimal consumption growth:

$$\hat{C} = \theta A - \rho \tag{10}$$

Now take time derivatives in (7) and note that s is constant while Y and b adjust, to obtain $\dot{C} = (1-s)(1+b)\dot{Y} - (1-s)Y\dot{b}$. Then divide by C as given in (7) to find:

$$\hat{C} = \hat{Y} - \frac{b}{1-b}\hat{b} \tag{11}$$

According to (3) output growth corresponds to capital growth $\hat{Y} = \hat{K}$. To derive capital growth divide (5) by K to obtain $\hat{K} = Y/K - C/K$. From (3) we have $Y/K = A$ and from (3) and (7) we have $C/K = (1-s)(1+b)A$. Insert these ratios into $\hat{K} = Y/K - C/K$ to reach:

$$\hat{Y} = \hat{K} = (s - b + sb)A \tag{12}$$

According to (10) consumption growth is constant. According to (11) and (12) consumption growth and output growth are constant if the deficit ratio stays constant $\hat{b} = 0$. Hence $\hat{b} = 0$ is the solution to the dynamic optimization problem. Now equate (10) and (12) to calculate the optimal level of the deficit ratio:

$$b^* = \frac{(s-\theta)A + \rho}{(1-s)A} \tag{13}$$

As a result we obtain:

Proposition 1. *There is an unique optimal deficit ratio. It depends on the saving ratio, on the rate of time preference, on the scale parameter, and on θ. An increase in the saving ratio leads to a rise in the optimal deficit ratio. The same holds for an increase in the discount rate. An increase in the scale parameter A or in θ leads to a fall in the optimal deficit ratio.*

Further analysis of (13) shows that the optimal deficit ratio is positive if $s > \theta - \rho/A$, and the optimal deficit ratio is negative if $s < \theta - \rho/A$. Put another way, if the saving ratio is high, then it is optimal to have a budget deficit. On the other hand, if the saving ratio is low, then it is optimal to have a budget surplus. Alternatively, the condition for a positive or negative deficit ratio might be formulated in the following way: if $\rho > (\theta - s)A$ we obtain $b^* > 0$, and if $\rho < (\theta - s)A$ we obtain $b^* < 0$. This means, if the discount rate is high it is optimal to have a budget deficit, and if the discount rate is low it is optimal to have a budget surplus.

Now assume the coherent case where the government knows the social marginal product of capital, i.e. $\theta = 1$. The optimal deficit ratio is $b^* = ((s-1)A - \rho)/((1-s)A)$. We obtain $b^* \gtrless 0$ if $\rho \gtrless (1-s)A$.

Next we assume equal weighting of current and future consumption, which means $\rho = 0$. In this case we obtain $b^* = (s-\theta)/(1-s)$. Assuming $\theta = 1$, we

Table 2.2. Time Preference, Optimal Deficit Ratio and Growth

	$\theta = 1$		$\theta = \alpha$	
ρ	b^*	$\hat{Y}$	b^*	$\hat{Y}$
0.00	−1.00	0.25	−0.22	0.075
0.01	−0.96	0.24	−0.18	0.065
0.02	−0.91	0.23	−0.13	0.055
0.03	−0.87	0.22	−0.09	0.045
0.04	−0.78	0.21	−0.04	0.035
0.05	−0.72	0.20	0	0.025
0.10	−0.56	0.15	0.22	−0.025
0.15	−0.33	0.1	0.44	−0.075
0.16	−0.29	0.09	0.49	−0.085
0.17	−0.24	0.08	0.53	−0.095
0.18	−0.2	0.07	0.57	−0.105
0.19	−0.16	0.06	0.63	−0.115
0.20	−0.11	0.05	0.67	−0.125
0.25	0.11	0.	0.89	−0.175

obtain an optimal deficit ratio of $b^* = -1$. This means that the government taxes away all income to accumulate capital. Growth is at the maximum and consumption is zero. Hence this policy is clearly undesirable for all generations. Now suppose $\theta = \alpha$. Then the optimal deficit ratio is $b^* = (s-\alpha)/(1-s)$, which is the same as in the neoclassical growth model. Insert b^* into (12) to obtain $\hat{Y} = \hat{K} = \alpha A$. Hence the growth rate corresponds to the interest rate, which is the golden rule condition. To exemplify how the optimal deficit depends on the saving ratio and the discount rate, consider the numerical example presented in Table 2.2. The calculations are based on the assumptions of $\alpha = 0.3$ and $A = 0.25$.

Next we analyse public debt. Divide (8) by public debt D and insert (3) to obtain debt growth $\hat{D} = bAK/D$. Insert the optimal deficit ratio to get:

$$\hat{D} = \frac{[(s-\theta)A+\rho]\,K}{(1-s)D} \tag{14}$$

Public debt growth is inversely related to the debt-capital ratio. Debt growth is constant if the deb-capital ratio is constant. In the steady state public debt grows at the same rate as capital, so the debt capital ratio is constant. Equate (12) and (14) to obtain the steady-state ratio of debt to capital:

$$\frac{D}{K} = \frac{(s-\theta)A+\rho}{(1-s)(\theta A-\rho)} \tag{15}$$

An increase in the saving ratio s or in time preference ρ leads to a rise in the debt-capital ratio.

2.4.2 Stability

The dynamics of consumption and capital are described by equations (10) and (14) in the previous subsection. It has been proved that consumption as well as capital and output always grow at the same constant rate:

$$\hat{C} = \hat{K} = \hat{Y} = \theta A - \rho \tag{16}$$

In Figure 2.23 the $\hat{K}$ line visualizes constant capital growth. The dynamics of public debt are given by:

$$\hat{D} = \frac{[(s-\theta)A+\rho]\,K}{(1-s)D} \tag{17}$$

The $\hat{D}$ line in Figure 2.23 shows debt growth. In the steady state, public debt grows at the same rate as capital. Hence at the intersection of the two growth lines the economy is in the steady state, where the debt-capital ratio stays constant. To the left of the steady state, the debt-capital ratio increases and to the right, the debt-capital ratio declines. As a result we obtain:

Proposition 2. *The steady state is stable.*

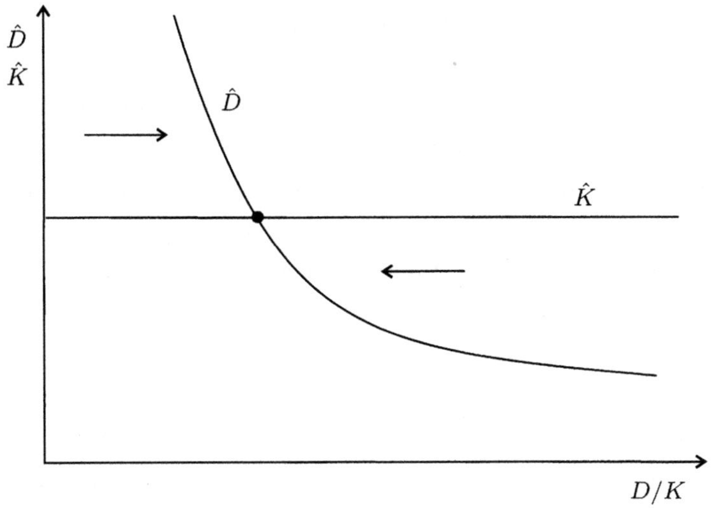

Figure 2.23.
Debt Growth and Capital Growth

2.4.3 Some Shocks

In this section we shall consider the process of adjustment induced by three shocks:

1) an increase in the saving ratio
2) an increase in productivity
3) an increase in the discount rate.

1) Increase in the saving ratio. At the beginning, the economy rests in the steady state. The budget deficit and public debt grow at the same rate as capital, output, consumption and investment. In this situation, households lift the saving ratio. As an immediate response, the government increases the deficit ratio so as to keep investment growing at the constant rate. Given the budget constraint, the government is able to reduce the tax rate. The increase in the saving ratio reduces consumption, and the decline in the tax rate increases consumption. Overall consumption remains unaffected. In the growth diagram, the $\hat{K}$ line remains unchanged, whereas the $\hat{D}$ line shifts to the right, cf. Figure 2.24.

In the medium run, the rise in the deficit ratio leads to an acceleration of debt growth. In contrast, the process has no influence on investment growth, capital growth and output growth. Since debt grows faster than capital, the debt-capital ratio increases. Therefore, owing to the budget constraint, the government must enhance the tax rate. The increase in debt income and the increase in the tax rate cancel each other out and, therefore, disposable income and consumption grow at the same rate as output.

Over time the economy moves towards a new steady state. The budget deficit and public debt grow at the same rate as capital and output. The ratio of public debt to capital reaches a higher level. Figure 2.25 shows the time path of the saving ratio and the deficit ratio. Figure 2.26 shows the path of the debt-capital ratio and Figure 2.27 depicts the time paths of debt and capital on a semilogarithmic scale.

2) Increase in productivity. Before the shock, the economy is in the steady state. The deficit and public debt grow at the same rate as capital, output and consumption. Then productivity goes up. Given the amount of capital, output and income both increase. Therefore savings go up as well. Due to higher growth prospects, the government reduces the deficit ratio. In the growth diagram, given in Figure 2.28, the $\hat{K}$ line moves upwards and the $\hat{D}$ line goes to the left. Capital and output growth increase immediately to the new steady-state level. In contrast, debt growth first declines and then intensifies gradually till it reaches the new steady-state level. As a consequence, the debt-capital ratio declines. In the new steady state, debt and capital grow at the same constant rate. Figure 2.29 illustrates the time paths of growth rates.

3) Increase in the discount rate. At the start, the economy is in a steady state. Public debt and capital grow at the same constant rate. Then suddenly the discount rate rises. As an immediate response, the government lifts the deficit ratio. In the growth diagram, the $\hat{K}$ line glides downwards and the $\hat{D}$ line goes to the right, cf. Figure 2.30. The shock immediately expands consumption and contracts investment. From then on, capital, output and consumption grow at a lower rate. Debt growth dwindles gradually. For that reason, the debt-capital ratio goes up. After a while, the economy converges to a new steady state where debt and capital grow at the same rate, so the debt-capital ratio is constant. Figure 2.31 illuminates the associated time paths on a semilogarithmic scale.

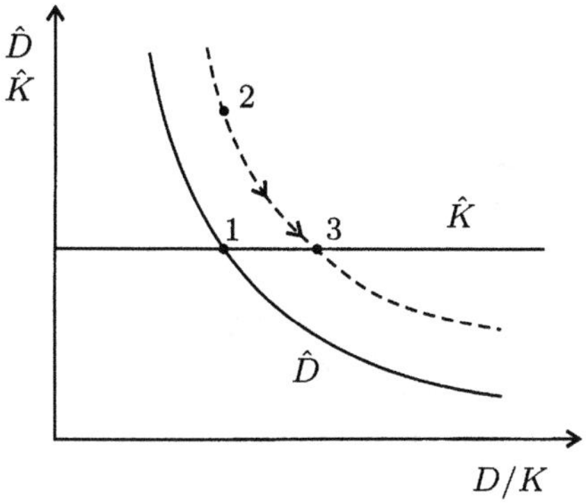

Figure 2.24.
Increase in Saving Ratio

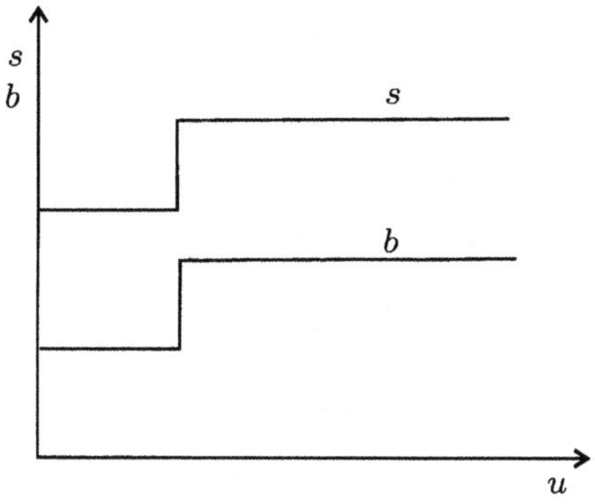

Figure 2.25.
Saving Ratio and Deficit Ratio

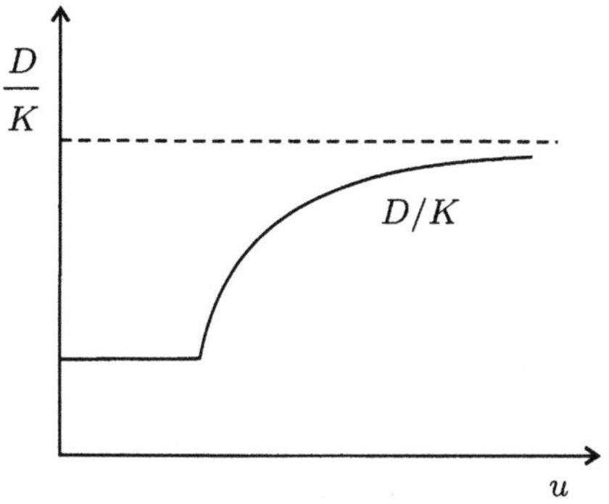

Figure 2.26.
Debt-Capital Ratio

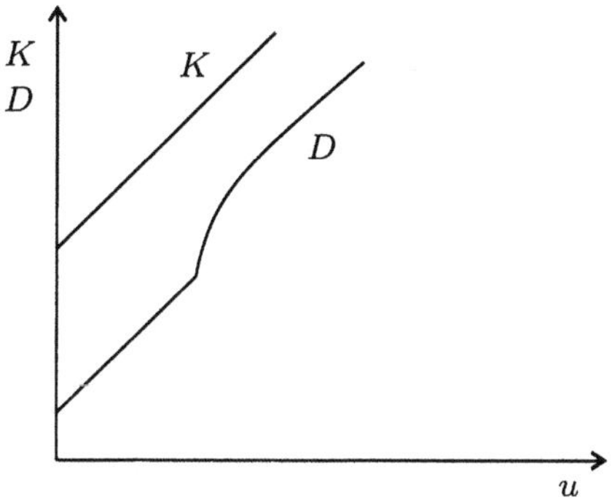

Figure 2.27.
Capital and Debt

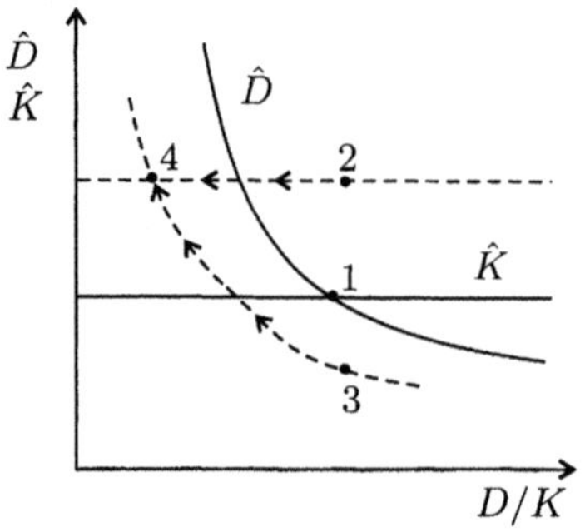

Figure 2.28.
Increase in Productivity

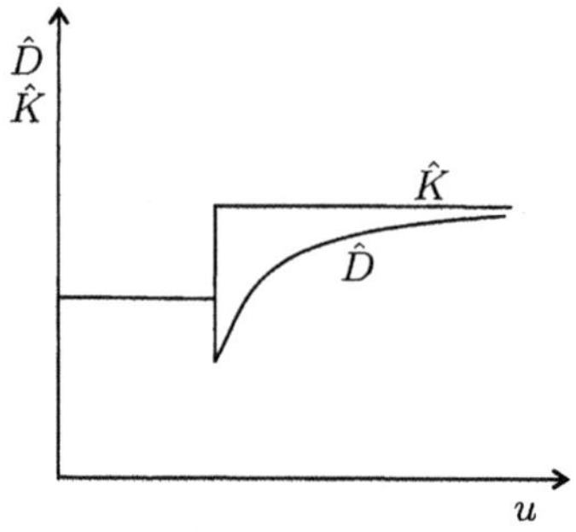

Figure 2.29.
Increase in Productivity

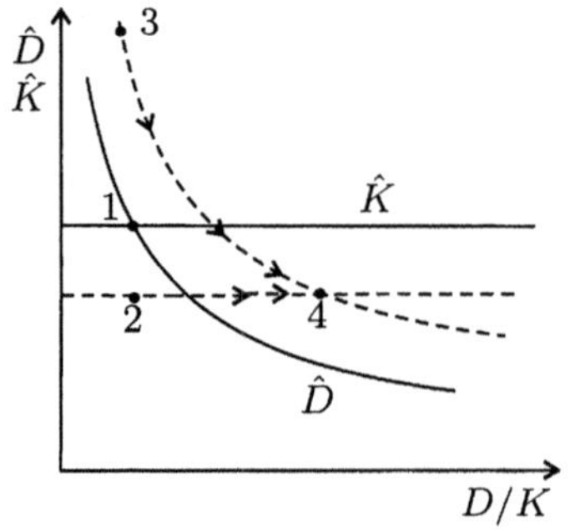

Figure 2.30.
Increase in Time Preference

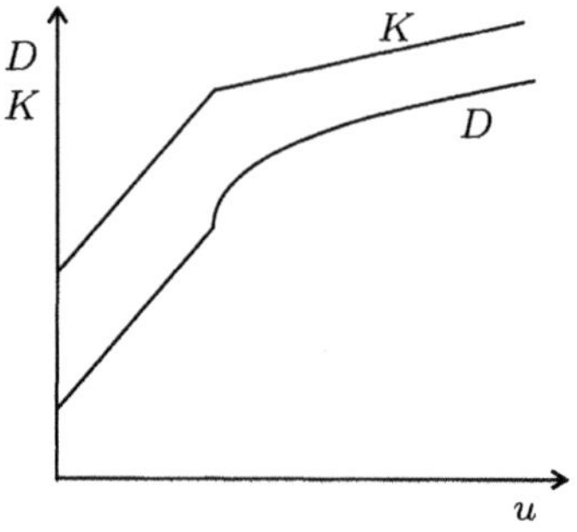

Figure 2.31.
Increase in Time Preference

2.4.4 Summary

The government optimizes the deficit ratio so as to maximize welfare over an infinite horizon. As a result, there is an optimal deficit ratio which is constant. It depends on the saving ratio and on the rate of time preference. An increase in the saving ratio or the rate of time preference leads to a rise in the optimal deficit ratio. If the saving ratio (rate of time preference) is high, then the optimal deficit ratio is positive. And if the saving ratio (rate of time preference) is low, then the optimal deficit ratio is negative. Due to the constant deficit ratio, capital, output and consumption grow at the same constant rate. Now suppose that the saving ratio increases. To counteract this, the government immediately increases the deficit ratio. As a consequence, capital growth, output growth and consumption growth remain unchanged.

3

The Overlapping Generations Model

3.1 Introduction

In this chapter we will analyse the growth effects of public debt in an overlapping generations model in the tradition of Diamond (1965). The basis model is presented in Blanchard and Fischer (1989). Public policy and welfare analysis in the overlapping generations model is described in Azariadis (1993) and in de la Croix and Michel (2002). In contrast to the Solow model, where a fixed saving ratio was assumed, the overlapping generations model derives the saving-ratio from intertemporal utility maximization of private agents within a finite horizon. The model has a long tradition for the analysis of public debt in neoclassical growth models. At first we have a look at the literature that assumes a fixed deficit ratio. Given a fixed deficit ratio, Carlberg (1984, 1985b, 1988) assumes that the government makes transfers. In contrast Michaelis (1989a) and Carlberg (1995) assume that the government either consumes or invests. As a result, in all the models of a fixed deficit ratio, there are two steady states if the deficit ratio stays below a critical level. However if the deficit ratio surpasses the critical level, then there is no steady state.

Now consider the literature on a fixed tax rate. Zee (1988) discusses an overlapping generations model of a growing economy with public consumption. The necessary condition of stability is that the net interest rate stays below the natural rate. But the interest rate is endogenous. Ihori (1988b), Michaelis (1989a) and Carlberg (1995) analyse the model of a fixed tax rate with government consumption. Necessary and sufficient conditions for the existence of a steady state are derived. As a rule, there will be no steady state.

As an exception, if the future consumption elasticity is very large and if the primary deficit ratio is extremely small, there will be two steady states. One of them is stable, the other is unstable. However, in general a fixed tax rate is not feasible in the long run. Schmid (1990) and Carlberg (1995) assume that the government fixes the tax per head. As a finding, there may exist two long-run equilibria, a stable one and an unstable one. However in general there will be no steady state. Hence, in neoclassical growth models there is a fundamental difference between the strategy of a fixed deficit ratio and a fixed tax rate.

Saint-Paul (1992) and Josten(2000a, 2000c) analyse public debt in overlapping generations models with endogenous growth. Saint-Paul (1992) and Josten (2000a) consider continuous-time overlapping generations models in the tradition of Blanchard (1985) and Yaari (1965). In Saint Paul an AK technology is assumed and Josten assumes endogenous growth through human capital formation. They concentrate on the steady state with a fixed debt-output ratio. In both models public debt reduces growth and welfare of future generations. Josten (2000c) considers a discrete time overlapping generations model with public debt. The government fixes the tax rate. As a result, there is a stable steady state if saving behaviour guarantees that without public debt the endogenous growth rate is above the interest rate. Otherwise no steady state exists.

In the following we will first analyse the model with the fixed deficit ratio and then the model with a fixed tax rate. In each section the first subsection presents the model and derives the steady state. The next subsection analyses stability. Finally the dynamics induced by shocks are considered.

3.2 Fixing the Deficit Ratio

3.2.1 The Model

First we consider the structure of production. A large number of identical firms denoted by i manufacture a single commodity Y_i by means of capital K_i and labour N_i. The production function is of the Cobb-Douglas type: $Y_i = AK_i^{\alpha}(EN_i)^{\beta}$, with $A > 0, \alpha > 0, \beta > 0, \alpha + \beta = 1$, and E as an exogenously given index of labour efficiency. Each firm maximizes profits $\Pi_i =$

$Y_i - rK_i - wN_i$ under perfect competition. Here Π_i denotes the profits of firm i, r the interest rate, and w the wage rate. Therefore each firm adjusts capital to equate the marginal product to the interest rate $\partial Y_i/\partial K_i = \alpha Y_i/K_i = r$, and labour is adjusted to equate the marginal product to the wage rate $\partial Y_i/\partial N_i = \beta Y_i/N_i = w$.

The aggregate production function is $Y = AK^\alpha(EN)^\beta$. Labour efficiency E depends on the amount of knowledge accumulated which comes from learning-by-doing. It is assumed that labour efficiency is proportional to capital per worker $E = K/N$ and is therefore endogenous for the economy. The aggregate production function simplifies to $Y = AK$. The markets for capital and labour are perfectly competitive. In each period, the supply of capital and labour is given exogenously. Due to competitive markets, the interest rate and the wage rate adjust to equate the supply and the demand of capital and labour. Hence, the interest rate corresponds to the marginal product of capital $r = \partial Y/\partial K = \alpha A$, and the wage rate corresponds to the marginal product of labour $w = \partial Y/\partial N = \beta Y/N$. Output Y can be devoted to consumption, investment and government purchases $Y = C + I + G$.

Now we take a look at the dynamics of public debt. The government spends a given proportion of national income on goods and services $G = gY$ with $g = const$. In addition, the government borrows a specified fraction of national income $B = bY$ with $b = const$. The budget deficit of this period adds up to the public debt of this period to give the public debt of the next period $D_{+1} = D + B$. The interest rate r has to be paid on public debt D, so that public interest is given by rD. The government levies a tax at the flat rate t on factor income and debt income $T = t(Y + rD)$. The government budget constraint is $B + T = G + rD$. Take account of the functional relationships to see $bY + t(Y + rD) = gY + rD$. The government fixes both the purchase ratio and the deficit ratio and has to accept interest payments on public debt. Then, the tax rate has to be adjusted accordingly.

Now we focus on individual saving decisions and resulting capital dynamics. Individuals live for two periods. In the first period of life they work and in the second they are retired. During the working period, the individual receives labour income, which he partly consumes and partly saves. The savings are used to buy government bonds and private bonds. During the retirement period, the individual earns interest on the bonds and sells the bonds altogether. The proceeds are entirely consumed, so nothing is bequeathed.

The utility u of the representative individual depends on his consumption in the working period c^1 and on his consumption in the retirement period c^2. The utility function is:

$$u = \gamma \log c^1 + \delta \log c^2 \tag{1}$$

with $\gamma > 0, \delta > 0$ and $\gamma + \delta = 1$. Here it is implicitly assumed that government purchases do not affect intertemporal allocation. Consequently, they do not enter the utility function.

The representative individual faces an intertemporal budget constraint. Net income in the working period is given by the net wage $(1-t)w$. It can be used for consumption in the working period and for savings s. Therefore the budget constraint in the first period of life is $(1-t)w = c^1 + s$. The individual earns the net interest rate $(1-t)r$ on savings. So consumption in the retirement period is $c^2 = [1 + (1-t)r]s$. As a consequence, the intertemporal budget constraint can be stated as:

$$c^1 + \frac{c^2}{1 + (1-t)r} = (1-t)w \tag{2}$$

The individual chooses present and future consumption so as to maximize utility subject to his budget constraint. Maximization of (1) under the restriction of (2) gives the consumption of a worker as $c^1 = (1-t)\gamma w$. Net labour income minus consumption gives the savings of the representative young individual $s = (1-t)w - c^1 = (1-t)\delta w$. The aggregate savings of the working generation are given by $S = sN$. Use $s = (1-t)\delta w$ and $w = \beta Y/N$ to obtain $S = (1-t)\beta\delta Y$. These savings of the young generation are used to finance public debt and private capital of the following period $D_{+1} + K_{+1} = S$. Accordingly, one can deduce $D_{+1} + K_{+1} = (1-t)\beta\delta Y$.

On this foundation, the model can be represented by a system of five equations:

$$Y = AK \tag{3}$$

$$r = \alpha A \tag{4}$$

$$D_{+1} + K_{+1} = (1-t)\beta\delta Y \tag{5}$$

$$D_{+1} = D + bY \tag{6}$$

$$bY + t(Y + rD) = gY + rD \tag{7}$$

Here $\alpha, \beta, \delta, b, g, A, D$, and K are exogenous, whereas r, t, D_{+1}, K_{+1}, and Y are endogenous.

For further analysis, it is convenient to consider growth factors. First, we look at the growth factor of public debt. Divide (6) by D to obtain $D_{+1}/D = bY/D$. Then replace output with the help of (3) and insert $x = D/K$ for the debt-capital ratio:

$$\frac{D_{+1}}{D} = 1 + \frac{bA}{x} \tag{8}$$

Now we analyse output growth. As it is obvious from (3), output growth corresponds to capital growth. To obtain the growth factor of capital we first have to solve for the endogenous tax rate. From (7) we observe $t = [(g-b)Y + rD]/[Y+rD]$. Replace Y by AK and r by αA to get $t = [(g-b)K + \alpha D]/[K + \alpha D]$. Finally divide numerator and denominator by K, and then substitute $x = D/K$ to obtain:

$$1 - t = \frac{1+b-g}{1+\alpha x} \tag{9}$$

Further insert (3) and (9) into (5), to reach $D_{+1} + K_{+1} = (1+b-g)\beta\delta AK/(1+\alpha x)$. Then replace debt in the next period with the help of (6), solve for K_{+1}, divide by K, and use $x = D/K$ to obtain the growth factor of capital:

$$\frac{K_{+1}}{K} = \left(\frac{(1+b-g)\beta\delta}{1+\alpha x} - b\right) A - x \tag{10}$$

The growth factor of capital as well as the growth factor of public debt depend on the debt-capital ratio. Both growth factors are constant if the debt-capital ratio is constant. Hence, in the steady state, public debt has to grow at the same rate as capital, so that the debt-capital ratio is constant. Now equate (8) and (10) to obtain:

$$1 + \frac{bA}{x} = \left(\frac{(1+b-g)\beta\delta}{1+\alpha x} - b\right) A - x \tag{11}$$

Analysis of (11) gives rise to the following proposition:

Proposition 1. *There is a critical deficit ratio b'. If the deficit ratio is below the critical level $b < b'$, then there are two steady states x_1 and x_2. In these steady states, debt and capital grow at the same rate, so the debt-capital ratio is constant. An increase in the deficit ratio leads to a rise in x_1, which matches the results obtained in the Solow model. On the other hand, an increase in deficit ratio reduces x_2. An increase in the deficit ratio that reduces the debt-capital ratio seems to be quite contradictory, suggesting that the second steady state will be unstable. If the deficit ratio exceeds a critical level $b > b'$, then there is no solution.*

Proof. Denote $p(x, b) = 1+x+bA/x$ and $q(x) = (1+b-g)\beta\delta A/(1+\alpha x)-bA$. In the steady state we have $p(x, b) = q(x, b)$. The function p has a minimum at $x_m = \sqrt{bA}$ where $p(x_m) = 1+2\sqrt{bA}$. The function q is declining monotonically with x. Figure 3.1 illustrates the two functions. Both functions are plotted for three levels of the deficit ratio $b_0 < b_1 < b_2$. For the levels b_0 and b_1 there are two crossings of p and q. For b_2 there is no solution. ■

To illustrate this, consider a numerical example with $\alpha = 0.3, \delta = 0.4, g = 0.2, A = 15$. The assumed value of the scale parameter A is much higher than in the Solow model. This reflects different time periods. In the overlapping generations model, the time period is 30 years. Notice that A is the inverse of the capital-output ratio. Hence, to obtain an estimate for A we have to aggregate output over 30 years. Table 3.1 shows the steady states as functions of the deficit ratio. In the numerical example the critical deficit ratio is $b = 0.034$. This means, if the deficit ratio is 3.4% or below, then there are two steady states. On the other hand, if the deficit ratio is above 3.4%, then there is no steady state. Hence a deficit ratio of above 3.4% implies that debt always grows faster than capital, and therefore the debt-capital ratio explodes.

Finally we consider growth factors. Inspection of (8) and (10) immediately reveals that in the steady state at the low debt-capital ratio, growth is high. And in the steady state at the high debt-capital ratio, growth is low.

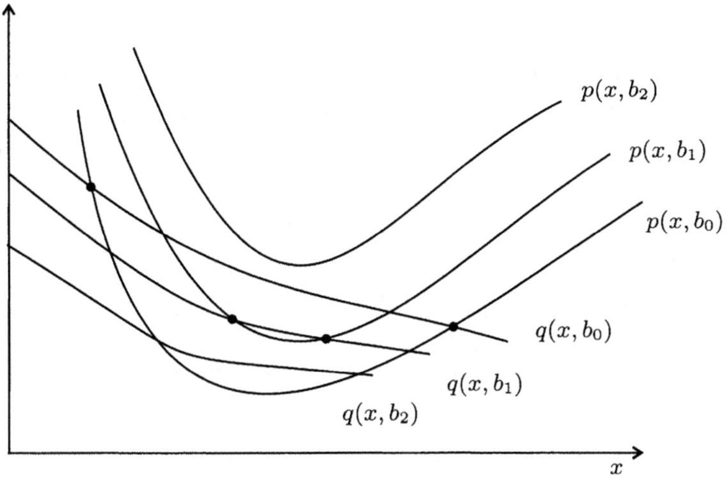

Figure 3.1.
Existence of Equilibria

Table 3.1. Deficit Ratio and Debt-Capital Ratio

b	x_1	x_2
0	0	1.377
0.01	0.071	1.218
0.02	0.165	1.037
0.03	0.318	0.799
0.034	0.461	0.622

3.2.2 Stability

The dynamics of the model are completely described by the two equations for the growth factors of public debt and capital. For convenience they are repeated here:

$$\frac{D_{+1}}{D} = 1 + \frac{bA}{x} \tag{12}$$

$$\frac{K_{+1}}{K} = \left(\frac{(1+b-g)\beta\delta}{1+\alpha x} - b\right) A - x \tag{13}$$

Both growth factors depend on the debt-capital ratio. First we consider public debt growth. As equation (12) shows, the growth factor of public debt goes to infinity when the debt-capital ratio approaches zero. For a very large debt-capital ratio, i.e. when x goes to infinity, the growth factor converges to one. Figure 3.2 displays the downwards-sloping DD line, representing equation (12). Equation (13) confirms that the growth factor of capital is a declining function of the debt-capital ratio. Thus the KK line, representing equation (13), is falling.

First consider the case where the deficit ratio stays below the critical level. Figure 3.2 presents the growth diagram. It illustrates that there are two steady states $x_1 < x_2$. At an initial debt-capital ratio below x_1, debt grows faster than capital. Therefore, the debt-capital ratio increases towards x_1. Given an initial debt-capital ratio between x_1 and x_2, capital grows faster than debt and the debt-capital ratio declines towards x_1. Given an initial debt-capital ratio above x_2, debt grows faster than capital. Therefore the debt-capital ratio increases. As a result we summarize:

Proposition 2. *The steady state at the low debt-capital ratio x_1 is locally stable, whereas the steady state at the high debt-capital ratio x_2 is unstable. As a conclusion, a fixed deficit ratio generally can be sustained. However, if the initial debt-capital ratio is very large, then the fixed deficit ratio cannot be sustained.*

Interestingly Rankin and Roffia (2002) find that in neoclassical growth models there is a maximum sustainable amount of public debt. Here, due to continuously growing capital, there is a maximum sustainable ratio of public debt to capital.

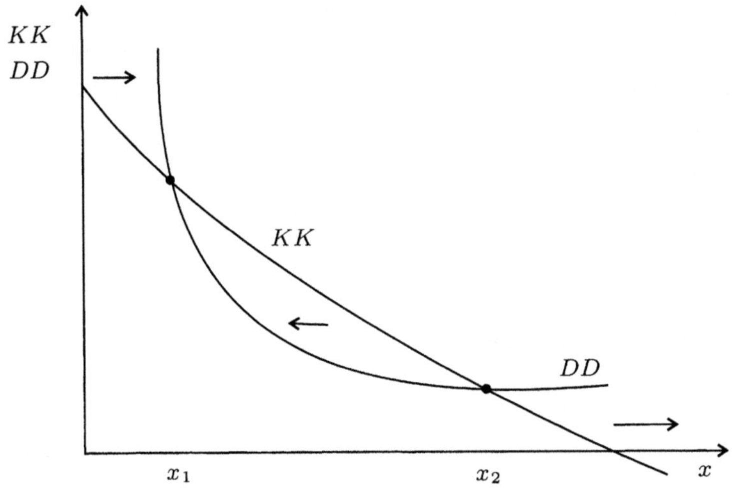

Figure 3.2.
Capital Growth and Debt Growth $b < b'$

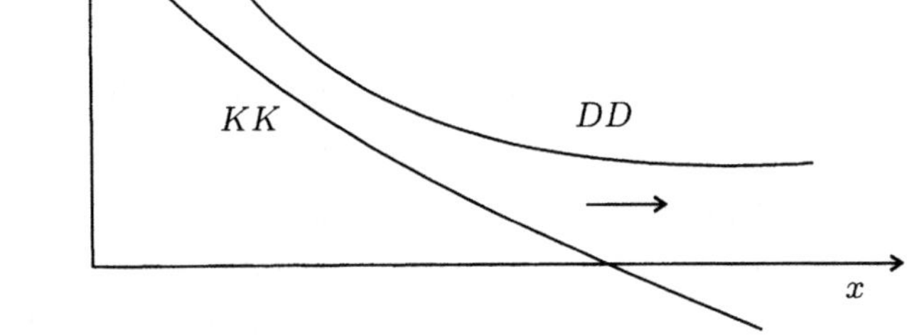

Figure 3.3.
Capital Growth and Debt Growth $b > b'$

Now consider the case where the deficit ratio exceeds the critical level, see Figure 3.3. Due to the high deficit ratio there is no crossing of the KK line and the DD line. Public debt growth always exceeds capital growth. The debt-capital ratio increases continuously. As a consequence capital growth and output growth decline continuously, become negative at some point of time and deteriorate further. This drives capital and output down to zero in finite time.

3.2.3 A Balanced Budget

Let us assume the government balances the budget $b = 0$. As Table 3.1 indicates there are two steady states. One of them has a debt-capital ratio of zero. The other has a positive debt-capital ratio. Now have a look at the dynamics. The growth diagram is shown in Figure 3.4.

To start with, consider public debt. For $b = 0$ the growth factor is always 1. Hence public debt stays constant. Therefore, the DD line displayed in the growth diagram is horizontal. Now we turn to capital dynamics. Capital growth declines with the initial debt-capital ratio. Hence the KK line in Figure 3.4 is falling. This gives rise to two cases. If the debt-capital ratio falls short of a critical level, then capital grows. However, if the initial debt-capital ratio exceeds a critical level, then there is a decay of capital. For constant debt, capital growth implies a falling debt-capital ratio, and a capital decay implies a rising debt-capital ratio. Hence, the growth diagram shows that the steady state with a zero debt-capital ratio is locally stable. In contrast, the steady state with a positive debt-capital ratio is unstable. In addition, we may conclude that a balanced budget can only be sustained if the initial debt-capital ratio is not too large.

This last conclusion differs from the Solow model. There a balanced budget can always be sustained, regardless of the initial debt-capital ratio. The underlying reason is that in the Solow model savings are made from all types of income at a uniform rate. In the overlapping generations model, the only savings are from wage income. A high initial debt-capital ratio implies high interest payments and, therefore, high interest income. Interest income is a source of savings in the Solow model but not in the overlapping generations model. This is why a high initial debt-capital ratio leads to instability in the

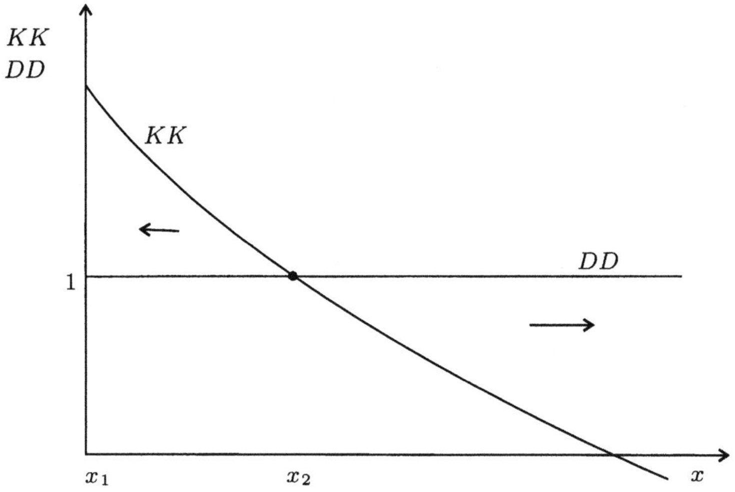

Figure 3.4.
Balanced Budget

overlapping generations model. To stabilize, the government has two options. The first is to run a budget surplus, at least temporarily. The second is to tax interest income at a higher rate than labour income.

3.2.4 An Increase in the Deficit Ratio

At the start the economy is in the steady state. The budget deficit and public debt grow at the same rate as capital and output. The initial steady state is marked as point 1 in Figure 3.5. Then the government increases the deficit ratio. The KK line shifts to the left and the DD line moves upwards. In the short run, due to the higher budget deficit, debt growth increases (point 2). At the same time, capital growth declines (point 3). This reduces output growth and budget deficit growth. In the medium run, due to lower deficit growth, debt growth declines. The debt-capital ratio increases. This reduces capital growth further. In the long run, debt growth and capital growth converge. In the new steady state (point 4), debt and capital grow at the same constant rate. Compared to the original steady state, capital growth and debt growth are reduced.

Now look at a numerical example. Initially, capital and output as well as the budget deficit and public debt grow at the same constant rate. Assume that the initial deficit ratio is 1%. As a result, the annual growth rate is 4.8%. Then the government increases the deficit ratio to 2%. In the short run, this increases debt growth to 6%. At the same time, it reduces capital growth, output growth and budget deficit growth to 4.6%. In the medium run, capital growth, output growth and budget deficit growth decline further. Due to the reduction in budget deficit growth, debt growth declines. In the long run, the growth rates converge. In the new steady state, capital, output, the budget deficit and public debt grow at the same constant rate of 4.5%. Figure 3.6 visualizes the time paths of capital growth and debt growth.

3.2.5 Summary

Capital growth and public debt growth depend on the deficit ratio and on the debt-capital ratio. Both growth rates stay constant if the debt-capital ratio is constant. In the steady state, public debt and capital grow at the same rate, so the debt-capital ratio and both growth rates are constant. There is a critical deficit ratio. First assume that the deficit ratio is below the critical level. In this case there are two steady states. One of them is locally stable, and the other is unstable. There is a critical initial debt-capital ratio. If the initial debt-capital ratio is below the critical level, the stable steady state will be reached. However, if the initial debt-capital ratio is above the critical level, then capital growth declines continuously, becomes negative at some point of time, and deteriorates further. Capital is driven to zero in finite time. Now assume that the economy is in the stable steady state. Consider an increase in the deficit ratio. First assume that the deficit ratio stays below the critical level. Then the increase in the deficit ratio leads to a new steady state. Capital growth and public debt growth are lower than in the original steady state. Second assume that the deficit ratio exceeds the critical level. In this case there is no steady state. Capital growth declines continuously and capital is driven to zero in finite time.

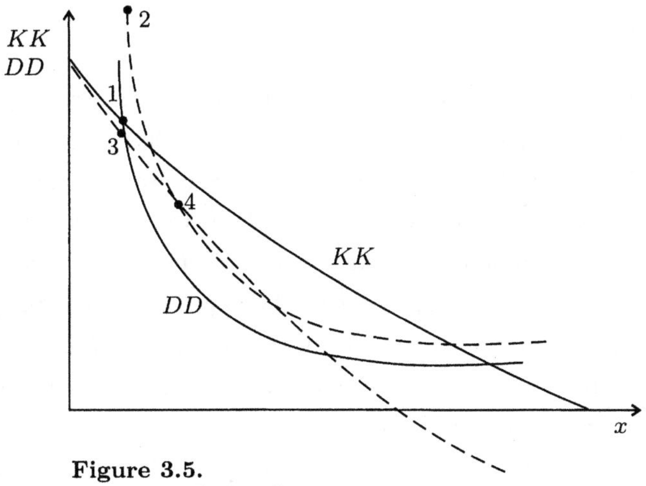

Figure 3.5.
Increase in Deficit Ratio

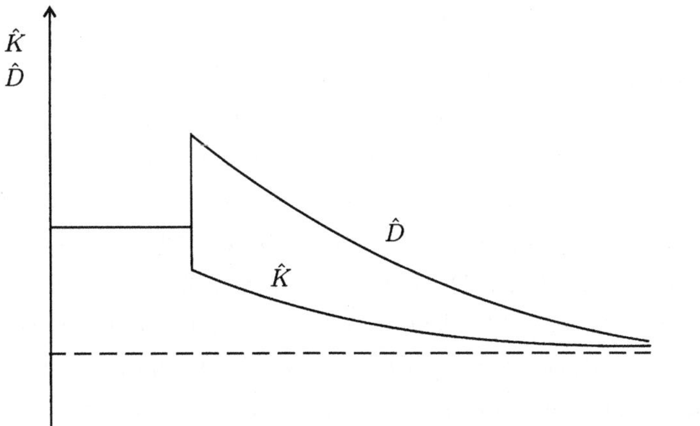

Figure 3.6.
Time Paths

3.3 Fixing the Tax Rate

3.3.1 The Model

We start out with budget dynamics. The government buys a certain proportion of the national product $G = gY$ with $g = const$ and has to pay interest r on public debt D. In addition, the government levies a proportionate tax on both factor income and debt income $T = t(Y + rD)$ with $t = const$. The budget deficit is given by the difference between government expenditures and tax proceeds $B = G + rD - T$. The budget deficit of this period adds to the public debt of this period to give the public debt in the next period $D_{+1} = D + B$. Insert the definition of the budget deficit to obtain public debt in the next period $D_{+1} = D + gY + rD - t(Y + rD)$.

The rest of the model is the same as in Section 3.2. Thus the model can be characterized by a system of four equations:

$$Y = AK \tag{1}$$

$$r = \alpha A \tag{2}$$

$$D_{+1} + K_{+1} = \beta\delta(1-t)Y \tag{3}$$

$$D_{+1} = D + gY + rD - t(Y + rD) \tag{4}$$

Here $\alpha, \beta, \delta, g, t, A, D$, and K and exogenous, while r, D_{+1}, K_{+1}, and Y are endogenous. Now it is suitable to analyse growth factors. Due to the proportional production function (1), output growth is always the same as capital growth. The interest rate stays constant, as seen in (2). Hence we have to consider the system of growth factors for debt and capital.

First, insert equations (1) and (2) into (4) and divide by debt D to obtain the growth factor of public debt stated in equation (5). Then use equations (1) and (2) in (3), subtract equation (4), divide by capital K, and rearrange to obtain the growth factor of capital, given in equation (6):

$$\frac{D_{+1}}{D} = 1 + (1-t)\alpha A + (g-t)\frac{AK}{D} \tag{5}$$

$$\frac{K_{+1}}{K} = [\beta\delta(1-t) - (g-t)]A - (1 + \alpha(1-t)A)\frac{D}{K} \tag{6}$$

Both growth factors depend on the debt-capital ratio $x = D/K$. In the steady state, debt grows at the same rate as capital, so the debt-capital ratio is constant. Equations (5) and (6) show that a constant debt-capital ratio implies constant debt growth and constant capital growth. In the main part of this section we concentrate on the question as to whether a steady state exists. Equate (5) and (6) and insert x to obtain:

$$1 + (1-t)\alpha A + (g-t)\frac{A}{x} = [\beta\delta(1-t) - (g-t)]\,A - (1 + \alpha(1-t)A)x \quad (7)$$

Obviously this is a quadratic equation in x. In the following, to avoid unnecessary complexity, we assume $t = 0$. Hence we ask, whether the government can provide goods and services without imposing a tax? Assume $t = 0$ and solve (7) for x to obtain:

$$x_{1,2} = \frac{(\beta\delta - \alpha - g)A - 1 \pm \sqrt{[(\beta\delta - \alpha - g)A - 1]^2 - 4(1 + \alpha A)gA}}{2(1 + \alpha A)} \quad (8)$$

A steady state will exist if either one or both of the solutions given in (8) are real and positive.

To analyse whether the solutions are real consider the reduced discriminant $U = [(\beta\delta - \alpha - g)A - 1]^2 - 4(1 + \alpha A)gA$. Whether U is positive or negative depends on the size of the government purchase ratio g. U becomes zero at:

$$g_{1,2} = \frac{1 + (\alpha + \beta\delta)A}{A} \mp \frac{2}{A}\sqrt{\beta\delta A(1 + \alpha A)} \quad (9)$$

Analysis of (9) shows that g_1 and g_2 are both real and positive with $g_1 < g_2$. The debt-capital ratio x is real and positive if and only if

$$\delta > \delta' = \frac{1 + \alpha A}{\beta A} \qquad \text{and} \qquad g \leq g_1$$

As a result we may state:

Proposition 1. *A steady state does exist if and only if the future consumption elasticity exceeds a critical and the government purchase ratio stay below a critical level. Given that these conditions are satisfied, there are two steady states. If either the government purchase ratio exceeds the critical level or* *the future consumption elasticity is below the critical level, there is no steady state.*

Proof. Evidently (8) can be written as $x_{1,2} = (P \pm \sqrt{U})/Q$, where $Q > 0$. In addition, the reduced discriminant of (8) can be stated as $U = (g - g_1)(g - g_2)$. This gives rise to four cases.

1) $g_1 < g < g_2$, then $U < 0$.

2) $g \leq g_1$ and $\delta < (1 + \alpha A)/\beta A$, then $U \geq 0$ and $x < 0$. P is negative. Now square $\sqrt{U} < P$ to confirm $x < 0$.

3) $g \leq g_1$ and $\delta > (1 + \alpha A)/\beta A$, then $U \geq 0$ and $x > 0$. In this case, P is positive. Next square $P > \sqrt{U}$ to verify $x_{1,2} > 0$.

4) $g \geq g_2$, then $U \geq 0$ and $x < 0$. Here P is negative. Finally square $\sqrt{U} < P$ to see $x < 0$. ■

To find out that the necessary level of δ is extremely high, we assume $\delta = \delta' = (1 + \alpha A)/\beta A$ and consider an economy without government activity. Hence we assume $g = t = D = 0$. In that case, capital growth is $\beta \delta A - 1$. Insert $\delta = \delta' = (1 + \alpha A)/\beta A$ to obtain $\beta \delta A - 1 = \alpha A$. Thus, the growth rate corresponds to the interest rate. For any $\delta > \delta'$ the growth rate exceeds the interest rate. This implies that the economy is dynamically inefficient. Empirical evidence suggests that this is not the case, see Abel, Mankiw, Summers, and Zeckhauser (1987) and Blanchard and Weil (2001).

To gain a better intuition for the results, we study a numerical example with $\alpha = 0.3$ and $A = 15$. Table 3.2 indicates the maximum purchase ratio that can be sustained for different levels of δ. The critical level of δ is $\delta' = 0.524$. Hence, for $\delta = 0.3$, $\delta = 0.4$ and $\delta = 0.5$ we have $g_1 = 0$. So only a balanced budget can be sustained. However, if $\delta = 0.6$, then $g_1 = 0.007$. Here two cases have to be distinguished. As long as the purchase ratio stays below 0.002, it will be feasible in the long run. Yet, as soon as it surpasses 0.002, it will not be sustainable any more. How do these results relate to an economy with a tax rate of $t = 0.2$? If we assume $\delta = 0.6$, then probably, a purchase ratio below 0.2002 can be sustained. In contrast, a purchase ratio above 0.2002 cannot be sustained.

As a main result, we may summarize as follows. From the empirical point of view, the interest rate is well above the growth rate. Hence, the rate of time preference is likely to be lower than the critical level. So a fixed tax rate

Table 3.2. Maximum Sustainable Purchase Ratio

δ	g_1
0.1	0
0.2	0
0.3	0
0.4	0
0.5	0
0.6	0.002
0.7	0.009

appears not to be feasible in the long run. On the other hand, there may be an exception to this rule. If both the future consumption elasticity is very high and the primary deficit ratio is extremely low, then a fixed tax rate is indeed feasible. Essentially, this emphasizes the importance of the results derived in the Solow model.

3.3.2 Stability

In this section, we return to an economy with taxation. The dynamics of debt and capital are described by the two growth equations given in the last section. For convenience they are repeated here:

$$\frac{D_{+1}}{D} = 1 + (1-t)\alpha A + (g-t)\frac{A}{x} \tag{10}$$

$$\frac{K_{+1}}{K} = [\beta\delta(1-t) - (g-t)]A - (1 + \alpha(1-t)A)x \tag{11}$$

Equation (10) shows that debt growth goes to infinity when the debt-capital ratio converges to zero. And when the debt-capital ratio becomes very large, i.e. goes to infinity, debt grows at the constant rate $(1-t)\alpha A$. In Figures 3.7 and 3.7 the DD lines visualizes the relation between the debt-capital ratio and debt growth. Equation (11) shows that capital grows at a constant rate if the debt-capital ratio is zero. An increase in the debt-capital ratio leads to a decline in capital growth. In Figures 3.7 and 3.8, the KK lines illustrate the effect of the debt-capital ratio on capital growth.

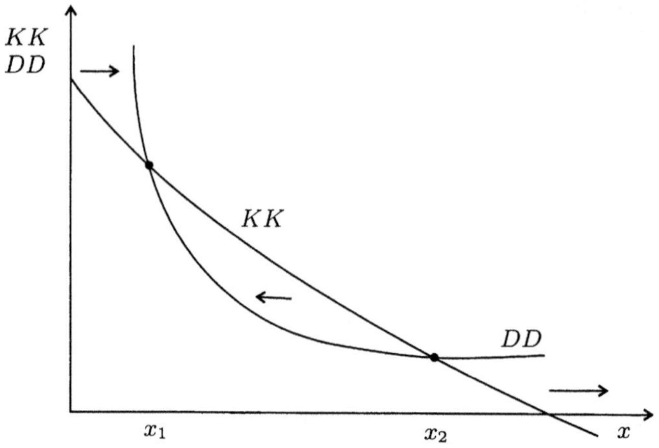

Figure 3.7.
Capital Growth and Debt Growth
Very Low Primary Deficit Ratio and Very Low Time Preference

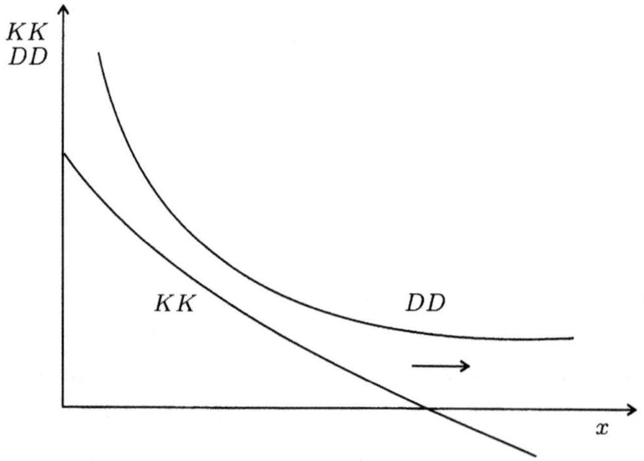

Figure 3.8.
Debt Growth and Capital Decay (Normal Case)

In Figure 3.7, it is assumed that the future consumption elasticity is very high and that the primary deficit is very low. In this case, the DD line and the KK line intersect twice. Hence there are two steady states. If the initial debt-capital ratio is below x_1, debt grows faster than capital. Therefore, the debt-capital ratio increases. For an initial debt-capital ratio between x_1 and x_2, capital grows faster than debt. Hence the debt-capital ratio declines. As a result, x_1 is locally stable. If, however, the initial debt-capital ratio is above x_2, then debt grows faster than capital. Hence the debt-capital ratio increases. As a result, x_2 is unstable. All this looks very similar to the case of a fixed deficit ratio. However, there is a major difference: in the case of a fixed deficit ratio, the two steady states are likely to occur. For a fixed tax rate, the two steady states only exist under very restrictive assumptions. The more likely case is exhibited in Figure 3.8. This case occurs when either the future consumption elasticity is not very high or if the primary deficit ratio is not very low. There is no intersection of the DD line and the KK line. Hence there is no steady state. Capital growth declines continuously. In contrast, debt growth remains positive.

3.3.3 Summary

Starting from a balanced budget, a tax cut leads to a budget deficit. Public debt results and begins to grow. Normally, public debt growth converges to a constant level, whereas capital growth declines continuously, becomes negative at some point of time, and deteriorates further. Capital is driven to zero in finite time. Only in a special case where the elasticity of future consumption is very high and the primary deficit ratio is extremely low, there is an exception. In this case there are two steady states. In these steady states, public debt and capital grow at the same constant rate. One of the steady states is stable and the other is not. As the fundamental result, a fixed tax rate generally cannot be sustained.

Part II

Human Capital and Innovations in the Closed Economy

4

The Augmented Solow Model

4.1 Introduction

This chapter considers human capital accumulation as the engine of economic growth as it is introduced in Lucas (1988) and Lucas (1993). Following Mankiw, Romer, and Weil (1992) we assume that households fix the saving ratio and the educational spending ratio. So we have an augmented Solow model. Buiter and Kletzer (1991, 1993), Zhang (1997) and Josten (2001) consider human capital in overlapping generations models of the open economy. In Buiter and Kletzer and in Zhang deficit financing policies that boost financial saving reduce the relative rate of human capital accumulation and labour productivity growth. Josten considers human capital in a small open economy. An increase in public debt that is used to redistribute every individual's tax burden from the youth to the middle age increases the steady state growth rate. Hence, in overlapping generations models of the open economy, public debt need not be harmful for growth. However, Josten (2000a) considers a continuous time overlapping generations model of a closed economy where human capital is the driving force of growth and shows that in this case public debt reduces growth. Now it is the question which of the results carries over to the augmented Solow model of the closed economy. In the following we will first consider the fixed deficit ratio and then we assume that the government fixes the tax rate.

4.2 Fixing the Deficit Ratio

4.2.1 The Model

Firms produce a single commodity Y by means of capital K and labour defined in efficiency units L. We assume a Cobb-Douglas technology with constant returns to scale $Y = AK^{\alpha}L^{\beta}$, where $A > 0, \alpha > 0$, $\beta > 0$ and $\alpha + \beta = 1$. Efficiency units of labour depend on human capital per worker and on the number of workers. Let H denote human capital and let N denote the number of workers. Then H/N is human capital per worker. Hence, efficiency units of labour depend on aggregate human capital $L = (H/N)N = H$. Consequently the production function might be stated as $Y = AK^{\alpha}H^{\beta}$. Output Y is used for consumption, investment, government purchases and spending on education $Y = C + I + G + Z$. Firms maximize profits $\Pi = Y - rK - wN$ under perfect competition. Here Π denotes profits, r the interest rate, and w the wage rate for a physical unit of labour. The interest rate agrees to the marginal product of capital $r = \partial Y/\partial K = \alpha Y/K$. An efficiency unit of labour is paid its marginal product $w_l = \partial Y/\partial L = \beta Y/L$. Since efficiency units depend on human capital we have $w_l = \beta Y/H$. Human capital per worker is H/N and therefore the wage of a worker is $w = w_l H/N = \beta Y/N$.

Now let us consider public debt dynamics. The government raises loans and levies an income tax in order to finance government purchases and the interest payments on public debt. The government spends a fixed share of national income on goods and services $G = gY$ with the purchase ratio $g = const.$ In addition the government borrows a specified proportion of national income $B = bY$ with the deficit ratio $b = const.$ The budget deficit in turn adds to public debt $\dot{D} = B$. The government pays the interest rate r on public debt D, so public interest amounts to rD. The government imposes a tax at the flat rate t on both factor income and debt income $T = t(Y + rD)$. Accordingly, the government budget constraint can be written as $B + T = G + rD$. Taking account of the behavioural functions, the identity can be reformulated in the following way $bY + t(Y + rD) = gY + rD$. In this equation, the purchase ratio and the deficit ratio are given, whereas the tax rate must be adjusted appropriately.

Next regard the dynamics of physical and human capital accumulation. Disposable income is the sum of factor income and debt income, net of taxes respectively $Y_d = Y + rD - T$. Households save a certain fraction of disposable income $S = sY_d$ with the saving ratio $s = const.$ In addition, households spend a fixed proportion of their disposable income on education $Z = zY_d$, with the education-spending ratio $z = const.$ A part of private savings is absorbed by public borrowing, the remainder is left for private investment $I = S - B$. Investment contributes to the accumulation of physical capital $\dot{K} = I$. Human capital is augmented by spending on education $\dot{H} = Z$. By backward substitution one obtains $\dot{K} = s(Y + rD - T) - B$ and $\dot{H} = z(Y + rD - T)$. Further note that with $B + T = G + rD$, $B = bY$ and $G = gY$ we obtain $\dot{K} = (1 + b - g)sY - bY$ and $\dot{H} = (1 + b - g)zY$. Taking all pieces together, the model can be represented by a system of six equations:

$$Y = AK^{\alpha}H^{\beta} \tag{1}$$

$$r = \alpha Y/K \tag{2}$$

$$\dot{K} = (1 + b - g)sY - bY \tag{3}$$

$$\dot{H} = (1 + b - g)zY \tag{4}$$

$$\dot{D} = bY \tag{5}$$

$$bY + t(Y + rD) = gY + rD \tag{6}$$

Here $\alpha, \beta, b, g, s, z, D$, and K are exogenous, while $r, t, \dot{D}$, $\dot{H}$, $\dot{K}$, and Y are endogenous.

The following analysis will be carried out in terms of growth rates. At first we consider physical capital growth. From (3) we have $\hat{K} = ((1 + b - g)s - b))Y/K$. Replace output with the help of (1) to obtain:

$$\hat{K} = [s(1 + b - g) - b]\, A\left(\frac{H}{K}\right)^{\beta} \tag{7}$$

Physical capital growth depends on the saving ratio, the government purchase ratio, the deficit ratio, and the physical-human capital ratio.

Now consider human capital growth. Divide (4) by human capital H to reach $\hat{H} = (1 + b - g)zY/H$. Then replace output with the help of (1) to obtain:

$$\hat{H} = z(1+b-g)A\left(\frac{K}{H}\right)^{\alpha} \tag{8}$$

Human capital growth depends on the education spending rate, the government purchase ratio, the deficit ratio, and the human-physical capital ratio.

Physical capital growth and human capital growth are constant if the physical-human capital ratio is constant. In the steady state, physical and human capital grow at the same constant rate, so the physical-human capital ratio is constant. Equate (7) and (8) to solve for the steady state physical-human capital ratio:

$$\frac{K}{H} = \frac{s(1+b-g)-b}{z(1+b-g)} \tag{9}$$

An increase in the saving ratio or in the government purchase ratio leads to a rise in the physical-human capital ratio, whereas an increase in the education-spending ratio or in the deficit ratio leads to a fall.

Now transform the production into growth rates $\hat{Y} = \alpha\hat{K} + \beta\hat{H}$ to note that the steady state condition $\hat{K} = \hat{H}$ implies that in the steady state, physical and human capital grow at the same rate as output $\hat{K} = \hat{H} = \hat{Y}$. Insert (9) into (7) or (8) to derive the steady state growth rate:

$$\hat{Y} = \hat{K} = \hat{H} = [z(1+b-g)]^{\beta}[s(1+b-g)-b]^{\alpha} A \tag{10}$$

As a result we obtain:

Proposition 1. *There is a critical deficit ratio b'. If the deficit ratio stays below the critical level there is a unique steady-state growth rate. If the deficit ratio exceeds the critical level then there is no steady state.*

Proof. If b exceeds $b' = (1-g)s/(1-s)$ we obtain $s(1+b-g)-b < 0$ and therefore (10) is not defined. ■

Interestingly the critical level b' here corresponds to the critical level in the AK model. Moreover the analysis of (10) gives the following proposition:

Proposition 2. *The steady-state growth rate depends on the saving ratio, the education-spending ratio, the government purchase ratio and the deficit ratio. An increase in either the saving ratio or the education-spending ratio leads to* *a rise in the growth rate. An increase in the government purchase ratio leads to a decline in the growth rate. And an increase in the deficit ratio leads to a decline in the growth rate if the deficit ratio exceeds a critical level* $b^{\#}$.

Proof. The effects of the saving ratio, the education-spending ratio and the government purchase ratio are obvious. The effect of the deficit ratio is given by:

$$\frac{d\hat{Y}}{db} = \frac{\beta\hat{Y}}{(1+b-g)} + \frac{(s-1)\alpha\hat{Y}}{s(1+b-g)-b}$$

Rearrange terms to obtain:

$$\frac{d\hat{Y}}{db} < 0 \text{ if } b > b^{\#} = \frac{(s-\alpha)(1-g)}{(1-s)}$$

■

Empirically the saving ratio is well below the capital elasticity $s < \alpha$ and therefore the critical level $b^{\#}$ is negative. Hence an increase in the deficit ratio will lead to a decline in output growth. Figure 4.1 illustrates the effect of the deficit ratio on output growth.

Next we analyse public debt. Use (5) to obtain public debt growth:

$$\hat{D} = \frac{bY}{D} \tag{11}$$

Public debt growth is constant if the debt-output ratio is constant. In the steady state, public debt grows at the same rate as output, so the debt-output ratio is constant. Equate (10) and (11) to obtain the debt-output ratio in the steady state:

$$\frac{D}{Y} = \frac{b}{[z(1+b-g)]^{\beta}[s(1+b-g)-b]^{\alpha} A} \tag{12}$$

Table 4.1 shows how the deficit ratio impinges on the physical-human capital ratio, the debt-output ratio and output growth. The assumed parameters are $\alpha = 0.3, \beta = 0.7, g = 0.2, s = 0.1,\ z = 0.1$ and $A = 0.25$.

Finally we take a look at the budget restriction which allows us to derive the tax rate. From (6) we obtain:

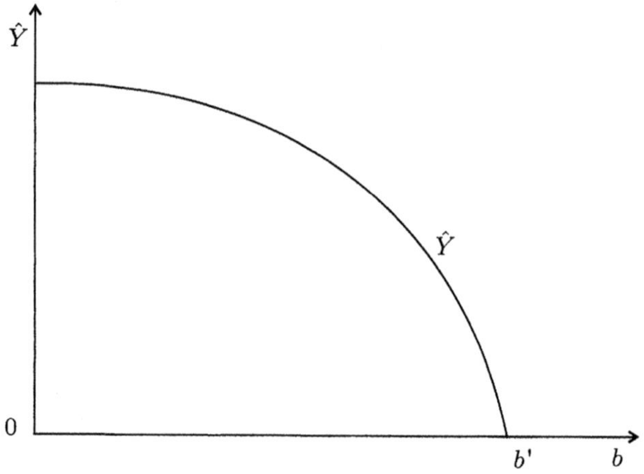

Figure 4.1.
Deficit Ratio and Output Growth

Table 4.1. The Long-Run Effects of the Budget Deficit

b	K/H	D/Y	$\hat{Y}$
0	1.0	0	0.02
0.01	0.877	0.514	0.0195
0.02	0.756	1.061	0.0188
0.03	0.639	1.654	0.0181
0.04	0.524	2.313	0.0173
0.05	0.412	3.071	0.0163
0.06	0.302	3.995	0.0150
0.07	0.195	5.252	0.0133
0.08	0.091	7.466	0.0107

$$t = \frac{(g-b)Y + rD}{(Y + rD)} = \frac{(g-b) + rD/Y}{(1 + rD/Y)} \tag{13}$$

Hence the tax rate depends on the government purchase ratio, the budget deficit ratio, the debt-output ration and the interest rate. Insert the production function (1) into (2) and simplify to get $r = \alpha A(H/K)^{\beta}$. Then insert the physical-human capital ratio given in (9) to obtain:

$$r = \alpha A \left(\frac{z(1+b-g)}{s(1+b-g) - b} \right)^{\beta} \tag{14}$$

According to (14), a boost in the deficit ratio drives up the interest rate. The underlying mechanism is that the budget deficit hinders physical capital accumulation, thus reducing the physical-human capital ratio and therefore raising the marginal product of physical capital. Moreover combine (12) and (14) to end up with the share of public interest in national income:

$$\frac{rD}{Y} = \frac{\alpha b}{[s(1+b-g) - b]} \tag{15}$$

Having laid this groundwork, we can try to find out the tax rate. Insert (15) into (13) and rearrange:

$$t = \frac{[s(1+b-g) - b]\,(g-b) + \alpha b}{s(1+b-g) - \beta b}$$

Interestingly the tax rate here is the same as in the AK model, see Chapter 2, Section 2.

4.2.2 Stability

The dynamics of the model can be represented by a system of three growth equations, for physical capital, for human capital and for public debt. First consider physical and human capital. The growth equations are:

$$\hat{K} = [s(1+b-g) - b)]\, A \left(\frac{H}{K} \right)^{\beta} \tag{16}$$

$$\hat{H} = z(1+b-g) A \left(\frac{K}{H} \right)^{\alpha} \tag{17}$$

Obviously physical and human capital growth, given in equation (16) and (17) respectively, are independent of public debt growth. In Figure 4.2 it is shown how physical and human capital growth depend on the physical-human capital ratio. In the steady state both types of capital grow at the same rate $\hat{K} = \hat{H}$. To the left of the steady state, physical capital grows faster than human capital. Hence, the physical-human capital ratio increases. To the right of the steady state, human capital grows faster than physical capital. Therefore the physical-human capital ratio declines. As a result, the steady state is stable.

Now consider public debt growth. The growth rate of debt is inversely related to the debt-output ratio. Public debt growth is constant if the debt-output ratio is constant. Hence, we have to consider the system of debt growth and output growth. Output growth is $\hat{Y} = \alpha\hat{K} + \beta\hat{H}$ and therefore the system can be represented by:

$$\hat{D} = \frac{bY}{D} \tag{18}$$

$$\hat{Y} = \alpha\left[s(1+b-g) - b)\right] A \left(\frac{H}{K}\right)^{\beta} + \beta z(1+b-g)A\left(\frac{K}{H}\right)^{\alpha} \tag{19}$$

In Figure 4.3 the $\hat{D}$ line represents equation (18) and the $\hat{Y}$ line represents equation (19). The steady state is at the intersection of the two lines. To the left of the steady state the debt-output ratio increases and to the right it

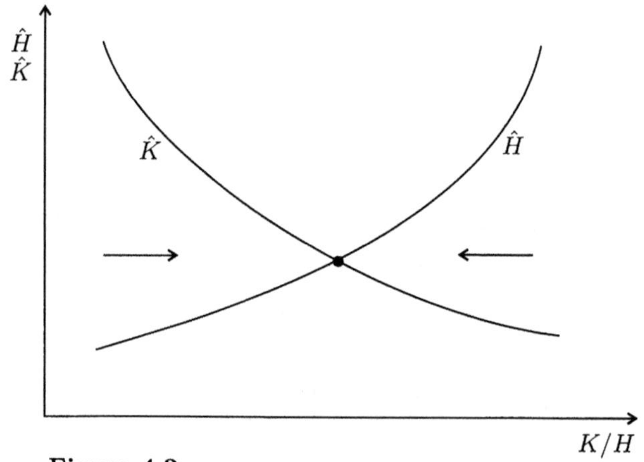

Figure 4.2.
Physical and Human Capital Growth

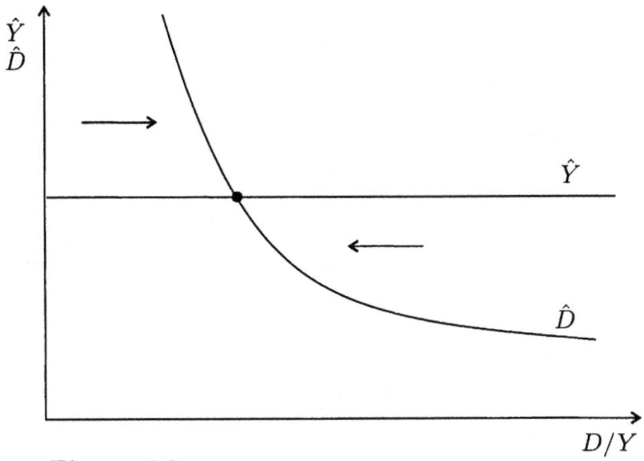

Figure 4.3.
Debt Growth and Output Growth

declines. Hence, the debt-output ratio converges to the steady state level. As a main result we may state:

Proposition 3. *The steady-state is stable.*

4.2.3 Some Shocks

Now we will consider the dynamics induced by some shocks. In particular we will consider

1) an increase in the deficit ratio ($b < b'$)
2) an increase in the deficit ratio ($b > b'$)
3) an increase in the government purchase ratio
4) an increase in the saving ratio
5) an increase in the education-spending ratio.

1) Increase in the deficit ratio ($b < b'$). In this situation there is a stable steady state. Before the increase in the deficit ratio, the economy is in the steady state. Physical and human capital grow at the same rate as output. The budget deficit and public debt grow at the same rate. Now the government increases the deficit ratio. First consider the dynamics of physical and human

capital. In Figure 4.4 the $\hat{K}$ line and the $\hat{H}$ line represent physical and human capital growth. Originally the economy is in the steady state marked as point 1. Due to the increase in the deficit ratio the $\hat{K}$ line moves downwards and the $\hat{H}$ line moves to the right. In the short run, physical capital growth declines and human capital growth increases, see points 2. Therefore, in the medium run, the physical-human capital ratio declines. This increases physical capital growth and reduces human capital growth. In the long run both converge to the same constant level, so the physical-human capital ratio is constant, see point 3. Figure 4.5 presents the time paths of physical and human capital growth.

Next consider output growth. Output growth depends on physical and human capital growth. In the short run, physical capital growth declines and human capital growth increases. Insert (16) and (18) into $\hat{Y} = \alpha\hat{K} + \beta\hat{H}$ to obtain:

$$\hat{Y} = \alpha\left[s(1+b-g)-b\right]A\left(\frac{K}{H}\right)^{-\beta} + \beta z(1+b-g)A\left(\frac{K}{H}\right)^{\alpha}$$

In the short run, the physical-human capital ratio is given and therefore we obtain:

$$\frac{d\hat{Y}}{db} = A\left(\frac{K}{H}\right)^{-\beta}\alpha(s-1) + A\left(\frac{K}{H}\right)^{\alpha}\beta z < 0$$

Insert the given physical-human capital ratio

$$\frac{K}{H} = \frac{s(1+b_0-g)-b_0}{z(1+b_0-g)}$$

with b_0 being the deficit ratio before the shock to obtain:

$$\frac{d\hat{Y}}{db} < 0 \quad \text{if} \quad \frac{s}{(1-s)} - \frac{b}{(1-s)(1+b-g)} < \frac{\alpha}{1-\alpha}$$

Empirically the saving ratio s is well below the capital elasticity α. Therefore, empirically, we have $s/(1-s) < \alpha/\beta$. So the short-run effect of an increase in the deficit ratio on output growth is likely to be negative.

Now consider the medium run dynamics. During the adjustment the physical-human capital ratio is declining monotonically. So we have to consider:

$$\frac{d\hat{Y}}{d(K/H)} = -\alpha\beta \left[s(1+b-g) - b) \right] A \left(\frac{K}{H} \right)^{-(1+\beta)} + \alpha\beta z(1+b-g) A \left(\frac{K}{H} \right)^{\alpha-1}$$

We obtain

$$\frac{d\hat{Y}}{d(K/H)} > 0 \quad \text{if} \quad \frac{K}{H} > \frac{s(1+b-g)-b}{z(1+b-g)}$$

The right hand side of the condition gives the ratio K/H in the new steady state. During transition K/H declines monotonically. So during transition we have $K/H > [s(1+b-g)-b]/z(1+b-g)$ and $d\hat{Y}/d(K/H) > 0$. And due to $d(K/H) < 0$ we have $d\hat{Y}/du < 0$. Figure 4.6 shows the time path of output growth.

Now we turn to the dynamics of the budget deficit and public debt. In the short run, the increase in the budget deficit leads to an increase in public debt growth. Then, in the medium run, output growth declines. This reduces budget deficit growth, which, in turn, reduces public debt growth. Finally public debt growth converges to output growth. Figure 4.7 shows the time path of public debt growth.

At the beginning there is a deficit ratio of $b = 0.01$. The budget deficit and public debt, as well as physical and human capital and output, grow at a rate of 1.95%. The government then increases the deficit ratio to $b = 0.02$. In the short run, physical capital growth declines to 1.70%. Human capital growth increases to 1.97%. Output growth, which depends on physical and human capital growth, declines to 1.89%. Public debt growth increases to 3.85%. The budget deficit grows at the same rate as output. In the medium run, this leads to a decline in debt growth. In the long run, public debt growth, physical capital growth, human capital growth and output growth converge. In the new steady state, they all grow at the rate of 1.88%.

2) Increase in the deficit ratio ($b > b'$). At the beginning the deficit ratio is below the critical level and the economy is in the steady state. Physical and human capital grow at the same constant rate. Output, the budget deficit and public debt grow at this rate as well. Then the government increases the

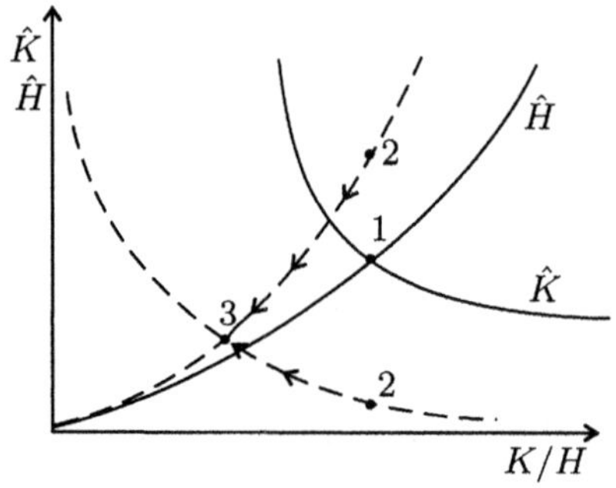

Figure 4.4.
Increase in Deficit Ratio

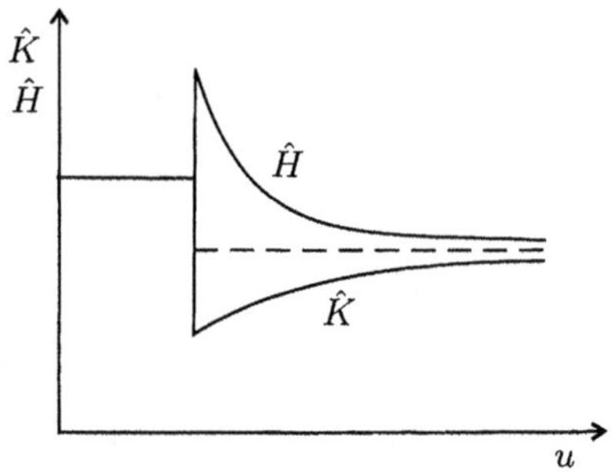

Figure 4.5.
Physical Capital Growth and Human Capital Growth

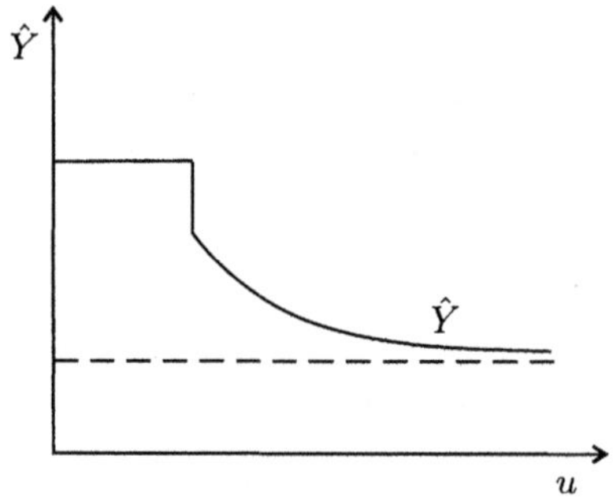

Figure 4.6.
Output Growth

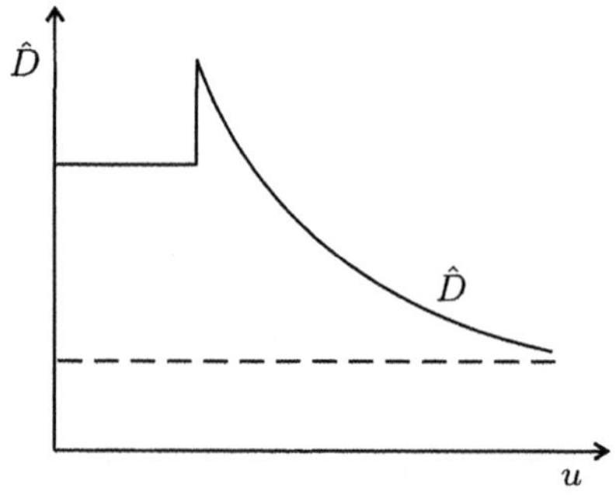

Figure 4.7.
Debt Growth

deficit ratio beyond the critical level b'. The growth diagram with physical and human capital is presented in Figure 4.8. The $\hat{K}$ line moves into the negative region, and the $\hat{H}$ line moves upwards. Hence, in the short run, physical capital growth becomes negative and human capital growth increases. As a consequence, output growth declines. Due to the increase in the deficit ratio, public debt growth increases.

In the medium run, the physical-human capital ratio increases. Reduced output growth leads to reduced savings and educational spending growth. Hence, human capital growth and physical capital growth decline. Therefore, output growth declines further and becomes negative at some point of time. Due to reduced output growth, budget deficit growth declines. Therefore, public debt growth declines as well. Over time, human capital growth and public debt growth converge to zero. However, physical capital growth and output growth are negative and decline continuously. As a result, physical capital and output are driven to zero in finite time. Figure 4.9 presents some time paths.

3) Increase in the government purchase ratio. Before the shock the economy is in the steady state. Then the government increases the purchase ratio. With a given budget deficit ratio this requires an increase in the tax rate. This reduces disposable income and therefore savings and educational spending decline. In the growth diagram, both, the $\hat{K}$ line and the $\hat{H}$ line move downwards, see Figure 4.10. In the short run, there is a decline in human capital growth and an even stronger decline in physical capital growth. In the medium run, human capital growth declines further while physical capital growth recovers. In the long run, physical capital, human capital and output grow at the same constant rate. The new steady state is at a higher physical-human capital ratio and at a lower growth rate than the original steady state. See Figure 4.11 for the time paths of human and physical capital growth.

Now we have a look at public debt. In the short run, the increase in the purchase ratio has no effect on the budget deficit. Therefore public debt growth does not change. However due to lower output growth, budget deficit growth is reduced. In the medium run, this reduces public debt growth. In the long run, public debt growth converges to output growth.

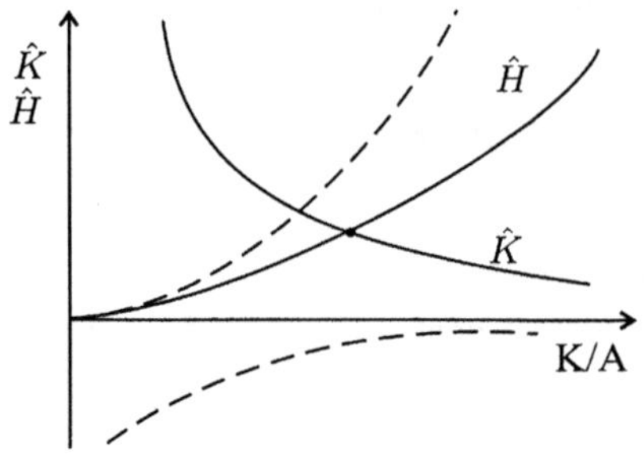

Figure 4.8.
Increase in Deficit Ratio
$(b > b')$

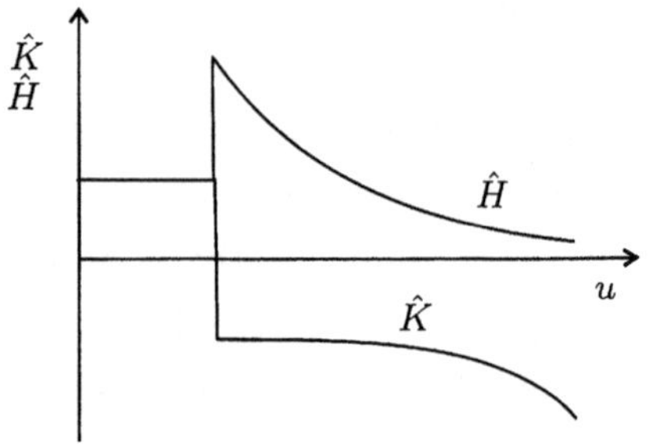

Figure 4.9.
Physical Capital Growth and Human Capital Growth

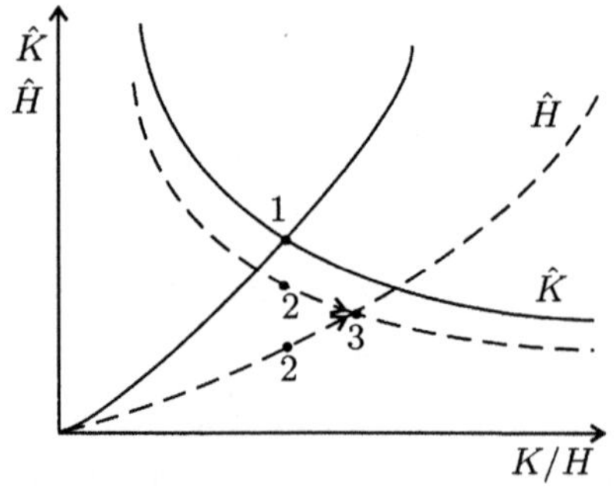

Figure 4.10.
Increase in Purchase Ratio

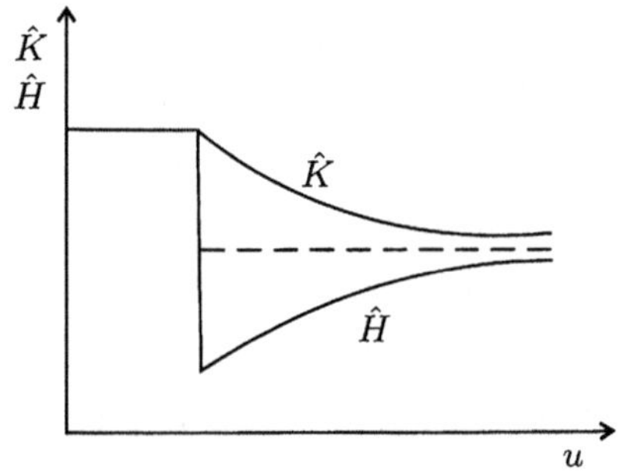

Figure 4.11.
Physical Capital Growth and Human Capital Growth

4) Increase in the saving ratio. Before the shock, the economy is in the steady state. Then the saving ratio rises. In the growth diagram the $\hat{K}$ line moves upwards and the $\hat{H}$ line is not affected, see Figure 4.12. In the short run, physical capital growth increases while human capital growth remains constant. Due to higher physical capital growth, output growth increases. In the medium run, higher output growth leads to higher education spending growth and therefore human capital growth increases gradually. In the long run, physical and human capital as well as output grow at the same constant rate.

Now look at public debt growth. In the short run, public debt growth is not affected. However, when output growth goes up, budget deficit growth also increases. This induces higher debt growth. In the long run, the budget deficit and public debt grow at the same rate as output. The debt-output ratio is constant. Compared to the steady state before the shock, public debt growth has increased and the debt-output ratio has decreased.

5) Increase in the education-spending ratio. Before the shock the economy is in the steady state. Then the education-spending ratio rises. In the growth diagram the $\hat{H}$ line moves upwards and the $\hat{K}$ line is not affected, see Figure 4.13. In the short run, human capital growth increases while physical capital growth remains constant. Due to higher human capital growth, output growth goes up. In the medium run, higher output growth leads to higher saving growth and therefore physical capital growth increases gradually. In the long run, physical and human capital as well as output grow at the same constant rate.

In the short run, public debt growth is not affected. However, when output growth goes up, budget deficit growth also increases. This induces higher debt growth. In the long run, the budget deficit and public debt grow at the same rate as output. The debt-output ratio is constant. Compared to the steady state before the shock, public debt growth has increased and the debt-output ratio has decreased.

4.2.4 Summary

As a result, physical capital growth, human capital growth and output growth depend on the deficit ratio and on the physical-human capital ratio. Public

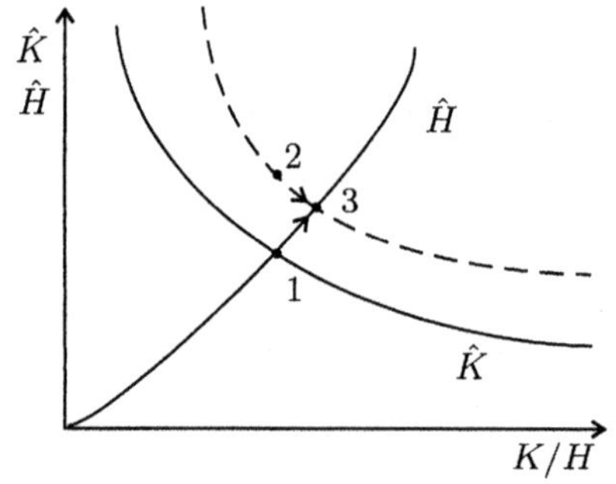

Figure 4.12.
Increase in Saving Ratio

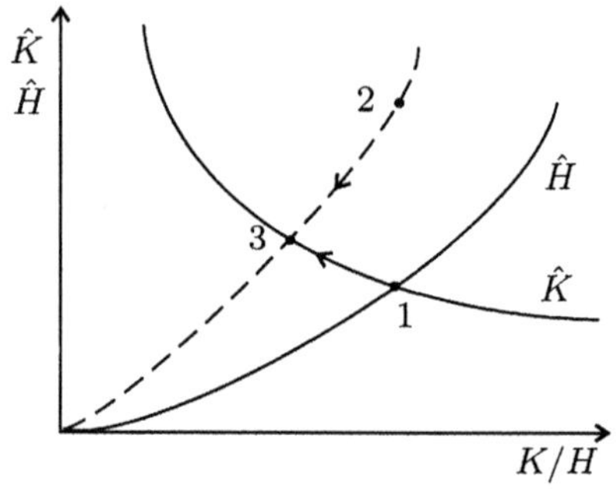

Figure 4.13.
Increase in
Education Spending-Ratio

debt growth depends on the deficit ratio and on the debt-output ratio. In the steady state all growth rates are constant and equal, so the physical-human capital ratio and the debt-output ratio are also constant. There is a critical deficit ratio. First assume that the deficit ratio is below the critical level. In this case, there is a stable steady state. An increase in the deficit ratio reduces the steady state growth rate. Now assume that the deficit ratio is increased above the critical level. In this case there is no steady state. In the short run, physical capital growth becomes negative. After some time output growth becomes negative. Both physical capital growth and output growth decline continuously and therefore physical capital and output are driven down to zero in finite time.

4.3 Fixing the Tax Rate

4.3.1 The Model

Firms produce a single commodity Y by means of physical and human capital. The production function is of the Cobb-Douglas type $Y = AK^{\alpha}H^{\beta}$, with $\alpha > 0, \beta > 0$ and $\alpha + \beta = 1$. Output Y is used for consumption, investment, government purchases and spending on education $Y = C + I + G + Z$. Firms maximize profits under perfect competition. Therefore, the interest rate agrees to the marginal product of capital $r = \alpha Y/K$ and the wage of a worker is $w = \beta Y/N$.

Let us look at budget dynamics. The government spends a constant proportion of national income on goods and services $G = gY$ with the purchase ratio $g = const.$ Additionally, the government imposes a proportionate tax on both factor income and debt income $T = t(Y + rD)$ with the tax rate $t = const.$ Government purchases plus public interest minus tax earnings correspond to the budget deficit $B = G + rD - T$. The budget deficit in turn adds to public debt $\dot{D} = B$. From this we obtain $\dot{D} = gY + rD - t(Y + rD)$.

The next point refers to investment and education dynamics. Disposable income is the sum of the after-tax factor and debt income $Y_d = (1-t)(Y+rD)$. Households save a constant proportion of disposable income $S = sY_d$ with the saving ratio $s = const.$ Savings finance public borrowing and investment $S = I + B$. Investment augments physical capital $\dot{K} = I$. Insert $I = S - B$ and use the behavioural functions to obtain $\dot{K} = s(1 - t)(Y + rD) - B$. Now insert $\dot{D} = B$ to establish $\dot{D} + \dot{K} = s(1 - t)(Y + rD)$. Households spend a fixed proportion of their disposable income on education $Z = zY_d$, with the education-spending ratio $z = const.$ Human capital is augmented by spending on education $\dot{H} = Z$. By backward substitution one obtains $\dot{H} = z(1 - t)(Y + rD)$.

On this foundation, the model can be characterized by a system of five equations:

$$Y = AK^\alpha H^\beta \tag{1}$$

$$r = \alpha Y/K \tag{2}$$

$$\dot{D} + \dot{K} = s(1 - t)(Y + rD) \tag{3}$$

$$\dot{H} = z(1 - t)(Y + rD) \tag{4}$$

$$\dot{D} = gY + rD - t(Y + rD) \tag{5}$$

Here $\alpha, \beta, g, s, t, z, A, D, H$, and K are exogenous, whereas r, $\dot{D}$,$\dot{H}$, $\dot{K}$, and Y are endogenous.

Now it is useful to analyse growth rates. Insert (2) and (5) into (3) and divide by capital K to obtain the growth rate of capital. Then insert (2) into

(4) divide by human capital H and rearrange to obtain human capital growth. Finally insert (2) into (5), divide by debt D and rearrange to obtain public debt growth:

$$\hat{K} = \left[s(1-t) - (g-t) - (1-s)(1-t)\alpha\frac{D}{K}\right]\frac{Y}{K} \tag{6}$$

$$\hat{H} = z(1-t)\left[1 + \alpha\frac{D}{K}\right]\frac{Y}{H} \tag{7}$$

$$\hat{D} = \left[(g-t)\frac{K}{D} + (1-t)\alpha\right]\frac{Y}{K} \tag{8}$$

Physical capital growth depends on the physical capital-output ratio and on the public debt-physical capital ratio. Human capital growth depends on the human capital-output ratio and on the public debt-human capital ratio. Public debt growth depends on the debt-output ratio and on the physical capital-output ratio. Physical capital growth, human capital growth and public debt growth are constant if these ratios are constant. The ratios are constant if growth rates are the same. Hence, in the steady state, physical capital, human capital, output and public debt have to grow at the same rate. The rest of this subsection will concentrate on the question of whether a steady state exists.

First consider physical capital growth and public debt growth. For notational simplicity we define the primary deficit ratio $h = g - t$ and the debt-physical capital ratio $x = D/K$. Insert these definitions into (6) and (8) and equate the two growth rates to achieve:

$$(s(1-t) - h) - (1-s)(1-t)\alpha x = h/x + (1-t)\alpha \tag{9}$$

The quadratic equation here is identical to the one obtained in the AK model, see Chapter 2, Section 3. Hence, as in the AK model there are two solutions for the debt-output ratio x if and only if:

$$s > \alpha \quad \text{and} \quad h \leq h_1 \tag{10}$$

As a result we state:

Proposition 1. *A steady-state debt-physical capital ratio does exist if and only if the saving ratio exceeds the capital elasticity and the primary deficit ratio stays below the critical level. If either of the two conditions is not fulfilled, then there is no steady state.*

Proof. See Chapter 2, Section 3. ∎

Now consider the dynamics of physical and human capital growth. Equate the two growth rates given in (6) and (8) to obtain:

$$\left[s(1-t)-(g-t)-(1-s)(1-t)\alpha\frac{D}{K}\right]\frac{Y}{K}=z(1-t)\left[1+\alpha\frac{D}{K}\right]\frac{Y}{H}$$

Now insert $h = g - t$, $x = D/K$ and $Y = AK^{\alpha}H^{\beta}$ to arrive at:

$$[s(1-t)-h-(1-s)(1-t)\alpha x]\,A\left(\frac{H}{K}\right)^{\beta}=z(1-t)\,[1+\alpha x]\,A\left(\frac{K}{H}\right)^{\alpha}$$

Rearrange to obtain the physical-human capital ratio in the steady state:

$$\frac{K}{H}=\frac{s(1-t)-h-(1-s)(1-t)\alpha x}{z(1-t)(1+\alpha x)} \tag{11}$$

The physical-human capital ratio depends on the public debt-physical capital ratio x. Hence if x does not stay constant, then the ratio K/H does not stay constant. Hence a steady state in the physical-human capital ratio requires a steady state in x. Given that the conditions in (10) are satisfied, there is a solution for x. In this case the denominator in (11) is positive. The numerator is always positive and so there is a constant positive physical-human capital ratio. We summarize the result:

Proposition 2. *If there is a steady-state debt-physical capital ratio, then there is also a steady-state physical-human capital ratio. If there is no steady-state debt-physical capital ratio then there is no steady-state physical-human capital ratio. The main result is that normally a steady state does not exist.*

4.3.2 A Tax Cut

In the following we will analyse the process of adjustment induced by a tax cut. We will assume that the saving ratio is below the capital elasticity $s < \alpha$, which is the empirically relevant case. Hence there will be no steady state.

At the beginning there is no public debt and the tax rate equals the government purchase ratio $t = g$, so the budget is balanced. The economy is in the steady state. Physical capital, human capital and output grow at the same

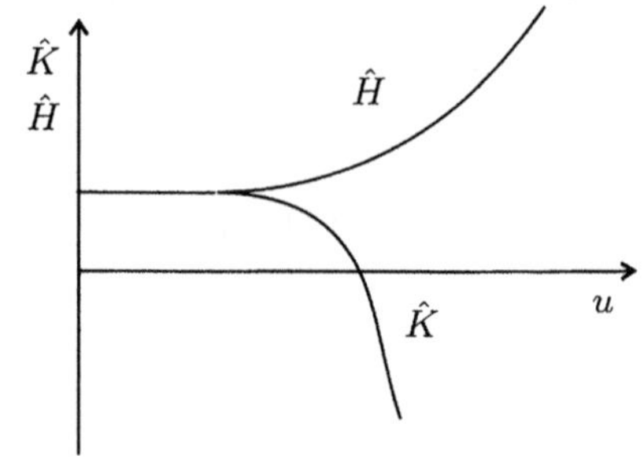

Figure 4.14.
Physical Capital Growth and
Human Capital Growth

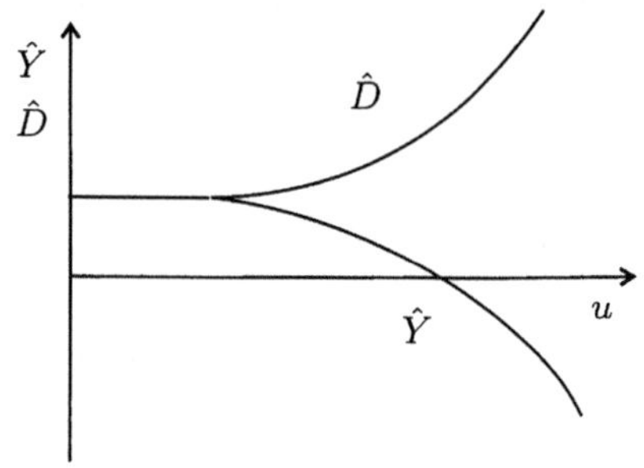

Figure 4.15.
Output Growth and
Public Debt Growth

constant rate. Then the government reduces the tax rate. As a consequence there is a budget deficit. Public debt comes into existence and begins to grow. The government has to pay interest on public debt. Since the tax rate is kept constant, the government has to increase the budget deficit to finance interest payment on public debt. Hence the budget deficit increases over time. This accelerates public debt growth.

In each point of time the budget deficit crowds out investment and therefore reduces physical capital growth. Reduced physical capital growth reduces output growth and drives up the interest rate. Reduced output growth leads to reduced saving and education spending growth. Reduced saving growth leads to lower physical capital growth and reduced education spending growth leads to reduced human capital growth. Therefore output growth declines even further. The interest rate goes up, due to reduced physical capital growth. The rising interest rate reinforces the process of rising budget deficits and accelerating public debt growth. Public debt growth increases over time. Physical capital growth and output growth decline, become negative at some point of time, and decline even further. Therefore physical capital is driven down to zero in finite time. Hence, the economy collapses. Figures 4.14 and 4.15 illustrate the time paths of growth rates.

Table 4.2. The Dynamic Effects of a Tax Cut

u	D	Y	K	H	$\hat{Y}$	$\hat{K}$	$\hat{H}$	$\hat{D}$
0	0	25	100	100	0.02	0.02	0.02	
1	2.3	25.5	101.5	102.1	0.0189	0.0150	0.0206	
2	5.3	25.9	102.9	104.2	0.0185	0.0136	0.0207	0.8331
3	9.1	26.4	104.1	106.4	0.0181	0.0118	0.0208	0.5507
4	14.2	26.9	105.1	108.7	0.0176	0.0096	0.021	0.4385
5	20.7	27.3	105.8	111.0	0.0169	0.0066	0.0213	0.38
6	29.3	27.8	106.1	113.4	0.0159	0.0027	0.0216	0.3458
7	40.5	28.2	105.8	115.9	0.0146	−0.0027	0.0221	0.3251
8	55.4	28.6	104.7	118.6	0.0127	−0.0103	0.0225	0.3132
9	75.4	28.9	102.5	121.4	0.0100	−0.0212	0.0233	0.308
10	102.7	29.0	98.7	124.4	0.0057	−0.0380	0.0244	0.309
11	141.0	28.9	92.4	127.6	−0.0016	−0.0661	0.026	0.3174
12	197.6	28.5	82.0	131.4	−0.0156	−0.1200	0.0287	0.3375
13	290.1	27.0	63.4	135.9	−0.0533	−0.2570	0.034	0.3838
14	528.9	16.9	11.6	143.8	−0.470	−1.6980	0.0567	0.6006
15		0	0					

Table 4.2 presents a numerical example for the dynamics induced by a tax cut. The assumed parameters are $\alpha = 0.3, \beta = 0.7, g = 0.2, s = 0.1$, $z = 0.1$ and $A = 0.25$. At the beginning the tax is given as $t = g = 0.2$. Then the tax is reduced to $t = 0.18$.

4.3.3 Summary

Starting from a balanced budget, a tax cut leads to a budget deficit. Public debt comes into existence and begins to grow. Public debt growth converges to a constant level. Physical capital growth and output growth decline continuously, become negative at some point of time and decline further. Physical capital and output decline to zero in finite time. There is an exception. If the saving ratio is very large a very small primary deficit can be sustained. In this case there is a steady state, in which physical capital, human capital, output, and public debt grow at the same rate.

5

The Romer Model

5.1 Introduction

In this chapter we analyse a model where economic growth is driven by endogenous technical progress. The production structure is of the type introduced in Romer (1987) and Romer (1990). Economic growth is driven by technical progress which comes from the development of new intermediate products. Intermediate products are developed in a research sector. Incentives for research are given by patents which guarantee profits for the development of new intermediate products. We will assume a constant saving ratio as in Bräuninger (2001). We will analyse how public debt impinges on the research activity and on economic growth. As in the other chapters, we first consider the fixed deficit ratio and then we turn to the fixed tax rate.

5.2 Fixing the Deficit Ratio

5.2.1 The Model

Production

First have a look at production. Production takes place in three sectors. The first sector uses labour and intermediate products to produce a homogenous final product. The second sector uses capital to produce intermediate products. And the third sector uses labour to invent new intermediate products. New intermediate products allow for a higher specialization in the production of the final product and therefore increase the efficiency in the first sector. Labour supply is given and normalized to 1. The wage is flexible and therefore there is full employment. Since labour can be used for research as well as for the production of the final product, the first and the third sector have to compete for workers. Let employment in the final product sector be L and employment in the research sector be $N = 1 - L$. An increase of employment in the first sector leads to higher output but to less research and to lower growth. So an important aspect of the model is to derive the proportion of workers employed in the two sectors.

Now we consider the sectors in more detail. In the first sector, firms use labour L and A intermediate products M_i to produce the final product Y. Following Ethier (1982) it is assumed that the production function is additive separable in intermediate products. Hence, intermediate products are neither perfect substitutes nor complements. In reality this need not be the case: new intermediate products could reduce or increase the productivity of existing intermediate products. Here we assume the average case, in which the productivity of each intermediate product is independent of all other intermediate products. At each point of time, the intermediate product number A is given. The production function is:

$$Y = L^{\beta} \sum_{i=1}^{A} M_i^{\alpha} \qquad \alpha + \beta = 1, \alpha, \beta > 0 \tag{1}$$

In the following we will show that each of the A intermediate products is used to the same amount M. So the production function might be written as $Y = AL^{\beta}M^{\alpha}$. Technical progress takes the form of new intermediate product inventions. Hence A increases and therefore the final product output goes up.

Let the price of Y be normalized to 1. Then profits are $\Pi = Y - wL - \Sigma_{i=1}^{A} P_i M_i$. Firms adjust labour and intermediate product input to equate the marginal product of labour to the wage w and the marginal product of an intermediate product to its price P_i. Hence, we have:

$$\frac{\partial Y}{\partial L} = \frac{\beta Y}{L} = w \qquad \text{and} \qquad \frac{\partial Y}{\partial M_i} = \alpha L^{\beta} M_i^{-\beta} = P_i \tag{2}$$

Intermediate products are produced by firms in the second sector. In this sector each firm buys one patent, which allows the production of one intermediate product. So the number of firms corresponds to the number of intermediate products. For simplicity we assume that intermediate products are produced solely by capital with a linear technology. Hence the production function is simply $M_i = K_i$. Profits Π_i are the difference between revenue and costs for capital and patents. Each patent has the price P_P and has an infinite lifetime. Firms finance the patent by credit on which they have to pay the interest rate r. Hence the costs of production are given by interest payments. The price of a patent might increase. Let $\dot{P}_P$ be the change in the patent price, then profits are $\Pi_i = \dot{P}_P + P_i M_i - rK_i - rP_P$. Each firm has one patent for one intermediate product and intermediate products are imperfect substitutes in the production of the final product. As a consequence, there is monopolistic competition in the intermediate product market. Each intermediate product demand function is given by its marginal product in final output production. Substitute the demand function (2) for the price to obtain:

$$\Pi_i = \dot{P}_P + \alpha L^\beta K_i^\alpha - rK_i - rP_P \tag{3}$$

Profit maximization leads to $\partial \Pi_i / \partial K_i = \alpha^2 L^\beta K_i^{\alpha-1} = r$. The interest rate is given for each of the A firms. However, for the economy we have a given capital stock and the interest rate adjusts to equate the demand for capital to the given stock of capital K. The A firms differ with respect to the intermediate product they use. All intermediate products are produced with the same technology. In addition, the demand functions for all A intermediate products are identical. Hence, optimal capital demand for all firms is the same and we have $K_i = K/A$. As a consequence, the interest rate is:

$$r = \alpha^2 L^\beta \left(\frac{K}{A}\right)^{\alpha-1} \tag{4}$$

Since all firms use the same amount of capital all intermediate products are produced to the same amount $M = M_i = K/A$ and therefore, all intermediate products have the same price. From (2) and (4) we obtain $P_i = r/\alpha$. With perfect competition the price would correspond to the marginal product r. Hence, due to monopolistic competition there is a higher price.

Finally we have to determine the price for a patent P_P. Naturally a patent can only be sold to a single firm. So firms in the intermediate product sector compete for patents. New firms will enter the market until the present value of future profits corresponds to the price of a patent. To obtain the present value of future profits we have to integrate (3) into the future. We assume static expectations which means $\dot{P}_P = 0$ and therefore the present value of future profits is $\Pi_{i,B} = \alpha L^\beta K_i^\alpha - rK_i - rP_P$. Now insert (4) for the interest rate and $K_i = K/A$. Then use the condition $\Pi_{i,B} = 0$ to solve for:

$$P_P = \frac{\beta}{\alpha}\frac{K}{A} \tag{5}$$

Here K/A is capital per intermediate product M, which gives intermediate product output. When intermediate product output increases, revenue obtained from the intermediate product will also increase. Therefore, the price for the patent necessary to produce the intermediate product increases.

The third sector is the research sector. Here N workers are used to develop new intermediate products. The output is the number of newly invented intermediate products $\dot{A}$. We assume that the productivity of labour depends on a constant λ and on the already existing product number A. Therefore the number of new inventions is:

$$\dot{A} = \lambda AN \tag{6}$$

Revenue of the sector is given by $P_P\dot{A}$ and the costs are wN, so profits are $\Pi_A = P_P\dot{A} - wN$. Profit maximization gives:

$$P_P\lambda A = w \tag{7}$$

Insert (5) to obtain the wage in the research sector. The number of workers is constant and normalized to 1. Workers are completely mobile between sectors and therefore the wage will equalize across sectors. Equate the wage in the final product sector given in (2) with the wage in the research sector given in (7) to obtain the proportion of workers in the final product sector:

$$L = \frac{\alpha Y}{\lambda K} \tag{8}$$

The proportion of workers in the final product sector L and the proportion of workers in the research sector $N = 1 - L$ depend on the endogenous ratio between final product output Y and capital K, and on the productivity parameters α and λ. Given the ratio Y/K, an increase in α implies a higher productivity of intermediate products. As a consequence, the demand for intermediate products increases and therefore the price goes up. This leads to a higher interest rate and the price of a patent declines. Therefore the wage of workers in the research sector declines. Due to the wage differential some workers will move into the final product sector, which equalizes the wage.

An increase in λ implies higher labour productivity in the research sector and therefore increases the wage in this sector. Labour mobility then leads to wage equalization. Finally notice that there is a critical capital-output ratio. When $K/Y \leq \alpha/\lambda$ then $L = 1$. This means, if the capital-output ratio falls below the critical level, then all labour is used for the final output production and no labour is used for research. In this case $\dot{A} = 0$, which means that there are no inventions.

Income and Wealth Dynamics

First we have a look at gross income. Output in the final product sector is Y. The wage income of workers in the final product sector is $wL = \beta Y$. Payments to the intermediate product sector are $\Sigma_{i=1}^{A} P_i M_i = \alpha Y$. Firms in the intermediate product sector pay the interest rate r on credits which are used to finance expenditures for capital and patents $rK + rP_P A$. Insert (4) and (5) to obtain $rK + rP_P A = \alpha Y$. At each point of time, the intermediate product sector takes up new credits to finance new capital and new patents. Expenditures for new patents $P_P \dot{A}$ go to the research sector. In the research sector, wages are $wN = P_P \dot{A}$. Households receive wage and interest income, so national income is $Y + P_P \dot{A}$.

Now let us consider the government budget. The government raises loans and it levies an income tax in order to finance government purchases and interest payments on public debt. It spends a fixed share of national income on goods and services $G = g(Y + P_P \dot{A})$ with the purchase ratio $g = const.$ Besides this, the government borrows a fixed proportion of income $B = b(Y + P_P \dot{A})$ with the deficit ratio $b = const.$ The budget deficit augments public debt $\dot{D} = B$. The government pays the interest rate r on public debt D, so interest on public debt amounts to rD. It also imposes a tax at the flat rate t on both factor income and debt income so tax revenue is $T = t(Y + P_P \dot{A} + rD)$. The government budget constraint can be written as $B + T = G + rD$. By using the behavioural functions, this identity can be reformulated in the following way $b(Y + P_P\dot{A}) + t(Y + P_P\dot{A} + rD) = g(Y + P_P\dot{A}) + rD$. Here, the purchase ratio and the deficit ratio are given, whereas the tax rate has to be adjusted.

Next we have a look at disposable income. Disposable income is the sum of factor income and debt income, net of taxes $Y_d = Y + P_P\dot{A} + rD - T$. Households save a constant fraction of their disposable income $S = sY_d$ with the saving ratio $s = const$. Household savings are partly absorbed by public borrowing. The rest is used as credits to firms. These are used to finance investment and expenditures for patents $I + P_P\dot{A} = S - B$. Investment augments capital $\dot{K} = I$. By using the savings function one obtains $\dot{K} + P_P\dot{A} = s(Y + P_P\dot{A} + rD - T) - B$. Further note $B + T = G + rD, B = b(Y + P_P\dot{A})$ and $G = g(Y + P_P\dot{A})$ to reach $\dot{K} + P_P\dot{A} = (1 + b - g)s(Y + P_P\dot{A}) - b(Y + P_P\dot{A})$.

The Growth Model

Summarizing the above, the model can be represented by a system of nine equations:

$$\dot{A} = \lambda A(1 - L) \tag{9}$$

$$Y = AM^{\alpha}L^{\beta} \tag{10}$$

$$r = \alpha^2 L^{\beta} M^{\alpha-1} \tag{11}$$

$$M = K/A \tag{12}$$

$$L = \frac{\alpha Y}{\lambda K} \tag{13}$$

$$P_P = \beta M/\alpha \tag{14}$$

$$b(Y + P_P\dot{A}) + t(Y + P_P\dot{A} + rD) = g(Y + P_P\dot{A}) + rD \tag{15}$$

$$\dot{D} = b(Y + P_P\dot{A}) \tag{16}$$

$$\dot{K} + P_P\dot{A} = [s(1 + b - g) - b](Y + P_P\dot{A}) \tag{17}$$

Here $\alpha, \beta, \lambda, b, g, s, A, D,$ and K are exogenous, while $r, t, \dot{A}, \dot{D}, \dot{K}, L, P_P, M$ and Y are endogenous.

Now it is useful to consider growth rates. At first insert (13) into (9) and divide by A to obtain intermediate product number growth:

$$\hat{A} = \lambda - \frac{\alpha Y}{K} \tag{18}$$

As a result, intermediate product number growth depends on the productivity parameters and on the capital-output ratio. There is a critical capital-output ratio. If the capital-output ratio becomes very small, i.e. $K/Y = \alpha/\lambda$, then all labour is used in the final product sector $L = 1$ and no labour is used in research $N = 0$. As a consequence, there are no new intermediate products and we have $\dot{A} = \hat{A} = 0$. Obviously in this case the model is different to the one presented here. For the moment we assume that the capital-output ratio is below the critical level. However, the capital-output ratio is endogenous and therefore we will derive the conditions for $K/Y > \alpha/\lambda$ later on.

Now consider capital growth. Insert (14) and (9) into (17), replace L with the help of (13), rearrange and divide by K to reach:

$$\hat{K} = [\beta + \alpha s(1 + b - g) - \alpha b]\frac{Y}{K} - [1 - s(1 + b - g) + b]\frac{\beta\lambda}{\alpha} \tag{19}$$

As a result, capital growth depends on the productivity parameters, the saving ratio, the government purchase ratio, the deficit ratio, and on the capital-output ratio.

Next have a look at public debt growth. Insert (14) and (9) into (16), replace L with the help of (13), divide by D and rearrange:

$$\hat{D} = b\left(\frac{\alpha Y}{D} + \frac{\beta\lambda K}{\alpha D}\right) \tag{20}$$

As a result, public debt growth depends on the deficit ratio, on the debt-capital ratio, and on the debt-output ratio.

Steady State

In the steady state, growth rates stay constant. This requires a constant capital-output ratio, a constant debt-capital ratio and a constant debt-output ratio. Notice that a constant capital-output ratio implies $\hat{Y} = \hat{K}$ and therefore, according to (13), a constant distribution of employment across sectors $\hat{L} = \hat{Y} - \hat{K} = 0$. Take the growth rate from the production function $Y = AM^\alpha L^\beta$ and notice $\hat{L} = 0$ to obtain $\hat{Y} = \hat{A} + \alpha\hat{M}$. From (12) we have $\hat{M} = \hat{K} - \hat{A}$. Insert this into $\hat{Y} = \hat{A} + \alpha\hat{M}$ and take account of $\hat{Y} = \hat{K}$

to obtain $\hat{Y} = \hat{A}$. As a result, in the steady state, capital, the intermediate product number, and final output grow at the same constant rate. Now use the condition $\hat{K} = \hat{A}$, equate (18) and (19), and solve for the capital-output ratio:

$$\frac{K}{Y} = \frac{\alpha\,(1 + \alpha s(1 + b - g) - \alpha b)}{\lambda\,(1 - \beta s(1 + b - g) + \beta b)} \tag{21}$$

Analysis of (21) shows:

Proposition 1. *There is a critical deficit ratio b'. If the deficit ratio exceeds the critical level, then the capital-output ratio falls below α/λ. In this case all labour is used in the final product sector ($L = 1$) and there is no research ($N = 0$).*

Proof. When b exceeds $b' = (1 - g)s/(1 - s)$ we obtain $K/Y = \alpha/\lambda$ and equation (13) gives $L = \alpha Y/(\lambda K) = 1$. ∎

Interestingly the critical level b' here corresponds to the critical level in the AK model and in the human capital model. Now assume that the deficit ratio stays below the critical level $b < b'$. Insert (21) into (18) or (19) to obtain the steady state growth rate:

$$\hat{Y} = \hat{K} = \hat{A} = \frac{\lambda(s(1 + b - g) - b)}{1 + \alpha s(1 + b - g) - \alpha b} \tag{22}$$

Proposition 2. *There is a unique steady-state growth rate. The growth rate is positive due to $b < b'$. It depends on the productivity parameters, on the saving ratio, on the government purchase ratio and on the deficit ratio. An increase in research productivity λ leads to a rise in the growth rate, whereas an increase in intermediate product productivity α leads to a decline in the growth rate. An increase in the saving ratio s leads to a rise in the growth rate, whereas an increase in the government purchase ratio g or in the deficit ratio b leads to a decline in the growth rate.*

Proof. The effects of λ and α are obvious. The other relevant differentials are:

$$\frac{d\hat{Y}}{ds} = \frac{\lambda(1+b-g)}{(1+\alpha s(1+b-g)-\alpha b)^2} > 0$$
$$\frac{d\hat{Y}}{dg} = \frac{-\lambda s}{(1+\alpha s(1+b-g)-\alpha b)^2} < 0$$
$$\frac{d\hat{Y}}{db} = \frac{(s-1)\lambda}{(1+\alpha s(1+b-g)-\alpha b)^2} < 0$$

■

The positive effect of research productivity is very intuitive. An increase in λ means that, given the same research input, more new intermediate products are developed. This increases the growth rate. But why do the saving ratio, the government purchase ratio and the deficit ratio influence the growth rate? To find the causality have a look at employment in the final product sector. Insert the ratio K/Y from (21) into (13) to obtain:

$$L = \frac{1-\beta s(1+b-g)+\beta b}{1+\alpha s(1+b-g)-\alpha b} \tag{23}$$

An increase in the saving ratio leads to a decline in the proportion of individuals employed in the final product sector and therefore to higher employment in the research sector. An increase in the deficit ratio or in the government purchase ratio reduces the proportion of those employed in research. To find the reason for the reallocation of employment, we have to consider the patent price. As shown in (14), the price P_P depends on the ratio K/A. To obtain this ratio we first substitute for output in (21), then we use $M = K/A$, and finally we insert (23) and rearrange:

$$\frac{K}{A} = \left(\frac{\alpha}{\lambda}\right)^{1/\beta}\left(\frac{1+\alpha s(1+b-g)-\alpha b}{1-\beta s(1+b-g)+\beta b}\right)^{\alpha/\beta} \tag{24}$$

An increase in the saving ratio or a decline in the deficit ratio leads to higher capital per intermediate product and therefore intermediate product output increases. This implies that producers in the intermediate goods sector are willing to pay a higher price for a patent. Therefore employment in the research sector increases. Table 5.1 shows how the proportion of workers in the final product sector and the growth rate depend on the deficit ratio. The assumed parameters are $\alpha = 0.3, \beta = 0.7, \lambda = 0.25, g = 0.2$ and $s = 0.1$.

Table 5.1. The Long-Run Effects of the Budget Deficit

b	L	$\hat{Y}$
0	0.922	0.0195
0.02	0.939	0.0152
0.04	0.957	0.0109
0.06	0.974	0.0065
0.08	0.992	0.0019

Now we consider the case where the deficit ratio exceeds the critical level $b > b'$. In this case we have $L = 1, N = 0$ and therefore $\dot{A} = 0$. The equation for capital accumulation (17) changes to $\dot{K} = [s(1 + b - g) - b]Y$. Insert the production function (10), while noting $M = K/A$ and $L = 1$ to obtain:

$$\hat{K} = [s(1 + b - g) - b]A^{\beta}K^{-\beta}$$

Due to $b > b'$ we have $s(1+b-g)-b < 0$ and $\hat{K} < 0$. Hence capital growth is negative. And what is more, since capital growth depends inversely on capital, capital growth declines continuously. This means there is no steady state.

Next we have a look at public debt. First we assume that the deficit ratio stays below the critical level $b < b'$. According to (20) public debt growth depends on the debt-output ratio and on the debt-capital ratio. However, in the steady state, we have the capital-output ratio given in (21). This can be used to express debt growth in terms of the debt-capital ratio:

$$\hat{D} = b\lambda \left(\frac{(1 - \beta s(1 + b - g) + \beta b)}{(1 + \alpha s(1 + b - g) - \alpha b)} + \frac{\beta}{\alpha} \right) \frac{K}{D} \tag{25}$$

In the steady state, public debt and capital grow at the same rate, so the debt-capital ratio is constant. Equate (22) and (25) to obtain the debt-capital ratio in the steady state:

$$\frac{D}{K} = \frac{b}{\alpha(s(1 + b - g) - b)} \tag{26}$$

Due to $b < b'$ there is a positive debt-capital ratio. An increase in the deficit ratio leads to a decline in the debt-capital ratio.

Now assume $b > b'$. In this case capital and output decline continuously. Therefore the budget deficit declines. This reduces public debt growth. So public debt becomes constant, while capital and output are driven down to zero.

5.2.2 Stability

Assume that the deficit ratio is below the critical level. The dynamics of the model are then described by the three growth equations, for capital, for the intermediate product number and for public debt. First consider capital and the intermediate product number. The growth equations are given in (18) and (19). Both growth rates depend on the capital-output ratio. To obtain a closed system we need to replace output. Output is given by the production function $Y = AM^{\alpha}L^{\beta}$. Insert the proportion of workers in the final product sector $L = \alpha Y/(\lambda K)$ and solve for $Y = A^{1/\alpha}M\left(\alpha/(\lambda K)\right)^{\beta/\alpha}$. Next insert $M = K/A$, then divide by K to reach:

$$\frac{Y}{K} = \left(\frac{\lambda K}{\alpha A}\right)^{-\beta/\alpha}$$

Insert this into the two growth equations (18) and (19) to obtain:

$$\hat{A} = \lambda - \alpha\left(\frac{\lambda K}{\alpha A}\right)^{-\beta/\alpha} \tag{27}$$

$$\hat{K} = [\beta + \alpha s(1+b-g) - \alpha b]\left(\frac{\lambda K}{\alpha A}\right)^{-\beta/\alpha} - [1 - s(1+b-g) + b]\frac{\beta\lambda}{\alpha} \tag{28}$$

In equations (27) and (28) it is assumed that the ratio K/A ensures positive growth. If K/A falls below the critical level we obtain $\hat{A} = 0$. Due to $b < b'$ we have $\beta + \alpha s(1+b-g) - \alpha b$ and therefore capital growth is negatively related to the ratio K/A.

Figure 5.1 shows the two growth lines. At the intersection, the economy is in the steady state where we have $\hat{A} = \hat{K}$. Here the ratio of K to A is given in equation (24). To the left of the steady state, capital grows faster than the intermediate product number, so the ratio K/A increases. To the right of the steady state, the intermediate product number grows faster than capital, so the ratio K/A declines. As a result, we see, that the steady state is stable.

Public debt growth depends on the debt-output ratio and on the debt-capital ratio. Now we take advantage of the fact that, given $b < b'$, the steady state of capital and intermediate product number growth will always be reached. This implies that the steady state capital-output ratio will be reached. This allows us to analyse public debt growth under the assumption that the steady state capital-output ratio is already reached. Insert (21) into (20) to obtain:

$$\hat{D} = b\lambda \left(\frac{1 - \beta s(1 + b - g) + \beta b}{1 + \alpha s(1 + b - g) - \alpha b} + \frac{\beta}{\alpha} \right) \frac{K}{D} \tag{29}$$

Debt growth depends inversely on the debt-capital ratio. In contrast, capital growth is independent of the debt-capital ratio. Figure 5.2 shows the two growth rates.

At the intersection of the two lines, debt and capital grow at the same rate. Hence, the economy is in the steady state. To the left of the steady state, debt growth exceeds capital growth, so the debt-capital ratio is rising. To the right of the steady state, capital growth exceeds debt growth, so the debt-capital ratio is falling. As a consequence, the steady state is stable. Summarizing the above, we find that both ratios K/A and D/K converge and so we may state:

Proposition 3. *The steady state is stable.*

5.2.3 Some Shocks

In the current section we shall trace out the processes of adjustment induced by four macroeconomic shocks in greater detail:

1) an increase in the deficit ratio ($b < b'$)
2) an increase in the deficit ratio ($b > b'$)
3) an increase in the purchase ratio
4) an increase in research productivity.

1) Increase in the deficit ratio ($b < b'$). This situation is characterized by a stable steady state. Initially the economy rests in the steady state. The budget deficit and public debt grow at the same rate as the intermediate product number, capital, and output. Now the government increases the deficit ratio. First consider the dynamics of capital growth and intermediate product

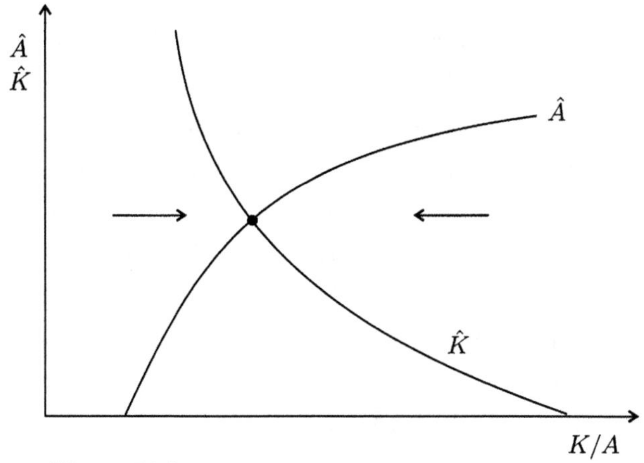

Figure 5.1.
Capital Growth and Intermediate Product Number Growth

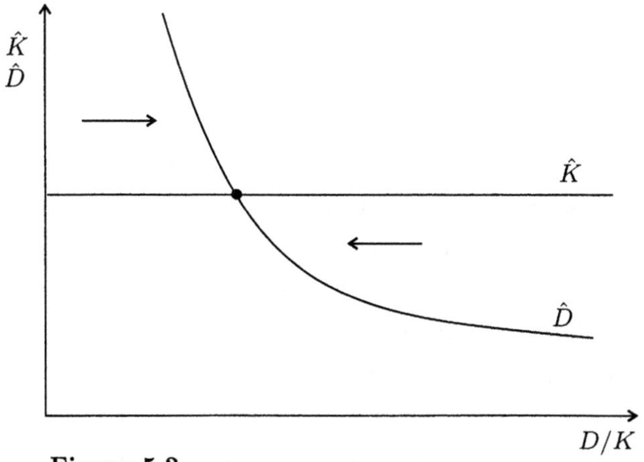

Figure 5.2.
Debt Growth and Capital Growth

number growth. Figure 5.3 shows the growth diagram. Originally the economy is in the steady state marked as point 1. Due to the increase in the deficit ratio, the $\hat{K}$ line moves downwards. In contrast, the $\hat{A}$ line is not affected. In the short run, capital growth declines as indicated by point 2. Intermediate product number growth, on the other hand, is not affected. Due to reduced capital growth, capital per intermediate product declines in the medium run. Intermediate product output $M = K/A$ declines and, therefore, the price of patents declines. As a consequence, less labour is used for research and intermediate product number growth declines. In the long run, capital growth and intermediate product number growth converge. Capital per intermediate product stays constant. Figure 5.4 presents the time path of capital growth and intermediate product number growth.

Now have a look at final output growth. In the short run, final output growth declines due to reduced capital growth. In the medium run, capital growth recovers. However, intermediate product number growth declines. From (10) we obtain $\hat{Y} = \hat{A} + \alpha\hat{M} + \beta\hat{L}$. Equation (12) gives $\hat{M} = \hat{K} - \hat{A}$ and (13) gives $\hat{L} = \hat{Y} - \hat{K}$. Insert these growth rates into $\hat{Y} = \hat{A} + \alpha\hat{M} + \beta\hat{L}$ and solve for $\hat{Y} = \beta(\hat{A} - \hat{K})/\alpha + \hat{K}$. Then insert intermediate product number growth and capital growth from (27) and (28) and rearrange to obtain:

$$\hat{Y} = \left(1 + \frac{\beta - \alpha}{\alpha}(1 - s(1 + b - g) + b)\right)\frac{\beta\lambda}{\alpha} - \left(\beta + \frac{\beta - \alpha}{\alpha}(\beta + \alpha s(1 + b - g) - \alpha b)\right)\left(\frac{\lambda K}{\alpha A}\right)^{-\beta/\alpha}$$

The term in brackets is positive due to $b < b'$. The ratio K/A is declining during adjustment and so final output growth increases during adjustment. In the long run, output growth corresponds to capital growth and intermediate product number growth. All growth rates are constant and the same. Compared to the original steady state, growth is reduced. The time path of output growth is presented in Figure 5.5.

Finally have a look at public debt growth. In the short run, the increase in the deficit ratio leads to an increase in the budget deficit and in public debt growth. Budget deficit growth corresponds to output growth. Therefore, in the medium run, budget deficit growth is reduced. This reduces public debt growth. In the long run, public debt growth corresponds to final output growth. Figure 5.6 shows the time path of public debt growth.

2) Increase in the deficit ratio ($b > b'$). Under these circumstances there is no steady state. At the start, let the economy be in a steady state with $b < b'$, so the economy grows at a constant rate. The budget deficit, public debt, capital, the intermediate product number and final output grow at the same constant rate. Then the government lifts the deficit ratio above the critical level. In the short run, as a reaction, investment becomes negative. This means that the $\hat{K}$ line moves into the negative region. In contrast, the $\hat{A}$ line is not affected. So capital growth becomes negative while intermediate product number growth is not affected. Due to capital decay, capital per intermediate product declines in the medium run. Intermediate product output $M = K/A$ declines and, therefore, the price of patents declines. Less labour is used for research and intermediate product number growth declines continuously. At some point of time, the intermediate product number stops to grow. Capital growth and output growth are negative and decline continuously. As a consequence, capital and output are driven to zero in finite time. Figure 5.7 illustrates the growth diagram with capital and intermediate product number growth. Figure 5.8 shows the corresponding time paths.

3) Increase in the purchase ratio. In this situation there is a stable steady state. At the beginning, the economy is in the steady state. Public debt, capital, the intermediate product number and output grow at the same constant rate. Then the government pushes up the purchase ratio. In the growth diagram, the $\hat{K}$ line shifts downwards and the $\hat{A}$ line is not affected. In the short run, on account of the budget constraint, the government has to raise the tax rate. This lowers savings and investment. Capital growth declines. As a consequence, intermediate product number growth and output growth also decline. The process of adjustment is similar to the one induced by an increase in the deficit ratio. Hence, output growth declines in the short run, then recovers in the medium run, and finally settles at a constant level which is below the original level. In the short run, public debt growth is constant. Then budget deficit growth declines due to reduced output growth. Therefore public debt growth declines. In the long run, the debt-capital ratio converges

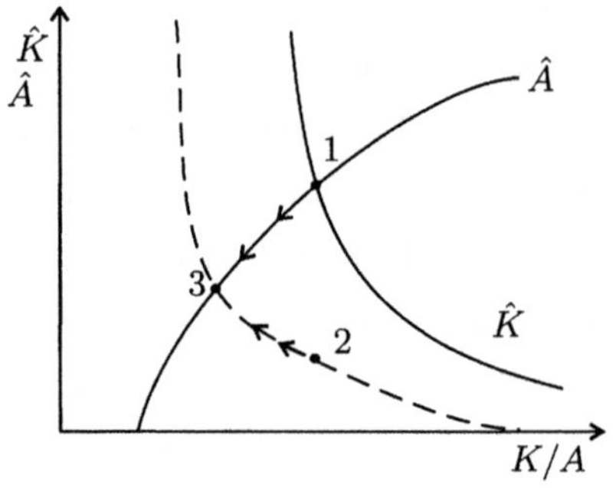

Figure 5.3.
Increase in Deficit Ratio

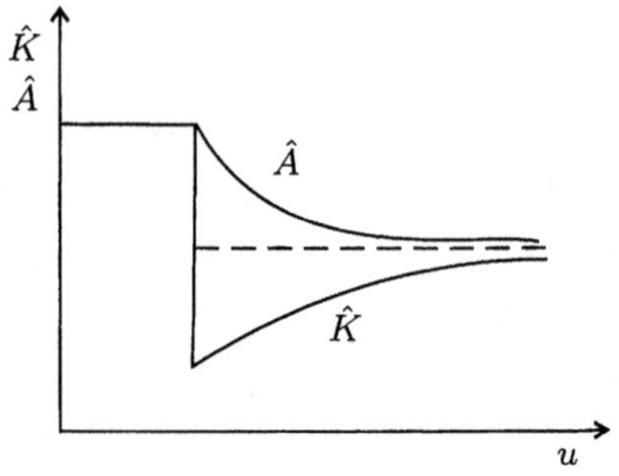

Figure 5.4.
Capital Growth and Intermediate Product Number Growth

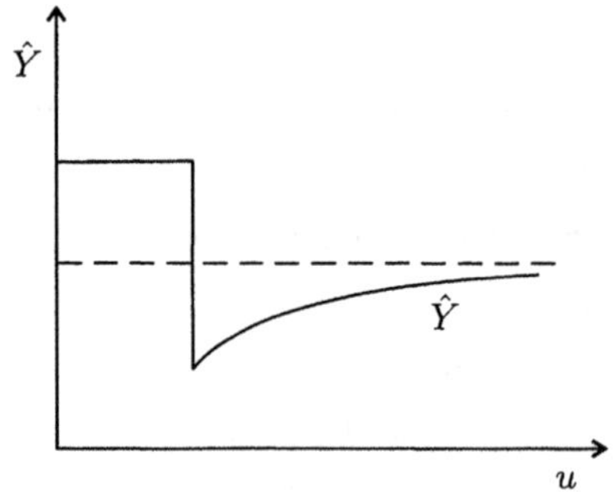

Figure 5.5.
Output Growth

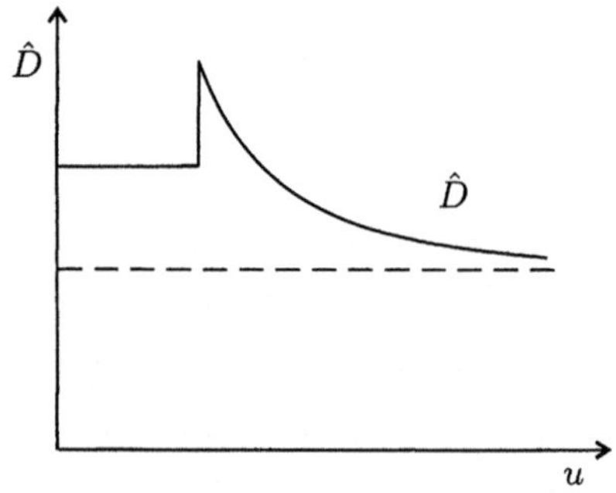

Figure 5.6.
Debt Growth

to a new steady state. In the new steady state, public debt and output grow at the same constant rate.

4) Increase in research productivity. Initially the economy rests in the steady state. The budget deficit and public debt grow at the same rate as the intermediate product number, capital, and output. Now research productivity λ increases. First consider the dynamics of capital growth and intermediate product number growth. Figure 5.9 shows the growth diagram. Originally the economy is in the steady state marked as point 1. Due to the shock, the $\hat{K}$ goes downwards and the $\hat{A}$ moves upwards. As a direct result, the number of new inventions goes up. To finance more new patents, firms have to borrow and therefore more savings are absorbed. This is why capital growth declines and intermediate product number growth goes up, see points 2. Capital per intermediate product declines and therefore each intermediate product is used less, and the price of patents declines. In due course labour is reallocated from research to final output production. More innovations and more labour used in the final product sector increase output growth. However, less use of each intermediate product leads to lower output growth. The total effect is that output growth goes up. Higher output growth leads to higher savings growth which allows higher capital growth. Therefore capital growth increases in the medium run. Final product number growth declines due to the reallocation of labour. In the long run, capital growth, final product number growth and output growth converge. Figure 5.10 shows the corresponding time paths.

Finally have a look at public debt. Output growth increases gradually from the original steady state to the new steady state. Budget deficit growth corresponds to output growth. As a result, public debt growth also increases gradually towards the new steady state.

5.2.4 Summary

As a result, capital growth depends on the deficit ratio. Capital growth and intermediate product number growth depend on the capital-output ratio. Public debt growth depends on the deficit ratio, on the debt-output ratio and on the debt-capital ratio. In the steady state, all growth rates are constant and the same, so the debt-capital ratio, the debt-output ratio and the capital-output ratio are constant. There is a critical deficit ratio. First assume that the deficit

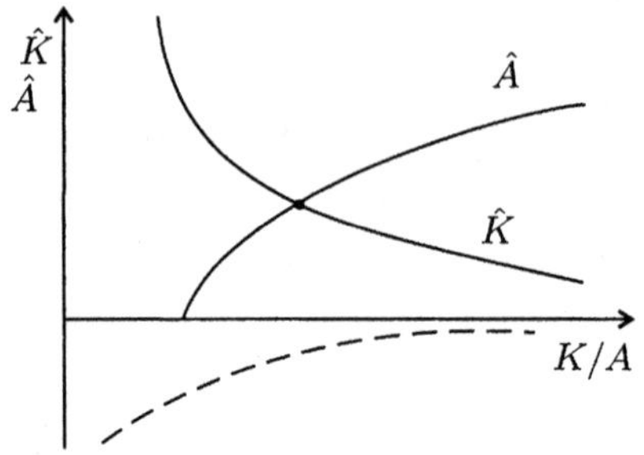

Figure 5.7.
Increase in Deficit Ratio
$(b > b')$

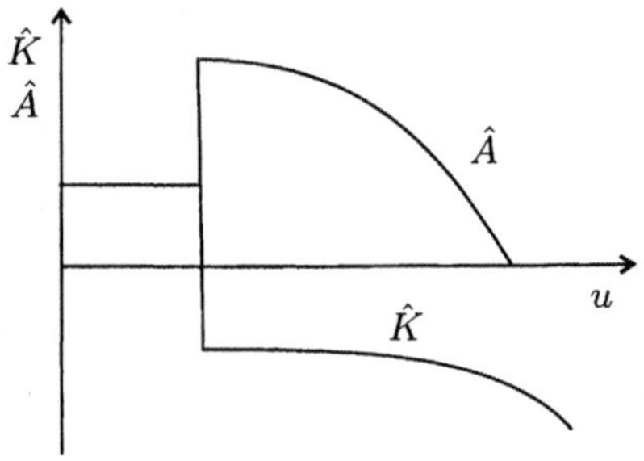

Figure 5.8.
Capital Growth and Intermediate Product Number Growth

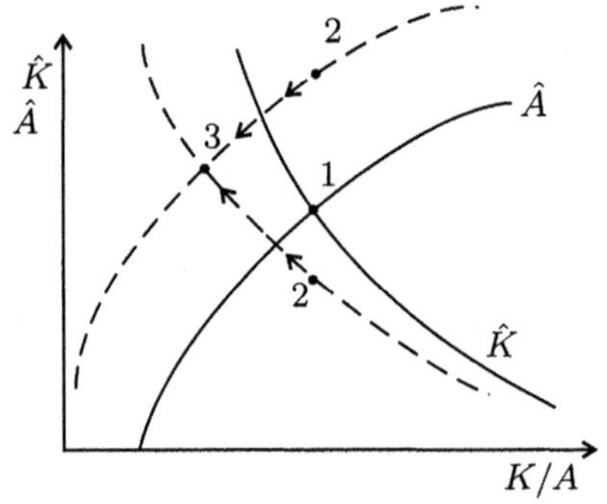

Figure 5.9.
Increase in Research Productivity

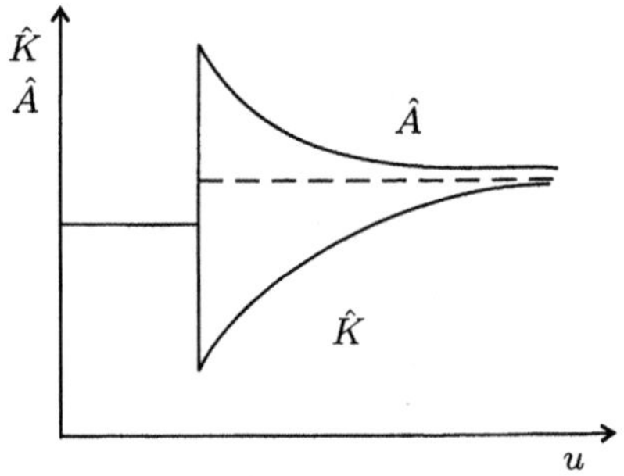

Figure 5.10.
Capital Growth and Intermediate Product Number Growth

ratio is below the critical level. In this case, there is a stable steady state. An increase in the deficit ratio reduces the steady state growth rate. Now assume that the deficit ratio is increased above the critical level. In this case, there is no steady state. In the short run, capital growth becomes negative. After some time, the intermediate product number stops to grow. Capital growth and output growth are negative and decline continuously. As a consequence, capital and output are driven to zero in finite time.

5.3 Fixing the Tax Rate

5.3.1 The Model

First we briefly review the structure of production. Production takes place in three sectors. In the first sector, firms use labour L and A intermediate products M_i to produce the final product Y. All intermediate products are used in the same amount M. This allows the production function to be stated as $Y = AL^\beta M^\alpha$. Technical progress increases the intermediate product number. Hence A increases and therefore final product output goes up. The price of Y is normalized to 1. Profits are $\Pi = Y - wL - \Sigma_{i=1}^{A} P_i M_i$, where w is the wage and P_i is the price of an intermediate product. Firms adjust labour and intermediate product input to equate the marginal product of labour to the wage $w = \partial Y/\partial L = \beta Y/L$ and the marginal product of an intermediate product to its price $P_i = \partial Y/\partial M_i = \alpha L^\beta M_i^{-\beta}$.

The second sector uses capital to produce intermediate products. Each firm buys one patent, which allows the production of one intermediate product. The production function is simply $M_i = K_i$, so one unit of capital transforms into one unit of an intermediate product. Profits Π_i are the difference between revenue and costs for capital and patents. Each patent has an infinite lifetime and has the price P_P. Firms finance the patent using credit on which they have to pay the interest rate r. Hence the costs of production are given by interest payments. The price of a patent might increase. Let $\dot{P}_P$ be the change in patent price, then profits are $\Pi_i = \dot{P}_P + P_i M_i - rK_i - rP_P$. The demand function for an intermediate product is given by its marginal product in the final product sector and so we have $\Pi_i = \dot{P}_P + \alpha L^\beta K_i^\alpha - rK_i - rP_P$. Profit maximization leads to $\partial \Pi_i/\partial K_i = \alpha^2 L^\beta K_i^{\alpha-1} = r$. Optimal capital demand for all firms is the same and so we have $K_i = K/A$, which implies that the interest rate is $r = \alpha^2 L^\beta (K/A)^{\alpha-1}$. Since all firms use the same amount of capital, all intermediate products are produced to the same amount $M = M_i = K/A$, and therefore they all have the same price $P_i = r/\alpha$. Finally we have to determine the price for a patent P_P. Firms in the intermediate product sector compete for patents which implies that the present value of future profits corresponds to the price of a patent, this gives $P_P = \beta K/(\alpha A)$. Here K/A is capital per intermediate product, which gives the intermediate product output M.

In the third sector N workers are used to develop new intermediate products. The number of newly invented intermediate products $\dot{A}$ depends on the research productivity of labour λ and on the already existing product number A, therefore we have $\dot{A} = \lambda A N$. Revenue of the sector is given by $P_P \dot{A}$ and the costs are wN, so profits are $\Pi_A = P_P \dot{A} - wN$. Profit maximization gives $P_P \lambda A = w$. The wage will equalize across sectors. Equate the wage in the final product sector with the wage in the research sector to obtain the proportion of workers in the final product sector $L = \alpha Y/(\lambda K)$. Finally notice that there is a critical capital-output ratio. When $K/Y \leq \alpha/\lambda$ then $L = 1$. This means, if the capital-output ratio falls below the critical level, then all labour is used for production of the final product and no labour is used for research. In this case $\dot{A} = 0$, which means that there are no inventions.

Now consider income and wealth dynamics. Output in the final product sector is Y. Wage income in the final product sector is $wL = \beta Y$. Payments to the intermediate product sector are $\Sigma_{i=1}^{A} P_i M_i = \alpha Y$. Firms in the intermediate product sector pay the interest rate r on credits which are used to finance expenditures for capital and patents $rK + rP_P A$. Insert (4) and (5) to obtain $rK + rP_P A = \alpha Y$. At each point of time, the intermediate product sector takes up new credits to finance new capital and new patents. Expenditures for new patents $P_P \dot{A}$ go to the research sector. In the research sector wages are $wN = P_P \dot{A}$. Households receive wage and interest income $Y + P_P \dot{A}$.

Now let us consider the government budget. The government spends a fixed share of national income on goods and services $G = g(Y + P_P \dot{A})$ with the purchase ratio $g = const.$ It imposes a proportionate tax on both factor income and debt income $T = t(Y + P_P \dot{A} + rD)$, with the tax rate $t = const.$

Government purchases plus interest payments on public debt rD minus tax earnings correspond to the budget deficit $B = G + rD - T$. By using the behavioural functions, this identity can be reformulated in the following way $B = g(Y+P_P\dot{A})+rD-t(Y+P_P\dot{A}+rD)$. The budget deficit augments public debt $\dot{D} = B$

Next we have a look at disposable income. Disposable income is the sum of factor income and debt income, net of taxes $Y_d = (1-t)(Y + P_P\dot{A} + rD)$. Households save a constant fraction of their disposable income $S = sY_d$ with the saving ratio $s = const$. Household savings are partly absorbed by public borrowing. The rest is used as credits to firms. These are used to finance investment and expenditures for patents $I+P_P\dot{A} = S-B$. Investment augments capital $\dot{K} = I$. By using the savings function one obtains $\dot{K}+P_P\dot{A}+\dot{D} = s(1-t)(Y + P_P\dot{A} + rD)$.

Summarizing the above, the model can be represented by a system of eight equations:

$$\dot{A} = \lambda A(1-L) \tag{1}$$

$$Y = AM^{\alpha}L^{\beta} \tag{2}$$

$$r = \alpha^2 L^{\beta} M^{\alpha-1} \tag{3}$$

$$M = K/A \tag{4}$$

$$L = \frac{\alpha Y}{\lambda K} \tag{5}$$

$$P_P = \beta M/\alpha \tag{6}$$

$$\dot{D} = g(Y + P_P\dot{A}) + rD - t(Y + P_P\dot{A} + rD) \tag{7}$$

$$\dot{K} + P_P\dot{A} + \dot{D} = s(1-t)(Y + P_P\dot{A} + rD) \tag{8}$$

Here $\alpha, \beta, \lambda, g, s, t, A, D$, and K are exogenous, while r, $\dot{A}$,$\dot{D}$, $\dot{K}$,L, P_P, M and Y are endogenous.

To start the analysis consider employment in the final product sector. Divide (2) by K and then insert (5) and solve for the capital-output ratio:

$$\frac{K}{Y} = \left(\frac{\lambda}{\alpha}\right)^{\beta/\alpha} M^{\beta/\alpha} \tag{9}$$

So employment in the final product sector is:

$$L = \left(\frac{\alpha}{\lambda}\right)^{1/\alpha} M^{-\beta/\alpha} \tag{10}$$

This allows to state the interest rate as:

$$r = \alpha^2 \left(\frac{\alpha}{\lambda}\right)^{\beta/\alpha} M^{-\beta/\alpha} \tag{11}$$

Now it is useful to consider growth rates. At first insert (10) into (1) and divide by A to obtain intermediate product number growth:

$$\hat{A} = \lambda - \alpha \left(\frac{\alpha}{\lambda}\right)^{\beta/\alpha} M^{-\beta/\alpha} \tag{12}$$

As a result, intermediate product number growth depends on the productivity parameters and on intermediate product output. There is a critical intermediate product output. If intermediate product output becomes very small, i.e. $M \leq (\alpha/\lambda)^{1/\beta}$, then all labour is used in the final product sector $L = 1$ and no labour is used in research $N = 0$. As a consequence, there are no new intermediate products and we have $\dot{A} = \hat{A} = 0$. Obviously, in this case, the model is different to the one presented here. For the moment we assume that intermediate product output is above the critical level. However, intermediate product output is endogenous and therefore we will derive the conditions for $M > (\alpha/\lambda)^{1/\beta}$ later on.

Now consider capital growth. Insert (1), (6), and (7) into (17) and replace L with the help of (5) to obtain $\dot{K} = (\beta + \alpha s(1-t) - \alpha(g-t))\,Y - (1 - s(1-t) + g - t)\beta\lambda K/\alpha - (1-s)(1-t)rD$. Next insert (11) for r, divide by K, and replace Y/K with the help (9) to reach:

$$\begin{aligned}\hat{K} = {} & (\beta + \alpha s(1-t) - \alpha(g-t)) \left(\frac{\alpha}{\lambda}\right)^{\beta/\alpha} M^{-\beta/\alpha} - \\ & (1 - s(1-t) + g - t)\frac{\beta}{\alpha}\lambda - (1-s)(1-t)\alpha^2 \left(\frac{\alpha}{\lambda}\right)^{\beta/\alpha} M^{-\beta/\alpha}\frac{D}{K}\end{aligned} \tag{13}$$

As a result, capital growth depends on the productivity parameters, on the saving ratio, on the government purchase ratio, on the tax rate, on intermediate product output and on the debt-capital ratio.

Finally consider public debt growth. Insert (1) and (6) into (7) to obtain $\dot{D} = (g-t)(Y + \beta\lambda K/\alpha - \beta Y) + (1-t)rD$. Divide by D, use $Y/D = Y/K \cdot K/D$, replace Y/K with the help of (9) and r by (11) to reach:

$$\hat{D} = (g - t)\left(\alpha\left(\frac{\alpha A}{\lambda K}\right)^{\beta/\alpha} + \frac{\beta\lambda}{\alpha}\right)\frac{K}{D} + (1-t)\alpha^2\left(\frac{\alpha}{\lambda}\right)^{\beta/\alpha} M^{-\beta/\alpha} \tag{14}$$

As a result, intermediate product number growth, capital growth and public debt growth depend on intermediate product output M.

For the growth rates to be constant, intermediate product output needs to be constant. Intermediate product output is constant if capital growth equals intermediate product number growth. Hence, a steady state requires $\hat{A} = \hat{K}$. Capital growth and public debt growth depend on the debt-capital ratio. For the growth rates to be constant, the debt-capital ratio needs to be constant. The debt-capital ratio is constant if public debt growth equals capital growth. Hence, a steady state requires $\hat{D} = \hat{K}$. Taking the two conditions together a steady state requires $\hat{A} = \hat{D} = \hat{K}$. To simplify the analysis we assume $t = 0$. Hence we ask, whether the government can provide goods and services without taxing income. Insert $t = 0$ and the debt-capital ratio $x = D/K$ into (12), (13) and (14) to obtain a system of three growth equations:

$$\hat{A} = \lambda - \alpha\,(\alpha/\lambda)^{\beta/\alpha} M^{-\beta/\alpha} \tag{15}$$

$$\hat{D} = (\alpha\,(\alpha/\lambda)^{\beta/\alpha} M^{-\beta/\alpha} + \beta\lambda/\alpha)g/x + \alpha^2\,(\alpha/\lambda)^{\beta/\alpha} M^{-\beta/\alpha} \tag{16}$$

$$\begin{aligned}\hat{K} = {} & \left(\beta + \alpha s - \alpha g - (1-s)\alpha^2 x\right)(\alpha/\lambda)^{\beta/\alpha} M^{-\beta/\alpha} \\ & -(1 - s + g)\beta\lambda/\alpha\end{aligned} \tag{17}$$

First equate intermediate product number growth and capital growth to obtain:

$$M^{-\beta/\alpha} = \frac{\lambda - \beta\lambda(s-g)}{\alpha\,(1 + \alpha(s - g - \alpha x(1-s)))}\left(\frac{\alpha}{\lambda}\right)^{-\beta/\alpha} \tag{18}$$

Intermediate product output depends on the debt-capital ratio. Intermediate product output stays constant, if the debt-capital ratio stays constant. An increase in the debt-capital ratio reduces intermediate product output. There is a critical debt-capital ratio. Intermediate product output is positive if $x < x' = [1 + \alpha(s-g)]/[\alpha^2(1-s)]$.

Now use (18) to replace $(\alpha/\lambda)^{\beta/\alpha} M^{-\beta/\alpha}$ in (16) and (17) and then equate debt growth and capital growth to obtain

$$
\begin{aligned}
&(\alpha\frac{\lambda-\beta\lambda(s-g)}{\alpha\left(1+\alpha(s-g-\alpha x(1-s))\right)}+\frac{\beta\lambda}{\alpha})\frac{g}{x} \\
&+\alpha^2\frac{\lambda-\beta\lambda(s-g)}{\alpha\left(1+\alpha(s-g-\alpha x(1-s))\right)} \\
=&\left(\beta+\alpha s-\alpha g-(1-s)\alpha^2 x\right)\frac{\lambda-\beta\lambda(s-g)}{\alpha\left(1+\alpha(s-g-\alpha x(1-s))\right)}- \\
&(1-s+g)\frac{\beta}{\alpha}
\end{aligned}
$$

After some tedious manipulations, it can be shown that this is a quadratic equation in the debt-capital ratio which has the solution:

$$
x_{1,2}=\frac{P\mp\sqrt{P^2-Q}}{R} \tag{19}
$$

with

$$
\begin{aligned}
P&=\left(\left(1-\beta s(1-g)\right)\lambda\alpha^2-\lambda+\beta\lambda\left(s-g\right)\right. \\
&\quad\left.+\left(\alpha\lambda+\beta+\alpha\beta(1-\lambda)\left(s-g\right)\right)\right)\left(1-s+g\right) \\
Q&=4\alpha^2\lambda\left(1-s\right)g\left(\lambda-\beta+\beta(1-\lambda)(s-g)\right) \\
R&=2\alpha^2\left(1-s\right)\left(\beta\left(1-s+g\right)-\lambda+\beta\lambda\left(s-g\right)\right)
\end{aligned}
$$

$x_{1,2}$ are steady state debt-capital ratios if they are real and positive. Whether $x_{1,2}$ are real and positive depends on the signs of P, Q and R. We have $Q<0$ and $R>0$ if

$$
\lambda<\beta\frac{1-s+g}{1-\beta(s-g)}>\beta
$$

In the following we assume that the condition holds. This can be justified as follows: Without government activity the growth rate is $\lambda s/(1+\alpha s)$. The growth rate is increasing in λ. Now assume $\alpha=0.3, s=0.1$ and that the growth rate without government activity is below 4%. Then, we have an upper limit of $\lambda<0.412$. And if the growth rate without government activity is 3%, then the upper limit is $\lambda<0.309$. In any case λ is far below β which is about 0.7.

Now, due to $Q<0$ both solutions $x_{1,2}$ are real and due to $Q<0$ and $R>0$ we have $x_1<0$ and $x_2>0$.

The solution for the debt-capital ratio given in (19) depends on the solution for intermediate product output given in (18), which was derived under the assumption that there is a constant debt-capital ratio that stays below a critical level, i.e. $x < x' = [1 + \alpha(s - g)]/[\alpha^2(1 - s)]$. Further analysis gives rise to the following proposition:

Proposition 1. *The debt-capital ratio given in (19) exceeds the critical level necessary to determine intermediate product output in (18). Therefore there is no steady state.*

Proof. The debt-capital ratio always exceeds the critical level required for a steady state:

$$\frac{P + \sqrt{P^2 - Q}}{R} > x' = \frac{1 + \alpha(s - g)}{\alpha^2(1 - s)}$$

Rearrange terms to obtain

$$\sqrt{P^2 - Q} > S - P$$

where $S = Rx' > 0$. Square both sides and rearrange to reach the condition $S(S - 2P) + Q < 0$. We have $Q < 0$, $S = 2\,(\beta\,(1 - s + g) - \lambda + \beta\lambda\,(s - g))$ $(1 + \alpha(s - g)) > 0$ and $S - 2P = -2\alpha\lambda\,((1 + \alpha)(1 - \beta s) + \beta g(1 + \alpha s)) < 0$. So the condition is fulfilled. ■

This result implies that intermediate product output declines continuously, and converges to zero. Therefore, the price for new patents, which is the incentive for research declines. As a consequence, the intermediate product number stops to grow $\hat{A} = 0$.

Now the question remains as to whether capital growth and public debt growth converge to zero. Use (7) and (8) insert the result $\dot{A} = 0$, and the simplifying assumption $t = 0$ to obtain:

$$\dot{D} = gY + rD \tag{20}$$

$$\dot{K} = (s - g)Y - (1 - s)rD \tag{21}$$

Due to $L = 1$ we have $Y = A^{\beta} K^{\alpha}$ and $r = \alpha^2\,(K/A)^{-\beta}$. Insert this into (20) and (21), divide by D and K respectively, note $Y/D = K/D \cdot Y/K$ and insert the debt-capital ratio $x = D/K$ to reach:

$$\hat{D} = g\left(\frac{K}{A}\right)^{-\beta} /x + \alpha^2 \left(\frac{K}{A}\right)^{-\beta} \tag{22}$$

$$\hat{K} = (s - g)\left(\frac{K}{A}\right)^{-\beta} - (1 - s)\alpha^2 \left(\frac{K}{A}\right)^{-\beta} x \tag{23}$$

Public debt growth and capital growth depend on the debt-capital ratio. An increase in the debt-capital ratio increases public debt growth and reduces capital growth. Now equate debt growth and capital growth and simplify:

$$g/x + \alpha^2 = (s - g) - (1 - s)\alpha^2 x$$

This is a quadratic equation in the debt-capital ratio which has the solution:

$$x_{1,2} = \frac{P \pm \sqrt{P^2 - Q}}{R} \tag{24}$$

with

$P = s - \alpha^2 - g$
$Q = 4(1 - s)\alpha^2 g > 0$
$R = 2(1 - s)\alpha^2 > 0$

$x_{1,2}$ need to be real and positive. They are real for $P^2 - Q > 0$. $P^2 - Q$ is a quadratic equation in the government purchase ratio. There are two solutions $g_{1,2}$ for $P^2 - Q = 0$ with $g_1 < g_2$. We obtain $P^2 - Q > 0$ for $g < g_1$ and for $g > g_2$. Further note $P > 0$ for $g < g_1$ and $P < 0$ for $g > g_2$. Hence we obtain three cases: 1) $g > g_2$: due to $P < 0$ we have $x_{1,2} < 0$. To see this square both sides in $P < \sqrt{P^2 - Q}$. 2) $g_2 > g > g_1$: we have $P^2 - Q < 0$ and there is no solution. 3) $g < g_1$: due to $P > 0$ we have $x_{1,2} > 0$. To see this square both sides in $P > \sqrt{P^2 - Q}$.

Hence, for $g < g_1$ there is a steady state debt-capital ratio for the system given in (22) and (23). Figure 5.11 shows the growth diagram for this case. There are two steady states, where public debt growth equals capital growth. To the left of the x_1, debt growth exceeds capital growth, so the debt-capital ratio is increasing. To the right of x_1, capital growth exceeds debt growth, so the debt-capital ratio is declining. To the right of x_2 debt growth exceeds capital growth, so the debt-capital ratio is increasing. As a result, the steady state x_1 is locally stable while the steady state x_2 is unstable. Now further analysis shows:

Proposition 2. *Two cases might arise: 1) If $g < g_1$ and the debt-capital ratio where $\hat{A} = 0$ occurs is below x_2, then the stable steady state x_1 is reached. In*

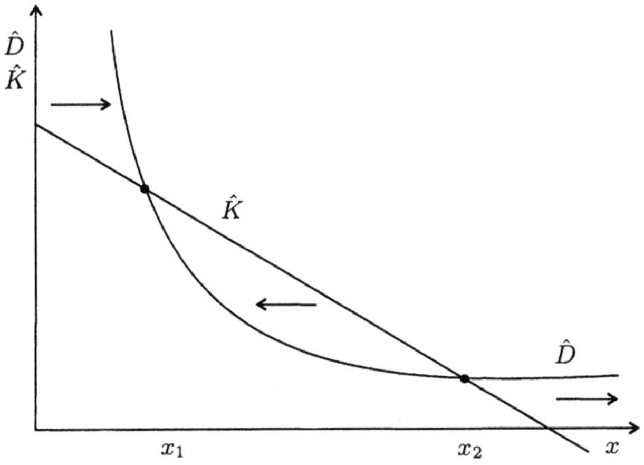

Figure 5.11.
Capital Growth and Debt Growth

this case, capital growth and public debt growth decline to zero. 2) If $g > g_1$ or if the debt-capital ratio where $\hat{A} = 0$ occurs is above x_2, then no steady state debt-capital ratio is reached. In this case, capital growth declines continuously, become negative at some point of time and declines further. This drives capital and output down to zero in finite time.

Proof. 1) If $g < g_1$ and the debt-capital ratio where $\hat{A} = 0$ occurs is below x_2, then the debt-capital ratio converges to x_1. Capital grows and therefore capital per intermediate product (K/A) increases over time. According to (22) and (23) capital growth and public debt growth decline to zero. 2) If $g > g_1$ or if the debt-capital ratio where $\hat{A} = 0$ occurs is above x_2, then debt growth always exceeds capital growth and so capital growth declines continuously, becomes negative at some point of time and declines further. This drives capital and output down to zero in finite time. ■

5.3.2 A Tax Cut

Now we will try to obtain some intuition for the process of adjustment induced by a tax cut. As we have seen, normally there is no steady state. Therefore we assume that at the beginning there is no public debt and the tax rate equals the government purchase ratio $t = g$, so the budget is balanced. The economy is in the steady state. The intermediate product number, capital and output grow at the same constant rate. Then the government reduces the tax rate which leads to a budget deficit. Public debt comes into existence and begins to grow. The government has to pay interest on public debt. Since the tax rate is kept constant, the government has to increase the budget deficit to finance interest payments on public debt. Hence the budget deficit increases over time. This accelerates public debt growth.

In each point of time, the budget deficit absorbs savings and reduces credits available for firms. This reduces investment and research activity. Capital growth and intermediate product number growth declines. Therefore output growth declines too. Reduced output growth leads to reduced saving growth which again leads to lower capital and intermediate product number growth. At some point of time, capital growth is negative and the intermediate product number stops to grow. Then capital growth declines further and so capital and output are driven down to zero in finite time.

5.3.3 Summary

Starting from a balanced budget, a tax cut leads to a budget deficit. Public debt comes into existence and begins to grow. Public debt reduces research activity and capital accumulation. Therefore, at first, intermediate product number growth, capital growth and output growth decline. At some point of time, the intermediate product number stops to grow and capital growth becomes negative. Then capital growth declines further. As a result, capital and output decline to zero in finite time.

Part III

The Open Economy with AK Production

6

The Solow Model of the Small Open Economy

6.1 Introduction

This chapter considers public debt in a small open economy. Most of the literature on endogenous growth in open economies concentrate on trade effects as introduced in Grossman and Helpman (1991). In these models there is no capital mobility. In contrast to this literature we allow for capital mobility and concentrate on intertemporal trade as in Buiter (1981) and Frenkel and Razin (1987). So opening the economy adds the dynamics of foreign debt growth. The production structure is assumed to be of AK type and households are assumed to save a constant fraction of their disposable income. The basic model, without public debt, is presented in Carlberg (1997).

Carlberg (1985a, 1988) contains a neoclassical Solow growth model with public consumption. The government fixes the deficit ratio. It is shown that there is an unique steady state. In addition there is an optimal deficit ratio. Carlberg (1993) reviews an overlapping generations model of a stationary economy with public consumption. The government fixes the tax rate. As a result, there exists no long-run equilibrium.

Allowing for endogenous growth, van der Ploeg (1996) examines government debt in a small open economy. The analysis is based on an overlapping generations model with imperfect capital mobility and adjustment costs. The government fixes the deficit ratio. It is shown that an increase in the deficit ratio reduces the growth rate and increases the foreign debt to income ratio. Josten (2001) considers endogenous growth through human capital accumulation in a small open economy. Physical capital is internationally mobile, but human capital is not. The government adjusts the tax to fix the ratio of public debt to human capital. An increase in this ratio, leads to a rise in the growth rate.

The rest of the chapter is structured the following way: The first section is on a fixed deficit ratio. In the first subsection it is shown that perfect capital mobility in an AK growth model leads to unrealistic capital flows. Therefore, we assume imperfect capital mobility. Two cases are considered in subsections 2 and 3. Firstly, we assume a high-productivity country and secondly we assume a low-productivity country. Section 2 considers the fixed tax rate. Again, the high- and the low-productivity country are considered.

6.2 Fixing the Deficit Ratio

6.2.1 Perfect Capital Mobility

A large number of identical firms produce a homogeneous commodity. Output Y_i depends on capital K_i and labour N_i input. The production function is of the Cobb-Douglas type: $Y_i = AK_i^\alpha(EN_i)^\beta$ with $\alpha > 0, \beta > 0$, $\alpha + \beta = 1$. $A > 0$ is a scale parameter and E is an exogenously given index of labour efficiency. Each firm maximizes profits $\Pi_i = Y_i - rK_i - wN_i$ under perfect competition. Here Π_i denotes profits of firm i, r the interest rate, and w the wage rate. As a consequence, each firm adjusts the input of capital so that the marginal product of capital equals the interest rate $\partial Y_i/\partial K_i = \alpha Y_i/K_i = r$ and the input of labour is adjusted to equate the marginal product of labour with the wage rate $\partial Y_i/\partial N_i = \beta Y_i/N_i = w$.

The aggregate production function is $Y = AK^\alpha(EN)^\beta$. It is assumed that labour efficiency is proportional to capital per worker $E = K/N$. Therefore, labour efficiency is endogenous for the economy. As a consequence, the production function simplifies to $Y = AK$. The private marginal product of capital is then given as αA. Labour is supplied inelastically and the total supply of labour N is given exogenously. The wage rate is given by the marginal product of labour $w = \beta Y/N$. Output Y can be devoted to consumption, investment, government purchases and exports $Y = C + I + G + H$.

We assume that the economy is small and open for capital mobility. The world interest rate is given $r^* = const.$ The domestic interest rate is equal to the private marginal product of capital $r = \alpha A$. Now, let us suppose that there is perfect capital mobility. Two cases might arise: In the first case, the world interest rate is above the domestic interest rate $r^* > r$. Then nobody would invest at home. There would be an extremely large capital outflow and the stock of capital would decline to zero. In the second case, the world interest rate is below the domestic interest rate $r^* < r$. Then there would be an extremely large capital inflow and the stock of capital would explode. Since this seems quite unrealistic, we assume imperfect capital mobility. We will consider two cases in turn. Firstly, we assume that the home country has a high productivity. So the marginal product of domestic capital exceeds the world interest rate. Secondly, we assume that the home country has a low productivity. So the world interest rate exceeds the marginal product of domestic capital.

6.2.2 The High-Productivity Country

Due to the high productivity, the marginal product of domestic capital exceeds the world interest rate $r = \alpha A > r^*$. As a consequence, there is a capital inflow and the country is an international debtor. However, the rest of the world is not willing to finance all the domestic assets and, therefore, a maximum is imposed on international credit. More precisely, the foreign debt F of the country is limited to a fixed proportion of domestic capital K. Let the maximum granted ratio of foreign debt to capital be $m < 1$. Due to the high domestic marginal product of capital, the constraint will always be binding, so that $F = mK$. This implies that the availability of international loans is limited and firms have to compete for international funds. As a consequence, they are willing to pay the private marginal product of capital as interest on foreign debt. Hence, interest payments amount to rF, where $r = \alpha A$.

Now we consider the public sector. The government raises loans and levies a tax on income in order to finance both government purchases and the interest payments on public debt. Government spending on goods and services is a fixed share of national income $G = gY$ with purchase ratio $g = const.$ In addition, the government borrows a fixed proportion of income $B = bY$ with deficit ratio $b = const.$ The budget deficit augments public debt $\dot{D} = B$. The government pays the interest rate r on public debt D, so that public interest amounts to rD. The government taxes income according to the residence principle. The income of domestic residents is factor income Y plus debt income rD minus interest payments on foreign debt rF. The tax is imposed at the flat rate t, so that the tax revenue is given as $T = t(Y + rD - rF)$. The government budget constraint can be written as $B + T = G + rD$. With the help of the behavioural functions, the identity can be reformulated in the following way $bY + t(Y + rD - rF) = gY + rD$. In this equation, the purchase ratio and the deficit ratio are given whereas the tax rate has to be adjusted.

Next we look at capital dynamics. Disposable income is the sum of debt income and domestic factor income, net of taxes respectively $Y_d = Y + rD - rF - T$. Households save a constant fraction of their disposable income $S = sY_d$ with saving ratio $s = const$. Given the government budget identity, tax payments are $T = G + rD - B$. Therefore disposable income is $Y_d = (1 - g + b)Y - rF$ and savings are $S = s(1 - g + b)Y - srF$. Savings finance a part of capital accumulation $\dot{K}$ and public borrowing $\dot{D}$. The other part is financed by international borrowing, which augments foreign debt $\dot{F}$. Hence, capital dynamics are given by $\dot{K} + \dot{D} = s(1 - g + b)Y - srF + \dot{F}$.

Summarizing the above, the model can be represented by a system of six equations:

$$Y = AK \tag{1}$$

$$r = \alpha A \tag{2}$$

$$F = mK \tag{3}$$

$$\dot{K} + \dot{D} = s(1 - g + b)Y - srF + \dot{F} \tag{4}$$

$$\dot{D} = bY \tag{5}$$

$$bY + t(Y + rD - rF) = gY + rD \tag{6}$$

Here α, b, g, m, s, A, D, and K are exogenous, while $r, t, \dot{D}, F, \dot{K}$, and Y are endogenous.

Now it is useful to analyse growth rates. From (1) and (3) it is immediately evident that output and foreign debt grow at the same rate as capital. From (3) it also follows that $\dot{F} = m\dot{K}$. Insert this into (4), replace the change in public debt by (5), and rearrange terms to obtain: $(1-m)\dot{K} = s(1-g+b)Y - bY - srF$.

Then insert (1), (2), and (3) to obtain: $(1+m)\dot{K} = s(1-g+b)AK - bAK - \alpha smAK$. Finally collect terms and divide by K to reach:

$$\hat{Y} = \hat{F} = \hat{K} = \frac{s(1-g+b-\alpha m)-b}{1-m}A \tag{7}$$

From here it follows:

Proposition 1. *The growth rate of output, of foreign debt and of capital is constant. It depends on the deficit ratio, on the government purchase ratio, on the saving ratio, on the scale parameter, and on the maximum ratio of foreign debt to capital. The growth rate declines when the deficit ratio or the government purchase ratio goes up and it increases when the saving ratio or the scale parameter rises.*

Further analysis of (7) shows that the growth rate is positive as long as the deficit ratio stays below a critical level:

$$b' = \frac{(1-g-\alpha m)s}{1-s} \tag{8}$$

All this is very similar to the closed economy. This is due to the fact that international borrowing is restricted by a domestic variable. With $m = 0$ equation (8) gives the critical deficit ratio of the closed economy. For any $m > 0$, the critical deficit ratio is below the level of the closed economy.

In addition, equation (7) reveals that the growth rate is an increasing function of the maximum ratio of foreign debt to capital m if the deficit ratio is below a critical level $b'' = (1-g-\alpha)s/(1-s)$. Comparison with (8) shows that the critical level for a positive effect of an increase in m is below the critical level b', i.e. $b'' < b'$. In that sense, we may conclude that international capital mobility increases growth and reduces the negative effect of government borrowing.

Now we analyse public debt. From(5) and (1) we derive public debt growth:

$$\hat{D} = \frac{bAK}{D} \tag{9}$$

As a result, public debt growth is determined by the deficit ratio, the scale parameter and the debt-capital ratio. Public debt growth is constant if the debt-capital ratio is constant. Hence in the steady state, public debt has to grow at the same rate as capital. Now equate (7) and (9) to find the debt-capital ratio in the steady state:

$$\frac{D}{K} = \frac{b(1-m)}{s(1+b-g-\alpha m)-b} \tag{10}$$

If the deficit ratio is below the critical level ($b < b'$), the debt-capital ratio is positive. When the deficit ratio goes up, the debt-capital ratio increases. An increase in the purchase ratio also leads to an increase in the debt-capital ratio. In contrast, a rise in the saving ratio causes a decline in the debt-capital ratio. And the same applies to an increase in the maximum ratio of foreign debt to capital.

If the deficit ratio exceeds the critical level, the debt-capital ratio is negative. An increase in public borrowing that leads to a reduction in the debt-capital ratio clearly suggests instability. And indeed, in that case public debt grows while capital declines. As a consequence the debt-capital ratio explodes.

Now assume $b < b'$. Then debt growth is a declining function of the debt-capital ratio. Capital growth and output growth are independent of the debt-capital ratio. As a consequence, the growth diagram is structurally identical to the growth diagram of a closed economy, see Part I, Chapter 2, Section 2. Hence, as in the closed economy, we may state:

Proposition 2. *The steady state is stable as long as the deficit ratio stays below the critical level.*

6.2.3 Some Shocks

Now we shall discuss the process of adjustment released by three shocks in greater detail:

- an increase in the budget deficit ratio
- an increase in the government purchase ratio
- an increase in the maximum ratio of foreign debt to capital.

1) An increase in the deficit ratio, granted $b < b'$. Assuming that the deficit ratio stays below the critical level, there is a stable steady state. Figure 6.1 shows the growth diagram. Initially the economy rests in the steady state marked as point 1. The budget deficit and public debt grow at the same rate as capital, output and foreign debt. Against this background, the government

enhances the deficit ratio. In Figure 6.1, the $\hat{K}$ line moves downwards and the $\hat{D}$ line moves to the right. As indicated by the points 2 and 3, public debt growth immediately increases and, at the same time, output growth declines. The arrows point out how public debt growth and output growth develop over time.

Now look at the process in more detail. In the short run, output does not respond. The increase in the deficit ratio leads to a higher budget deficit and, therefore, public debt growth increases. The budget deficit crowds out investment. As a consequence, capital growth and output growth decline. Since output expands at a lower rate, foreign debt grows at a lower rate too. Due to the increase in the deficit ratio, the government is able to cut the tax rate, thereby lifting consumption. In the medium run, reduced output growth leads to a decline in tax revenue growth and the increase in public debt growth leads to faster interest payment growth. Both require an increase in the tax rate. Higher taxes reduce consumption and higher interest income increases consumption. Overall consumption grows at the same rate as output. Due to lower output growth there is lower budget deficit growth. This reduces public debt growth. As time proceeds, public debt growth converges to capital growth. In the new steady state, marked as point 4 in Figure 6.1, the debt-capital ratio is constant. The budget deficit and public debt grow at the same rate as capital, output and foreign debt.

2) An increase in the purchase ratio. In this situation there is a stable steady state. At the beginning, the economy is in the steady state. Public debt, capital and foreign assets grow at the same rate, see point 1 in Figure 6.2. Then the government pushes up the purchase ratio. In the diagram, the $\hat{K}$ line shifts downwards. In the short run, on account of the budget constraint, the government has to raise the tax rate. This lowers savings and investment. Therefore, capital growth and output growth decline (point 2). Due to the limit on international borrowing, foreign debt also expands at a lower rate. Reduced output growth leads to reduced deficit growth. In the medium run, this reduces public debt growth, and in the long run, public debt growth converges to output growth. In the new steady state (point 3), the debt-capital ratio is constant.

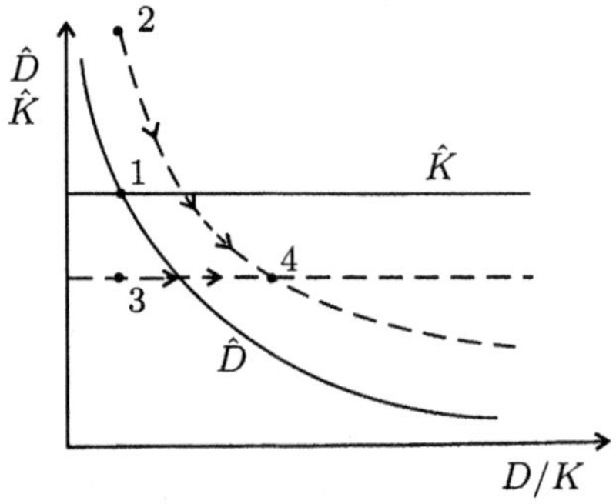

Figure 6.1.
Increase in the Deficit Ratio

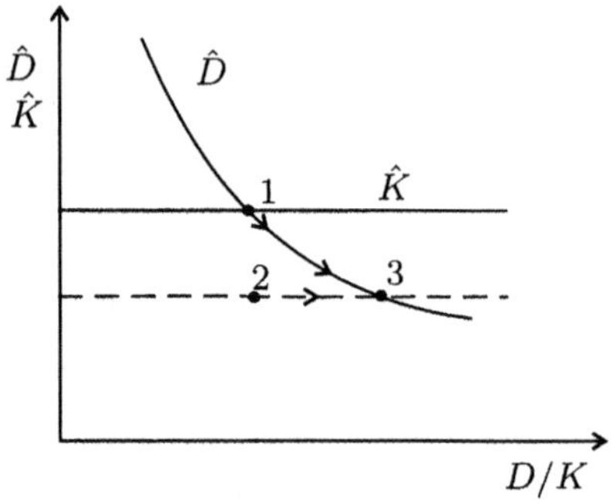

Figure 6.2.
Increase in the Purchase Ratio

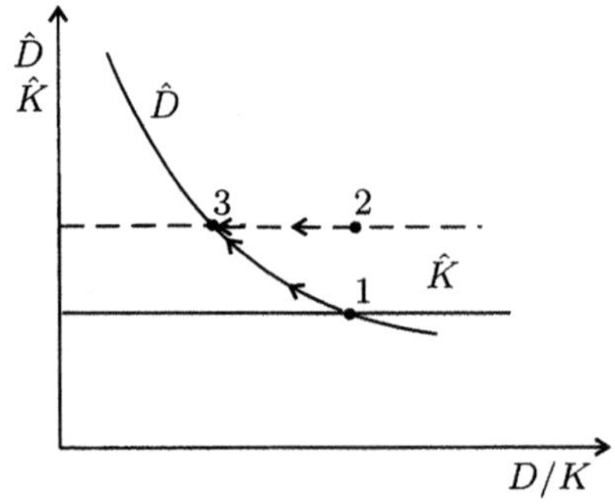

Figure 6.3.
Increase in Maximum
Foreign Debt-Capital Ratio

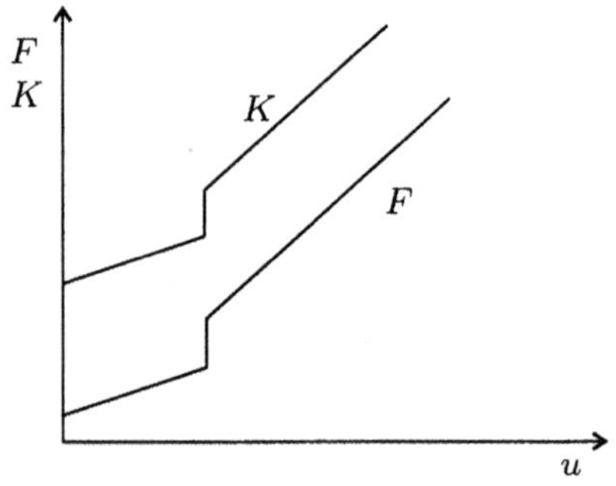

Figure 6.4.
Increase in Maximum
Foreign Debt-Capital Ratio
(Time Paths)

3) An increase in the maximum ratio of foreign debt to capital. At the start the economy rests in the steady state, marked as point 1 in Figure 6.3. Then m goes up. In the growth diagram, the $\hat{K}$ line moves upwards. Hence, capital growth and output growth increase (point 2). Public debt growth accelerates gradually. Asymptotically the economy tends to a new steady state (point 3). The post-shock growth rates are above the pre-shock levels and the debt-capital ratio is below its pre-shock value.

Now we look at the process of adjustment in more detail. At the moment where the constraint on foreign borrowing is relaxed, there is an immediate capital inflow. Foreign debt and capital increase instantaneously by the same amount. Due to a higher capital stock, output goes up. The increase in output and income leads to higher consumption, to higher savings and to a higher budget deficit. Higher savings increase investment and capital growth. The higher budget deficit leads to higher public debt growth. However, public debt growth accelerates only gradually towards the new long-run level. In contrast, capital growth immediately increases to the steady-state level. Therefore, capital grows at a higher rate than public debt during transition. As a consequence, the debt-capital ratio declines. Figure 6.4 shows the time paths of capital and foreign debt on a semilogarithmic scale.

6.2.4 The Low-Productivity Country

Here we assume that the marginal product of domestic capital is below the world interest rate $r < r^*$. As a consequence, the country holds foreign assets F and the income of domestic residents exceeds the sum of domestic factor and debt income by an interest inflow of r^*F. We assume that domestic residents regard wealth held in the form of bonds of domestic firms or the government as more secure than international bonds. Therefore, they limit foreign assets even though these give a higher rate of return. Let the maximum ratio of foreign to domestic assets be $m < 1$. Then, foreign assets will be limited to $F = m(D + K)$.

The public sector is described the same way as in the previous section. The only difference is that the income of domestic residents now exceeds factor and debt income. Therefore, tax revenue is $T = t(Y + rD + r^*F)$. The government budget constraint is $B + T = G + rD$, which can be stated as

$bY + t(Y + rD + r^*F) = gY + rD$. Again, the purchase ratio and the deficit ratio are given, whereas the tax rate has to be adjusted.

Disposable income is the sum of factor income, public debt income and the interest inflow, net of tax respectively $Y_d = Y + rD + r^*F - T$. Households save a constant fraction of their disposable income $S = sY_d$ with saving ratio $s = const.$ Given the government budget identity, tax payments are $T = G + rD - B$. Therefore, disposable income is $Y_d = (1 - g + b)Y + r^*F$ and savings are $S = s(1-g+b)Y + sr^*F$. Savings finance public borrowing, foreign asset accumulation, and capital accumulation $\dot{D} + \dot{F} + \dot{K} = s(1-g+b)Y + sr^*F$.

Summarizing the above, the model can be represented by a system of six equations:

$$Y = AK \tag{11}$$

$$r = \alpha A \tag{12}$$

$$F = m(D + K) \tag{13}$$

$$\dot{D} + \dot{F} + \dot{K} = s(1 - g + b)Y + sr^*F \tag{14}$$

$$\dot{D} = bY \tag{15}$$

$$bY + t(Y + rD) = gY + rD \tag{16}$$

Here $\alpha, b, g, m, r^*, s, A, D$, and K are exogenous, while $r, t, \dot{D}, F, \dot{K}$, and Y are endogenous.

Now it is useful to analyse growth rates. From (11) and (13) it is immediately evident that output grows at the same rate as capital. To obtain capital growth, note that (13) implies $\dot{F} = m(\dot{D} + \dot{K})$ and use this together with (15) in (14) to replace the accumulation of foreign assets and public debt $(1 + m)\dot{K} = s(1 + b - g)Y - b(1 + m)Y + sr^*F$. Next insert (11), (12), and (13) to attain $(1 + m)\dot{K} = s(1 + b - g)AK - b(1 + m)AK + msr^*(D + K)$. Finally collect the terms and divide by K to yield:

$$\hat{K} = \frac{s(1 - g + b)A}{1 + m} - bA + msr^* + msr^* \frac{D}{K} \tag{17}$$

The growth rate of capital is an increasing function of the debt-capital ratio. The reason is that, given the stock of capital, an increase in public debt implies higher domestic assets. An increase in domestic assets implies that households are also willing to hold more foreign assets. These give a higher rate of return than domestic assets. This is why savings and capital accumulation increase.

Next we analyse public debt. Divide (15) by D and substitute output with the help of (11) to reach public debt growth:

$$\hat{D} = \frac{bAK}{D} \tag{18}$$

Public debt growth is a declining function of the debt-capital ratio. Public debt growth and capital growth are constant if the debt-capital ratio is constant. Hence, in the steady state, public debt has to grow at the same rate as capital. To solve for debt-capital ratio the steady state, equate (17) and (18) to obtain:

$$\frac{bAK}{D} = \frac{s(1-g+b)A}{1+m} - bA + msr^* + msr^* \frac{D}{K} \tag{19}$$

For notational simplicity define:

$$z \equiv \frac{s(1-g+b)A}{1+m} - bA + msr^* \qquad \text{and} \qquad x \equiv \frac{D}{K}$$

Using these definitions, (19) can be restated as:

$$\frac{bA}{x} = z + msr^* x \tag{20}$$

which is a quadratic equation in the debt-capital ratio. The solution is:

$$x_{1,2} = \frac{1}{2msr^*}\left[-z \pm \sqrt{z^2 + 2msr^* bA}\right]$$

Both solutions are real, one of them is negative and one of them is positive. So we have:

Proposition 3. *There is a unique steady-state ratio of debt to capital. An increase in the deficit ratio increases the debt-capital ratio.*

Proof. The debt-capital ratio is

$$x = \frac{1}{2msr^*}\left[-z + \sqrt{z^2 + 2msr^* bA}\right] \tag{21}$$

Take the derivative with respect to b:

$$\frac{\partial x}{\partial b} = \frac{1}{2msr^*}\left[-\frac{\partial z}{\partial b} + \frac{1}{\sqrt{z^2 + 2msr^* bA}}\left(z\frac{\partial z}{\partial b} + msr^* A\right)\right]$$

with $\partial z/\partial b = sA/(1+m) - A < 0$.

Obviously $\partial x/\partial b > 0$ holds true if the term in brackets is positive. Take this term, multiply it by the radical, and rearrange to obtain the condition:

$$\left[z - \sqrt{z^2 + 2msr^*bA}\right] \frac{\partial z}{\partial b} + msr^*A > 0$$

Due to $msr^*A > 0$ and $\partial z/\partial b < 0$ a sufficient condition is $z < \sqrt{z^2 + 2msr^*bA}$. Square both sides to see that this always holds true. ■

To obtain the steady-state growth rate we have to insert (21) into either growth equation (17) or (18). Let us consider capital growth. An increase in the deficit ratio has a direct negative effect on capital growth. However, it also increases the debt-capital ratio, which has a positive effect on capital growth. The direct effect dominates and, therefore, we may state:

Proposition 4. *An increase in the deficit ratio reduces capital growth.*

Proof. Using the definitions of x and z, the growth rate of capital given (17) can be written as $\hat{K} = z + msr^*x$. Now insert the solution of x given in (21) and simplify to obtain:

$$\hat{K} = \frac{1}{2}\left[z + \sqrt{z^2 + 2msr^*bA}\right]$$

The effect of a change in the deficit ratio is given by:

$$\frac{\partial \hat{K}}{\partial b} = \frac{1}{2}\left[\frac{\partial z}{\partial b} + \frac{1}{\sqrt{z^2 + 2msr^*bA}}\left(z\frac{\partial z}{\partial b} + msr^*A\right)\right]$$

with

$$\frac{\partial z}{\partial b} = \frac{sA}{1+m} - A < 0$$

At $b = 0$ we find:

$$\left.\frac{\partial \hat{K}}{\partial b}\right|_{b=0} = \left[\frac{sA}{1+m} - A + \frac{msr^*A}{2z}\right]$$

Insert z at $b = 0$ to see that $msr^*A/(2z) < 0.5$. Then the derivative is negative for any $s < 0.5(1+m)$. Since this is empirically fulfilled, we assume the condition holds true. Hence we have $\partial K/\partial b|_{b=0} < 0$. Now take the second derivative:

$$\frac{\partial^2 K}{\partial b^2} = -\frac{1}{4}\left(\frac{z(\partial z/\partial b + 2msr^* A)^2}{(z^2 + 2msr^* bA)\sqrt{z^2 + 2msr^* bA}}\right) < 0$$

Hence, for any $b > 0$ the derivative is $\partial K/\partial b < 0$. ■

Finally, note that foreign assets are proportional to the sum of capital and public debt. This implies that in a steady state, where debt and capital grow at the same rate, foreign assets will grow at this rate as well.

6.2.5 Stability

The dynamics are described by the two growth equations repeated here for convenience:

$$\hat{K} = \frac{(1+b-g)sA}{1+m} - bA + msr^* + msr^* \frac{D}{K} \tag{22}$$

$$\hat{D} = \frac{bAK}{D} \tag{23}$$

Capital growth increases in proportion to the debt-capital ratio. Debt growth is inversely related to the debt-capital ratio. Figure 6.5 shows the two growth lines.

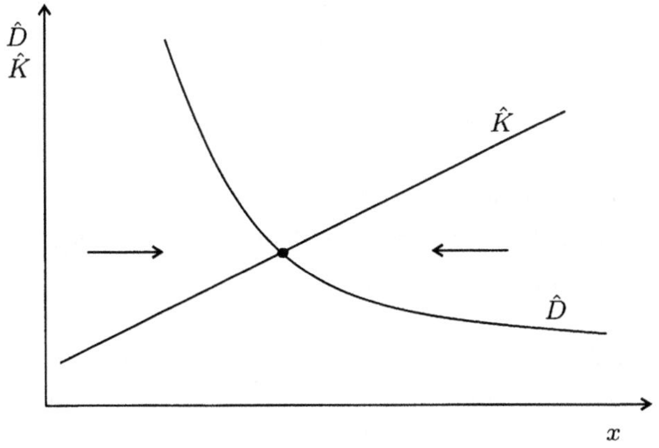

Figure 6.5.
Capital Growth and Debt Growth

There is a unique steady state at the intersection of the two lines. To the left of the steady state, debt grows faster than capital. And to the right of the steady state, capital grows faster than debt. As a results we my state:

Proposition 5. *The steady state is stable.*

6.2.6 Some Shocks

In this section we will explore the process of adjustment initiated by three shocks:

- an increase in the budget deficit ratio
- an increase in the government purchase ratio
- an increase in the maximum ratio of foreign to domestic assets.

1) Increase in the deficit ratio. In the growth diagram the $\hat{K}$ line moves to the right and the $\hat{D}$ line moves upwards. The new steady state is at a higher debt-capital ratio and at a lower growth rate, see Figure 6.6. Now we consider the process of adjustment. At the time of the increase in the deficit ratio, debt growth increases and capital growth declines. Foreign assets are dependent upon domestic assets. Take time derivatives from $F = m(D + K)$ to obtain $\dot{F} = m\dot{D} + m\dot{K}$. Then divide by F and insert $F = m(D + K)$ on the right hand side to reach $\hat{F} = \dot{D}/(K + D) + \dot{K}/(K + D)$. Finally expand the fractions on the right by D and K respectively, and use $x = D/K$ to obtain:

$$\hat{F} = \frac{x}{1+x}\hat{D} + \frac{1}{1+x}\hat{K} \tag{24}$$

In the short run, the debt-capital ratio x is constant. The short-run effect of an increase in b on the growth rates of debt and capital can be derived from (22) and (23) of the previous section:

$$\frac{\partial \hat{K}}{\partial b} = \frac{sA}{1+m} - A \qquad \text{and} \qquad \frac{\partial \hat{D}}{\partial b} = \frac{A}{x} \tag{25}$$

Insert (25) into (24) to obtain the effect on foreign asset growth:

$$\frac{\partial \hat{F}}{\partial b} = \frac{sA}{(1+x)(1+m)} > 0 \tag{26}$$

Hence, at the moment of the shock there is a positive effect on foreign assets growth. To summarize the short-run effects: At the moment where the deficit ratio goes up, capital growth declines, while debt growth and foreign asset growth increase.

Due to the lower capital growth, output growth declines as well. Therefore, the budget deficit grows at a lower rate. In the medium run, this reduces debt growth. As a consequence, domestic assets grow at a lower rate. Due to the restriction on the holdings of foreign assets, their growth rate falls as well. In the long run, all three growth rates become constant and the same again. See Figure 6.7 for the time paths of growth rates.

Now consider a numerical example. At the start, the economy is in the steady state. Let the deficit ratio be given with 1%. Then, public debt, capital and foreign assets grow at the same constant rate of 1.3%. Now the government increases the deficit ratio to 2%. In the short run, this increases debt growth to 2.7%. At the same time, capital growth declines to 1.1%, and foreign asset growth increases to 1.4%. The budget deficit grows at the rate of 1.1%. In the medium run, debt growth declines and capital growth increases. Domestic asset growth and foreign asset growth both decline. In the long run, the growth rates converge. In the new steady state, public debt, capital and foreign assets and grow at the same constant rate of 1.2%.

2) Increase in the government purchase ratio. In the growth diagram the $\hat{K}$ line moves to the right. The new steady state is at a higher debt-capital ratio and implies lower capital growth and public debt growth. At the moment of the increase in the purchase ratio, capital growth declines while debt growth remains constant. Due to reduced capital growth, output and foreign assets grow at a lower rate. Deficit growth corresponds to output growth. In the medium run, lower deficit growth leads to a decline in debt growth. Finally, the debt-capital ratio becomes constant again. The growth rates of public debt, capital and foreign assets are constant and the same again.

3) Increase in foreign assets. Domestic households are willing to hold a higher proportion of their wealth in the form of foreign assets. This increase in m moves the $\hat{K}$ line upwards, while the $\hat{D}$ line remains unaffected, see Figure 6.8. In the new steady state, debt and capital grow at a higher rate.

Let us look more closely into the process of adjustment. At the moment the shock occurs, capital is reduced and foreign assets are increased by the same amount. Due to the higher rate of return on foreign assets, income goes up.

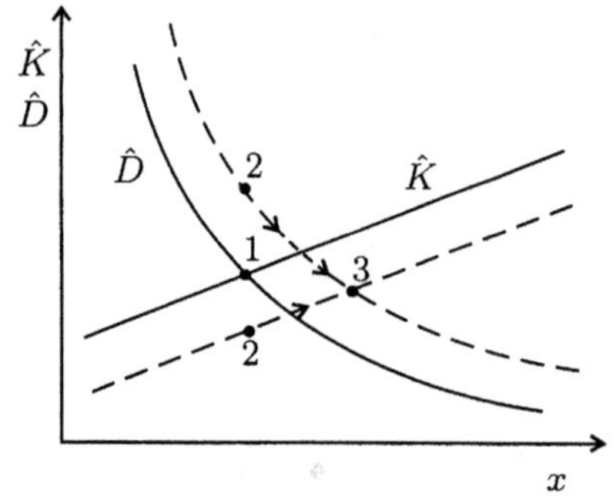

Figure 6.6.
Increase in the Deficit Ratio

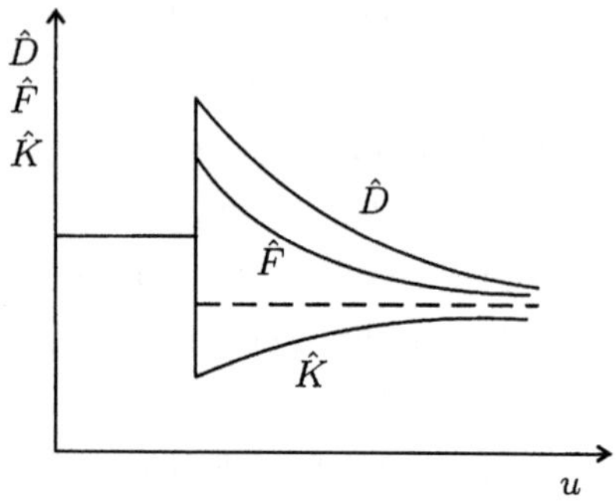

Figure 6.7.
Increase in the Deficit Ratio
(Time Paths)

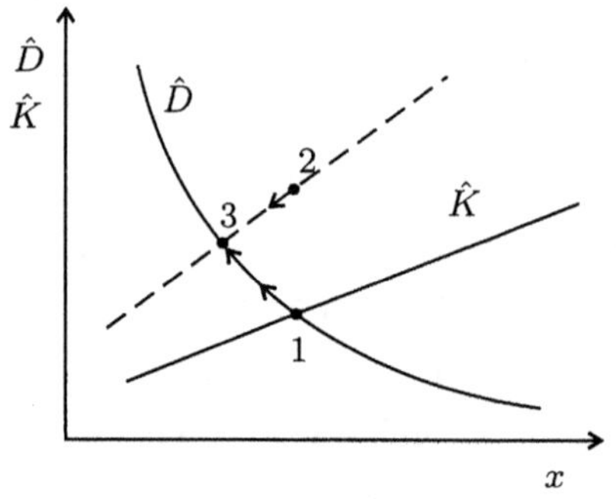

Figure 6.8.
Increase in Maximum
Foreign Asset-Capital Ratio

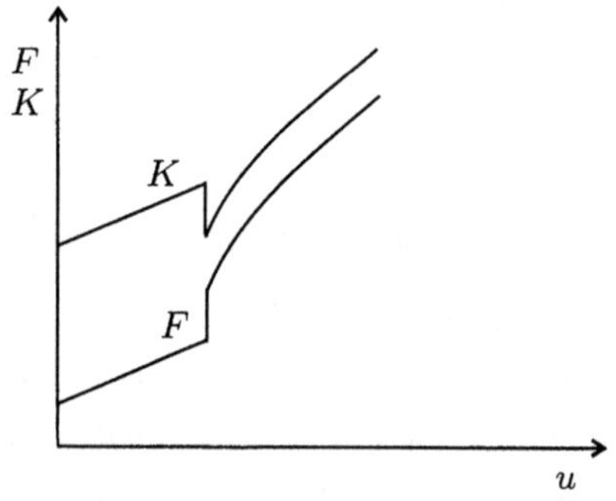

Figure 6.9.
Increase in Maximum
Foreign Asset-Capital Ratio
(Time Paths)

Therefore, savings rise and capital grows at a higher rate. Debt growth starts to accelerate gradually. Since capital growth exceeds debt growth, the debt-capital ratio declines. Then, capital growth declines and debt growth increases. Finally, the growth rates become constant and the same again. Figure 6.9 visualizes the time paths of capital and foreign assets on a semilogarithmic scale.

6.2.7 Summary

Two cases might arise. In the first case, the country has a high productivity. Therefore the domestic interest rate is below the world interest rate, and the country is an international debtor. The rest of the world puts a maximum on the ratio of foreign debt to capital. As a result, capital, output and foreign debt grow (or decline) at the same constant rate. The growth rate depends on the deficit ratio. An increase in the deficit ratio reduces capital growth, output growth and foreign debt growth. In the steady state, public debt and capital grow at the same constant rate. There is a critical deficit ratio. If the deficit ratio is below the critical level, there will be a steady state that proves to be stable. If the deficit ratio is above the critical level, there will be no steady state. Public debt growth is positive, while capital growth, output growth and foreign debt growth are negative.

In the second case, the country has a low productivity. Therefore, the domestic interest rate exceeds the world interest rate and the country is an international creditor. Domestic residents put a maximum on the ratio of foreign to domestic assets. As a result, capital growth and output growth as well as public debt growth depend on the deficit ratio and on the debt-capital ratio. Foreign asset growth depends on capital growth and on public debt growth. In the steady state, public debt and capital grow at the same constant rate. There is a steady state that proves to be stable. In the steady state, foreign assets grow at the same rate as capital, output and public debt. An increase in the deficit ratio reduces the steady-state growth rate.

6.3 Fixing the Tax Rate

6.3.1 The High-Productivity Country

We will now analyse the strategy of a fixed tax rate for a highly productive small open economy. Production is characterized the same way as in previous sections. The marginal product of domestic capital is above the world interest rate $r = \alpha A > r^*$. There is a capital inflow, and the country is an international debtor. It is assumed that the rest of the world limits international credit. However, the rest of the world is not willing to finance all the domestic assets and, therefore, a maximum is imposed on international credit. More precisely, the foreign debt F of the country is limited to a fixed proportion of domestic capital K. Let the maximum granted ratio of foreign debt to capital be $m < 1$. The constraint is always binding, so that $F = mK$. Hence, the availability of international loans is limited and firms compete for international funds. Therefore, they are willing to pay the private marginal product of capital as interest on foreign debt. Hence, interest payments amount to rF, where $r = \alpha A$.

Let us look at budget dynamics: The government spends a fixed fraction of national income on goods and services $G = gY$ with purchase ratio $g = const.$ Furthermore, it levies a proportionate tax on the income of domestic residents. The income of domestic residents is given by factor income plus debt income, minus interest payments on foreign debt. Therefore, tax revenue is $T = t(Y + rD - rF)$ with tax rate $t = const.$ The primary budget deficit is hY, where h is the primary deficit ratio. Given the budget constraint, we have $hY = gY - t(Y - rF)$. The primary budget deficit plus after tax interest payments gives us the budget deficit $B = hY + (1 - t)rD$. The budget deficit in turn adds to public debt $\dot{D} = B$. From this we obtain $\dot{D} = hY + (1 - t)rD$.

The next point refers to investment dynamics. Disposable income is made up of factor income and debt income, net after tax respectively, $Y_d = (1 - t)(Y + rD - rF)$. Households save a given share of disposable income $S = sY_d$ with saving ratio $s = const.$ Savings finance a part of capital accumulation $\dot{K}$ and public borrowing $\dot{D}$. International borrowing finances the remainder and augments foreign debt $\dot{F}$. Hence, capital dynamics are given by $\dot{K} + \dot{D} = s(1 - t)(Y + rD - rF) + \dot{F}$.

Summarizing the above, the model can be represented by a system of six equations:

$$Y = AK \tag{1}$$

$$r = \alpha A \tag{2}$$

$$F = mK \tag{3}$$

$$\dot{K} + \dot{D} = s(1-t)(Y + rD - rF) + \dot{F} \tag{4}$$

$$\dot{D} = hY + (1-t)rD \tag{5}$$

$$hY = gY - t(Y - rF) \tag{6}$$

Here α, g, m, s, t, A, D, and K are exogenous, while $h, r, \dot{D}, F, \dot{K}$, and Y are endogenous.

Now we are going to analyse growth rates. Note from (3) $\dot{F} = m\dot{K}$ and insert this together with (1), (2), (3) and (5) into (4) to substitute for the endogenous variables, rearrange and divide by K to obtain the growth rate of capital. Then use (1) to substitute for output in (5) and divide by D to find the growth rate of public debt:

$$\hat{K} = \frac{[s(1-t)(1-\alpha m) - h]\, A}{1-m} - \frac{(1-s)(1-t)\alpha A}{1-m}\frac{D}{K} \tag{7}$$

$$\hat{D} = hA\frac{K}{D} + (1-t)\alpha A \tag{8}$$

Both growth rates depend on the debt-capital ratio. Both growth rates are constant, if the debt-capital ratio is constant. So in the steady state, public debt grows at the same rate as capital. The rest of this section will focus on the question as to whether a steady state exists. Insert $x = D/K$ into (7) and (8) and equate the two growth rates to achieve:

$$(1-m)[h/x + (1-t)\alpha] = s(1-t)(1-\alpha m) - h - (1-s)(1-t)\alpha x \tag{9}$$

The solution to this quadratic equation is:

$$x_{1,2} = \frac{P \pm \sqrt{P^2 - Q}}{R} \tag{10}$$

with

$$P = s(1-t)(1-\alpha m) - h - (1-m)(1-t)\alpha$$
$$Q = 4(1-m)(1-s)(1-t)\alpha h$$
$$R = 2(1-s)(1-t)\alpha$$

There are two conditions for the solution to be real and positive:

$$s > s' = \frac{(1-m)\alpha}{(1-\alpha m)} \qquad \text{and} \qquad h < h_1$$

So we are able to state:

Proposition 1. *A steady state does exist if and only if the saving ratio exceeds a critical level and the primary deficit ratio stays below the critical level. Given that these conditions are satisfied, there are two steady states. If either the deficit ratio exceeds the critical level or the saving ratio is below the critical level, there is no steady state.*

Proof. In equation (10), Q and R are always real and positive. P is a declining function of h, i.e. $P' < 0$. For $s = s'$, we obtain $P = 0$ for $h = 0$. If $s > s'$, then P is positive for low levels of h and negative for high levels of h, and we observe $P = 0$ at $h = h' = (1-t)s - (1-m)(1-t)\alpha/(1-\alpha m) > 0$. Obviously P^2 is at minimum at $P = 0$. The solutions $x_{1,2}$ are real if $P^2 - Q > 0$. Since $P^2 - Q$ is a quadratic equation in h, it has two solutions $h_{1,2}$ for $P^2 - Q = 0$. For $h < h_1$ and for $h > h_2$ we have $P^2 - Q > 0$. This gives rise to four cases:

1) $s < s'$: In this case P is negative. Due to $P < 0$, both solutions are negative, i.e. $P + \sqrt{P^2 - Q} < 0$. To see this, square both sides in $-P > \sqrt{P^2 - Q}$.

2) $s > s'$ and $h_1 < h < h_2$: We have $P > 0$ but $P^2 - Q < 0$, and therefore both solutions are complex.

3) $s > s'$ and $h < h_1$: We have $P > 0$ and $P^2 - Q > 0$. Due to $P^2 - Q > 0$ the solutions are real. And due to $P > 0$ both solutions are positive, i.e. $P - \sqrt{P^2 - Q} > 0$. To see this, square both sides in $P > \sqrt{P^2 - Q}$.

4) $s > s'$ and $h > h_2$: We have $P < 0$ and $P^2 - Q > 0$. Due to $P^2 - Q > 0$ the solutions are real. But due to $P < 0$, both solutions are negative, i.e. $P + \sqrt{P^2 - Q} < 0$. To see this, square both sides in $-P > \sqrt{P^2 - Q}$. ∎

The structure of the two growth equations is identical to the closed economy, see Part I, Chapter 2. Therefore, if the saving ratio is above the critical level and the deficit ratio is below the critical level, then one of the two steady states is stable, and the other is unstable. However, if either the saving ratio is below the critical level or the deficit ratio is above the critical level, there will be no steady state. In this case, capital growth declines continuously, becomes negative at some point of time, and deteriorates further. Capital is driven to zero in finite time.

All this is very similar to the closed economy. In fact, for $m = 0$ we have the closed economy. However, openness in the form of $m > 0$ implies that the conditions for the existence of the two steady states are less restrictive. Table 6.1 gives an impression of how maximum foreign borrowing affects the conditions. The first column gives the assumed value of m. The second column gives the minimum required saving ratio s', given $\alpha = 0.3$. If $s = s'$, then the maximum primary deficit ratio is $h_1 = 0$. The third column gives the maximum primary deficit ratio for different levels of m under the assumption of $s = 0.3 > s'$.

Table 6.1. Critical Levels

m	s	h
0	0.3	0
0.1	0.278	0.0004
0.2	0.255	0.0019
0.3	0.231	0.0045
0.4	0.205	0.0086
0.5	0.177	0.0147
0.6	0.146	0.0234
0.7	0.114	0.0359
0.8	0.079	0.0549
0.9	0.041	0.0871

6.3.2 The Low-Productivity Country

Now we assume that the marginal product of domestic capital falls short of the world interest rate $r < r^*$. The marginal product of domestic capital is $r = \alpha A$. For ease of exposition, let the world interest rate be $r^* = \mu\alpha\mathrm{A}$ with $\mu > 1$. As a consequence of its low productivity, the country holds foreign assets F, and the income of domestic residents exceeds the sum of domestic factor and debt income by an interest inflow of r^*F. We assume that domestic residents regard wealth held in the form of bonds of either domestic firms or the government as more secure than foreign assets. Therefore they limit foreign assets, even though they give a higher rate of return. Let the maximum ratio of foreign to domestic assets be $m < 1$. Then foreign assets will be limited to $F = m(D + K)$.

Let us look at budget dynamics. The government spends a fixed fraction of national income on goods and services $G = gY$ with purchase ratio $g = const.$ Furthermore, the government levies a proportionate tax on the income of domestic residents. The income of domestic residents is given by factor income, debt income and interest earnings on foreign assets. Therefore, tax revenue is $T = t(Y + rD + r^*F)$ with tax rate $t = const.$ Government purchases plus public interest minus tax earnings represent the budget deficit $B = G + rD - T$. The budget deficit in turn adds to public debt $\dot{D} = B$. From this we obtain $\dot{D} = gY + rD - t(Y + rD + r^*F)$.

The next point refers to investment dynamics. Disposable income is made up of factor income, debt income and interest earning on foreign assets, net after tax respectively, $Y_d = (1-t)(Y+rD+r^*F)$. Households save a given share of disposable income $S = sY_d$ with saving ratio $s = const.$ Savings finance capital accumulation $\dot{K}$, public borrowing $\dot{D}$ and foreign asset accumulation $\dot{F}$. Hence, capital dynamics are given by $\dot{K}+\dot{D}+\dot{F} = s(1-t)(Y+rD+r^*F)$.

Summarizing the above, the model is captured by six equations:

$$Y = AK \tag{11}$$

$$r = \alpha A \tag{12}$$

$$r^* = \mu r \tag{13}$$

$$F = m(K + D) \tag{14}$$

$$\dot{K} + \dot{D} + \dot{F} = s(1-t)(Y + rD + r^*F) \tag{15}$$

$$\dot{D} = gY + rD - t(Y + rD + r^*F) \tag{16}$$

Here $\alpha, \mu, g, m, s, t, A, D$, and K are exogenous, while $r, r^*, \dot{D}, F, \dot{K}$, and Y are endogenous.

First, we consider public debt growth. Insert (13) and (14) into (16) to substitute for the world interest rate and foreign assets $\dot{D} = (g-t)Y + (1-t)rD - \mu mrt(D+K)$. Then collect terms and replace Y and r with the help of (11) and (12) to obtain $\dot{D} = (g - t - \alpha\mu mt)AK + (1 - t - \mu mt)\alpha AD$. The factor $(g - t - \alpha\mu mt)$ gives the deficit to output ratio at zero debt. Denote this as the primary deficit ratio $h = g - t - \alpha\mu mt$ so that we have $\dot{D} = hAK + (1 - t - \mu mt)\alpha AD$. Now divide by debt D and insert the debt-capital ratio $x = D/K$ to obtain public debt growth:

$$\hat{D} = \frac{hA}{x} + (1 - t - \mu mt)\alpha A \tag{17}$$

To derive capital growth, first note $\dot{F} = m(\dot{D} + \dot{K})$ from (14), and then use (11), (12), (13), and (14) in (15) to substitute for output, the domestic and the world interest rate, and foreign assets. Then subtract $\dot{D} = hAK + (1 - t - \mu mt)\alpha AD$, rearrange and divide by K. Finally, insert the debt-capital ratio $x = D/K$ to obtain:

$$\hat{K} = \frac{[s(1-t)(1+\alpha\mu m) - (1+m)h]A}{1+m} + \frac{[s(1-t)(1+\mu m) - (1+m)((1-t) - \mu mt)]\alpha Ax}{1+m} \tag{18}$$

Both, capital growth and debt growth depend on the debt-capital ratio. In the steady state, public debt grows at the same rate as capital, so the debt-capital ratio is constant. Equations (17) and (18) show that in this case capital growth and debt growth are constant. To find the steady state, equate the two growth rates given in (17) and (18):

$$\frac{[s(1-t)(1+\alpha\mu m)-(1+m)h]}{1+m} + \frac{[s(1-t)(1+\mu m)-(1+m)(1-t-\mu mt)]\alpha x}{1+m} = \frac{h}{x} + (1-t-\mu mt)\alpha \tag{19}$$

This is a quadratic expression in the debt-capital ratio. The solution is:

$$x_{1,2} = \frac{P \pm \sqrt{P^2 - Q}}{R} \tag{20}$$

with

$$P = s(1-t)(1+\alpha\mu m) - (1+m)(h + (1-t-\mu mt)\alpha)$$
$$Q = 4((1+m-s(1+\mu m))(1-t) - \mu mt(1+m))\alpha(1+m)h$$
$$R = 2((1+m-s(1+\mu m))(1-t) - \mu mt(1+m))\alpha$$

The solutions $x_{1,2}$ are steady states if they are both real and positive. So we obtain:

Proposition 2. *Four cases may arise:*

1) If the saving ratio is below a critical level s', there is no solution. The critical level of the saving ratio is:

$$s' = \frac{(1+m)(1-t-\mu mt)\alpha}{(1-t)(1+\alpha\mu m)}$$

2) If the saving ratio is above a critical level s'', there is a unique positive solution. The critical level of the saving ratio is:

$$s'' = \frac{(1+m)(1-t-\mu mt)}{(1-t)(1+\mu m)}$$

3) If the saving ratio is between the two critical levels $s' < s < s''$, and the deficit ratio exceeds a critical level h_1, then there is no solution.

4) If the saving ratio is between the two critical levels $s' < s < s''$, and the deficit ratio stays below a critical level h_1, then there are two solutions.

Proof. For $s < s''$ we observe $R > 0$ and $Q > 0$. For $s > s''$ we observe $R < 0$ and $Q < 0$.

First, we consider $s < s''$, $R > 0$, and $Q > 0$. For $s < s'$ we obtain $P < 0$ for any $h > 0$. For $s > s'$ we obtain $P = 0$ for $h = h' = s(1-t)(1+\alpha\mu m)/(1+m) - (1-t-\mu mt)\alpha > 0$. Then P is positive for low levels of h and negative for high levels of h. At $h = h'$ we obtain $P = 0$. Consequently, P^2 has its minimum at $h = h'$. The solutions $x_{1,2}$ are real if $P^2 - Q > 0$. Since $P^2 - Q$ is a quadratic equation in h, it has two solutions $h_{1,2}$ to $P^2 - Q = 0$. For $h < h_1$ and for $h > h_2$ we have $P^2 - Q > 0$. Four cases arise:

1) $s < s'$: We observe $P < 0, Q > 0$ and $R > 0$. Due to $P < 0$ both solutions are negative, we have $P + \sqrt{P^2 - Q} < 0$. To see this, square both sides in $-P > \sqrt{P^2 - Q}$.
2) $s' < s < s''$ and $h < h_1$. We have $P > 0, Q > 0, R > 0$ and $P^2 - Q > 0$. Due to $P^2 - Q > 0$ the solutions are real. And due to $P > 0$ and $R > 0$ both solutions are positive, i.e. $P - \sqrt{P^2 - Q} > 0$. To see this, square both sides in $P > \sqrt{P^2 - Q}$.
3) $s' < s < s''$ and $h > h_2$: We have $P < 0, Q > 0, R > 0$ and $P^2 - Q > 0$. Due to $P^2 - Q > 0$ the solutions are real. But due to $P < 0$ and $R > 0$ both solutions are negative, i.e. $P + \sqrt{P^2 - Q} < 0$. To see this, square both sides in $-P > \sqrt{P^2 - Q}$.
4) $s' < s < s''$ and $h_1 < h < h_2$. We have $P > 0, Q > 0, R > 0$, but due to $P^2 - Q < 0$ both solutions are complex.

Now assume $s > s''$: We have $P < 0, R < 0$ and $Q < 0$. Due to $Q < 0$ we have $P^2 - Q > 0$ and therefore both solutions are real. Due to $P < 0$ we have $P - \sqrt{P^2 - Q} < 0$ and $P + \sqrt{P^2 - Q} > 0$. To see this, square both sides in $-P < \pm\sqrt{P^2 - Q}$ and note $Q < 0$. ■

Figures 6.10 to 6.12 show the growth diagrams for the different cases. The $\hat{D}$ line shows that public debt growth is a declining function of the debt-capital ratio. The $\hat{K}$ line represents capital growth. In Figure 6.10 a normal saving ratio is assumed ($s < s'$). In this case there is no steady state, and the debt-capital ratio explodes. In Figure 6.11 it is assumed that the primary deficit is low and the saving ratio is high but not extraordinarily high ($s' < s < s''$). In this case there are two steady states. The steady state at the high debt-capital ratio is unstable, and the steady state at the low debt-capital ratio is locally stable. In Figure 6.12, it is assumed that the saving ratio is extraordinarily high. In this case, capital growth is an increasing function of the debt-capital ratio, and the $\hat{K}$ line slopes upwards. As Figure 6.12 illustrates there is a unique and stable steady state.

Table 6.2 assumes $\alpha = 0.3, t = 0.2$ and $\mu = 2$ and shows how the two critical levels of the saving ratio depend on m. As a result, we see that even with high capital mobility (high m) the case of a saving ratio $s > s''$ is very unlikely. In contrast, empirically, the saving ratio is below the critical level s'. Hence, empirically relevant is the case where there is no steady state.

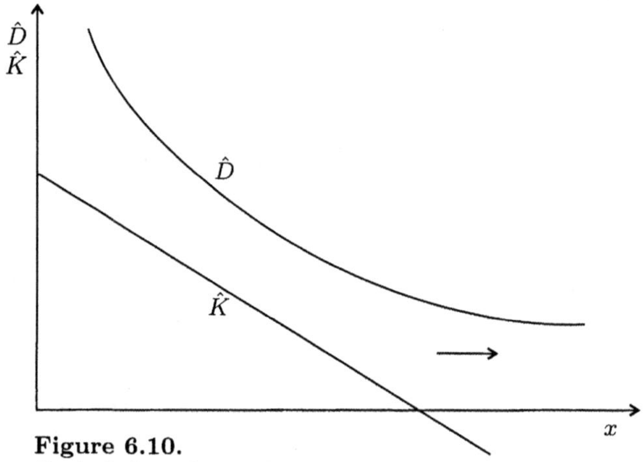

Figure 6.10.
Capital Growth and Debt Growth
Normal Saving Ratio or High Deficit

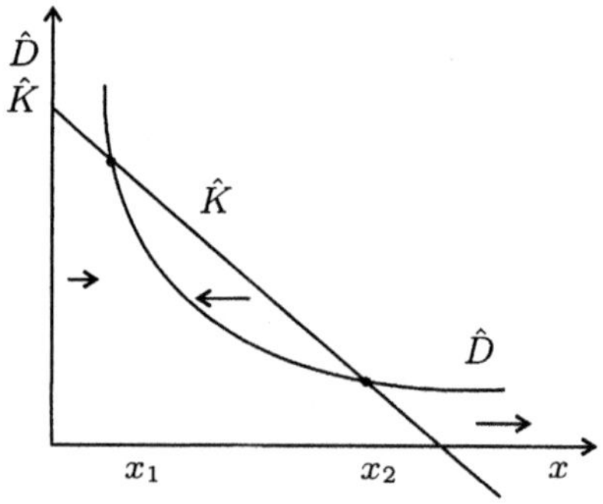

Figure 6.11.
Growth Diagram
High Saving Ratio, Low Deficit

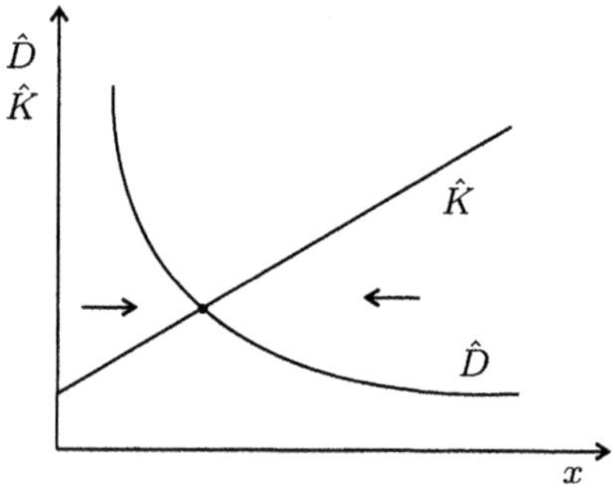

Figure 6.12.
Growth Diagram
Extremely High Saving Ratio

Table 6.3 shows the maximum sustainable primary budget deficit given a saving ratio in the interval $s' < s < s''$ The first column gives the assumed value of m. The second column gives the critical primary deficit ratio for a saving ratio of $s = 0.2$, and the third column gives the critical level of h, given that $s = 0.3$.

6.3.3 Summary

Starting from a balanced budget, a tax cut leads to a budget deficit. Public debt emerges and begins to grow. Public debt growth converges to a certain level, while capital growth and output growth decline continuously, become negative at some point of time, and deteriorate further. Capital and output are driven to zero in finite time. Only if the saving ratio is very high and the deficit is very low, there will be two steady states. In these steady states, public debt and capital grow at the same rate. One of the steady states is stable, and the other is unstable. Still, as an essential result a fixed tax rate normally cannot be sustained.

Table 6.2. Critical Saving Ratios

m	s'	s''
0	0.3	1
0.1	0.296	0.871
0.2	0.289	0.771
0.3	0.281	0.691
0.4	0.271	0.622
0.5	0.260	0.563
0.6	0.247	0.509
0.7	0.234	0.460
0.8	0.219	0.415
0.9	0.204	0.373

Table 6.3. Maximum Sustainable Primary Deficits

m	h $(s = 0.3)$	h $(s = 0.4)$
0	0	0.0009
0.1	0	0.0010
0.2	0	0.0012
0.3	0	0.0013
0.4	0	0.0017
0.5	0.0002	0.0021
0.6	0.0003	0.0026
0.7	0.0006	0.0031
0.8	0.0009	0.0038
0.9	0.0013	0.0045

7

The Solow Model of a Two-Country World

7.1 Introduction

In this chapter we will explore the cross country effects of public debt. The basic assumptions are that the production structure is again of AK type and that households save a constant fraction of their disposable income. The basic model, without public debt, is presented in Carlberg (1997).

At the start, let us have a look at the literature on public debt in a world economy made up of two countries. Schmid (1988, 1990) introduces public consumption in an overlapping generations model of a growing economy as it is developed in Buiter (1981). The government fixes the tax per head. Stability analysis by phase diagrams shows that there are possibly two steady states. One of them is stable, the other is unstable. Carlberg (1993) relies on an overlapping generations model of a stationary economy with public consumption. The government fixes the tax rate. There is no long-run equilibrium, hence this strategy cannot be sustained. Carlberg (1995) considers a Solow model of a growing economy. The government either fixes the budget deficit per head or the tax per head. In the case where the government fixes the budget deficit per head, there are normally two steady states. An increase in the budget deficit in either country reduces capital per head and output per head in both countries. If the deficit ratio exceeds a critical level, then there is no steady state. In the case where the government fixes the tax per head there is normally no steady state. Only if the saving ratio is very large, then a very small primary deficit can be sustained.

Endogenous growth in a two country world is analysed in Buiter and Kletzer (1991) and in Alogoskoufis and van der Ploeg(1991, 1993). Buiter and Kletzer (1991) consider a three period overlapping generations model where endogenous growth comes from human capital accumulation. Physical capital is internationally mobile but human capital is not. The analysis concentrates on the steady state in which the government adjusts taxes to keep the public debt-human capital ratio constant. This implies a fixed deficit ratio. An increase in the deficit ratio reduces physical capital accumulation but fosters human capital accumulation and, therefore, output growth. As a result, the two countries may permanently differ in growth rates. Alogoskoufis and van der Ploeg (1991, 1993) analyse public debt in a continuous-time overlapping generations model. In their 1991 paper it is assumed that the government fixes the deficit ratio, while in their 1993 paper the government balances the budget intertemporally. In both papers, endogenous growth comes from externalities in physical capital accumulation. Physical capital is internationally mobile and, therefore, the growth rates are equalized across countries. However, there might be permanent differences in output levels. It is shown that an increase in the deficit ratio in one of the countries reduces output growth in both countries. In addition it leads to an increase in that country's foreign debt to output ratio while it leads to an increase in the other country's foreign asset to output ratio.

The two following sections analyse the fixed deficit ratio and the fixed tax rate respectively. In each section the first subsection presents the model, the second analyses stability, the third goes into the dynamics of adjustment and the fourth summarizes the results.

7.2 Fixing the Deficit Ratio

7.2.1 The Model

There are two countries denoted by $i = 1, 2$. In each of these countries there is a large number of identical firms. Each firm ι in country i produces a homogeneous commodity $Y_{i,\iota}$ by means of capital $K_{i,\iota}$ and labour $N_{i,\iota}$. The firm production function is of the Cobb-Douglas type: $Y_{i,\iota} = AK^{\alpha}_{i,\iota}(EN_{i,\iota})^{\beta}$, where $A > 0$ is a scale parameter, $\alpha > 0, \beta > 0, \alpha + \beta = 1$, and E is an exogenously given index of labour efficiency. Each firm maximizes profits $\Pi_{i,\iota} = Y_{i,\iota} - rK_{i,\iota} - wN_{i,\iota}$,under perfect competition. Here $\Pi_{i,\iota}$ denotes the profits of firm ι in country i, r the interest rate, and w the wage rate. As a consequence, each firm adjusts the input of capital, so that the marginal product of capital equals the interest rate $\partial Y_{i,\iota}/\partial K_{i,\iota} = \alpha Y_{i,\iota}/K_{i,\iota} = r$. Likewise the input of labour is adjusted to equate the marginal product of labour with the wage rate $\partial Y_{i,\iota}/\partial N_{i,\iota} = \beta Y_{i,\iota}/N_{i,\iota} = w$.

The aggregate production function in country i is $Y_i = AK_i^{\alpha}(EN_i)^{\beta}$, where K_i and N_i are the aggregate amounts of capital and labour used in country i. Labour efficiency E depends on the amount of knowledge accumulated which is proportional to capital. It is assumed that knowledge diffuses immediately all over the world. Therefore, labour efficiency in both countries is proportional to average capital per worker $E = (K_1 + K_2)/(N_1 + N_2)$. Capital is perfectly mobile throughout the world, and the markets for capital and labour are perfectly competitive. At each point of time, the amount of capital is given. Labour is immobile and supplied inelastically in both countries. We assume that both countries are of the same size $N_1 = N_2$. Due to competitive markets, the interest rate and the wage rate adjust to equate the supply and the demand of capital and labour. Hence, the interest rate corresponds to the marginal product of capital $r = \partial Y/\partial K = \alpha A$ and the wage rate corresponds to the marginal product of labour $w = \partial Y/\partial N = \beta Y/N$. Due to symmetry of firms, equal labour supply in both countries and perfect capital mobility, the aggregate capital used in the two countries will be the same $K_1 = K_2$. As a consequence, the aggregate production functions simplify to $Y_i = AK_i$. Output Y can be devoted to consumption, investment, government purchases, and exports $Y_i = C_i + I_i + G_i + X_i$.

Next we look at income. Domestic residents earn the interest rate r on foreign assets F_i, so that the interest inflow is rF_i. Disposable income is made up of factor income, public interest and the interest inflow, net of tax respectively $Y_{d,i} = Y_i + rD_i + rF_i - T_i$. To determine tax payments, consider the dynamics of public debt. In each country the government raises loans and levies an income tax in order to finance both government purchases and the interest payments on public debt. Each government spends a fixed share of national income on goods and services $G_i = g_i Y_i$ with purchase ratio $g_i = const.$ Besides this, governments borrow a fixed proportion of income $B_i = b_i Y_i$ with deficit ratio $b_i = const$. Budget deficits augment public debt $\dot{D}_i = B_i$. Both governments pay the interest rate r on public debt D_i, so public interest payments amount to rD_i. Governments impose a tax at the flat rate t_i on the income of domestic residents. Tax revenue is $T_i = t_i(Y_i + rD_i + rF_i)$. The government budget constraints can be written as $B_i + T_i = G_i + rD_i$. By using the behavioural functions, the identities can be reformulated in the following way $b_i Y_i + t_i(Y_i + rD_i + rF_i) = g_i Y_i + rD_i$. In these equations, the purchase ratios and the deficit ratios are given, whereas the tax rates have to be adjusted.

Households save a constant fraction of their disposable income $S_i = sY_{d,i}$ with the saving ratio $s = const$ and of the same size in both countries. Private savings serve to finance public borrowing, the accumulation of foreign assets, and the accumulation of capital $\dot{D}_i + \dot{F}_i + \dot{K}_i = S_i = s_i(Y_i + rD_i + rF_i - T_i)$. Now use $B_i + T_i = G_i + rD_i$, $B_i = b_i Y_i$ and $G_i = g_i Y_i$ to obtain $\dot{D}_i + \dot{F}_i + \dot{K}_i = (1 + b_i - g_i)sY_i + srF_i$.

Summarizing the above, the model can be represented by a system of eleven equations:

$$Y_i = AK_i \tag{1}$$

$$r = \alpha A \tag{2}$$

$$\dot{D}_i + \dot{F}_i + \dot{K}_i = (1 + b_i - g_i)sY_i + srF_i \tag{3}$$

$$\dot{D}_i = b_i Y_i \tag{4}$$

$$b_i Y_i + t_i(Y_i + rD_i + rF_i) = g_i Y_i + rD_i \tag{5}$$

$$K_1 = K_2 \tag{6}$$

$$F_1 = -F_2 \tag{7}$$

Here $\alpha, b_i, g_i, s, A, D_i, F_i$, and K_i are exogenous, while $r, t_i, \dot{D}_i, \dot{F}_i, \dot{K}_i$, and Y_i are endogenous.

Now the analysis is carried out in terms of growth rates. To start with, consider capital growth. First, take the sum over equation (3), while noting that both countries use the same amount of capital $K_1 = K_2$ and that the foreign assets of country 1 are the foreign debt of country 2, to get $2\dot{K}_i =$

$(2+b_1+b_2-g_1-g_2)sY_i-\dot{D}_1-\dot{D}_2$. Then insert (4) and substitute for output with the help of (1) to obtain:

$$\hat{K}_i=[(2+b_1+b_2-g_1-g_2)s-(b_1+b_2)]\frac{A}{2} \tag{8}$$

As a result we may summarize:

Proposition 1. *Capital growth in both countries is constant and the same. It depends on both deficit ratios, on both purchase ratios, on the saving ratio, and on the scale parameter. An increase in either deficit ratio causes a decline in capital growth and the same holds for an increase in either purchase ratio. An increase in the saving ratio or in the scale parameter leads to a rise in capital growth.*

The obvious reason for a negative effects of the deficit ratios on growth rates is that a budget deficit in either country reduces capital formation in both countries. The growth rates are positive if the sum of the two deficit ratios stays below a critical level:

$$b_1+b_2<b'=\frac{s(2-g_1-g_2)}{1-s} \tag{9}$$

Given $b_1=b_2$ and $g_1=g_2$ we obtain the condition of the closed economy. If the deficit ratio in country 2 is below the critical level of the closed economy, then the deficit of country 1 might exceed the critical level and there is still positive capital growth.

Now look at public debt growth. The growth rates are immediately derived from (4) and (1):

$$\hat{D}_i=\frac{b_iAK_i}{D_i} \tag{10}$$

Public debt growth in each country depends on the deficit ratio and on the debt-capital ratio of that country. It is independent of the deficit ratio of the other country. Public debt growth is constant if the debt-capital ratio is constant. Therefore, in the steady state, public debt and capital have to grow at the same rate. Equate (8) and (10) to find the steady-state ratios of public debt to capital:

$$\frac{D_i}{K_i} = \frac{2b_i}{(2 - g_1 - g_2)s - (1 - s)(b_1 + b_2)} \tag{11}$$

The steady-state ratios of public debt to capital depend on both deficit ratios, on both purchase ratios and on the saving ratio. An increase in the own deficit ratio causes an increase in the debt-capital ratio and an increase in the deficit ratio of the other country also leads to a rise in the debt-capital ratio. And the same holds for an increase in either purchase ratio. An increase in the saving ratio leads to a decline in the debt-capital ratio.

Finally, consider foreign assets of country 1. Rearrange equation (3) to obtain: $\dot{F}_1 = (1 + b_i - g_i)sY_1 + srF_1 - \dot{D}_1 - \dot{K}_1$. Then use (4), (8), and $\dot{K}_1 = \hat{K}_1 K_1$ to replace the changes in public debt and capital and simplify:

$$\dot{F}_1 = -\frac{[(1 - s)(b_1 - b_2) + (g_2 - g_1)]Y_1}{2} + srF_1 \tag{12}$$

Then divide by F_1 to obtain foreign asset growth:

$$\hat{F}_1 = -\frac{[(1 - s)(b_1 - b_2) + (g_2 - g_1)]AK_1}{2F_1} + sr \tag{13}$$

Foreign asset growth depends on the difference in deficit ratios, on the difference in purchase ratios, and on the ratio of foreign assets to capital. In the steady state, foreign assets grow at the same rate as capital. Hence, in the steady state, the ratio of foreign assets to capital is constant. Equate foreign asset growth to capital growth to obtain the steady-state ratio of foreign assets to capital:

$$\frac{F_1}{K_1} = \frac{(1 - s)(b_1 - b_2) + g_2 - g_1}{2\alpha s - (2 - g_1 - g_2)s + (1 - s)(b_1 + b_2)} \tag{14}$$

To simplify the analysis and to concentrate on the consequences of public debt, we assume $g = g_1 = g_2$. The ratio of foreign assets to capital is then given by:

$$\frac{F_1}{K_1} = -\frac{(1 - s)(b_1 - b_2)}{2s(1 - \alpha - g) - (1 - s)(b_1 + b_2)} \tag{15}$$

The denominator is positive as long as the sum of the budget deficit ratios stays below a critical level:

$$b_1 + b_2 < b'' = \frac{2s(1 - \alpha - g)}{1 - s} \tag{16}$$

First, assume that the sum of the deficit ratios is below the critical level b'' Then the denominator in (15) is positive. In that case $b_1 > b_2$ implies $F_1 < 0$ and $F_2 > 0$. Hence, we may state:

Proposition 2. *The high-deficit country will be an international debtor. Conversely the low-deficit country will be an international creditor. Let country 1 be the high deficit country. Then a rise in the deficit ratio in country 1 causes a rise in the ratio of foreign debt to capital in country 1 and a rise in the ratio of foreign assets to capital in country 2. A rise in the deficit ratio in country 2 causes a decline in the ratio of foreign debt to capital in country 1 and a decline in the ratio of foreign assets to capital in country 2.*

Now assume that the sum of the deficit ratios is above the critical level b''. In that case $b_1 > b_2$ implies $F_1 > 0$ and $F_2 < 0$. Hence, the high-deficit country would be an international creditor and the low-deficit country would be an international debtor. This seems contradictory and suggests instability.

Finally, compare the two critical levels for the sums of the deficit ratios. Comparison (9) and (16) shows $b'' < b'$. Hence, the potential instability of the foreign-asset ratio occurs even though the sum of the deficit ratios still allows positive capital growth and output growth.

7.2.2 Stability

Dynamics of the model are completely described by the three growth equations for capital, public debt and foreign assets. To concentrate on public debt, we analyse the case where both countries have the same purchase ratio $g = g_1 = g_2$. In that case the growth equations simplify to:

$$\hat{K}_i = [2s(1-g) - (1-s)(b_1 + b_2)]A/2 \tag{17}$$

$$\hat{D}_i = b_i Y_i / D_i \tag{18}$$

$$\hat{F}_1 = -(1-s)(b_1 - b_2)AK_1/(2F_1) + sr \tag{19}$$

Equation (17) shows that capital growth is constant and independent of public debt and foreign assets. According to equation (18) public debt growth depends on the debt-capital ratio, and according to equation (14) foreign asset growth depends on the ratio of foreign assets to capital.

Figure 7.1 shows the growth lines of capital and public debt for the two countries. It is assumed that the deficit ratio of country 1 exceeds the deficit ratio of country 2, and that the sum of the two deficit ratios stays below the critical level b'. The steady states are at the intersections of the $\hat{D}_i$ lines with the $\hat{K}_i$ line. To the left of the steady states, public debt growth exceeds capital growth, so the debt-capital ratio increases. To the right of the steady states, capital growth exceeds public debt growth, so the debt-capital ratio declines. Hence, the steady states are stable.

Figure 7.2 shows the growth lines of capital and foreign debt. It is assumed that the sum of the two deficit ratios stays below the critical level b''. At the intersection of the $\hat{F}_1$ line and the $\hat{K}_1$ line, the ratio of foreign debt to capital is in the steady state. To the left of the steady state, foreign debt grows faster than capital, and to the right, capital grows faster than foreign debt. Hence, the steady state is stable.

Now consider the case where the sum of the deficit ratios exceeds the critical level b'' but stays below the critical level b'. In this case there is still positive capital growth. The growth diagram with public debt and capital is structurally identical to Figure 7.1. However, the growth diagram with foreign debt and capital is now different, see Figure 7.3. Capital growth is below $sr = s\alpha A$. In contrast, foreign debt growth never falls below sr. As a consequence, there is no crossing of the $\hat{K}$ line and the $\hat{F}$ line. That means, capital grows and so does foreign debt. However, foreign debt growth always exceeds capital growth. This is why the ratio of foreign debt to capital in country 1 grows exponentially. And, as a mirror image, the ratio of foreign assets to capital in country 2 also grows exponentially.

Figure 7.4 shows $\hat{D}_i$ lines and the $\hat{K}_i$ line for the case where the sum of the deficit ratios exceeds the critical level b'. Due to high deficit ratios, capital growth is negative. Hence there is a continuous decline of capital. Public debt growth is positive in both countries. As a result, the debt-capital ratio explodes in both countries. To summarize:

Proposition 3. *If the sum of the deficit ratios stays below both critical levels, the foreign debt-capital ratio and the public debt-capital ratio converge to their steady-state levels.*

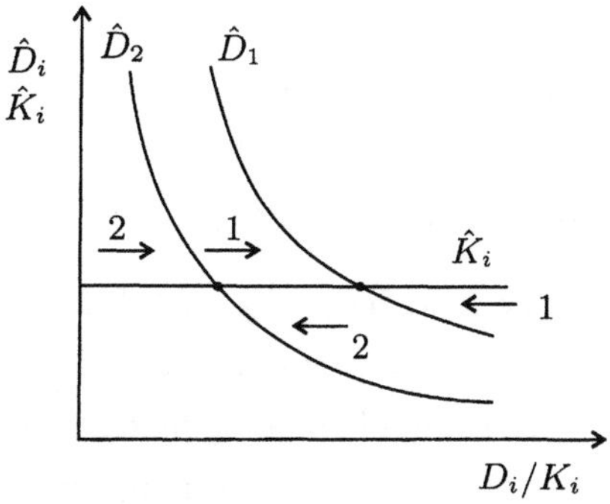

Figure 7.1.
Capital and Public Debt

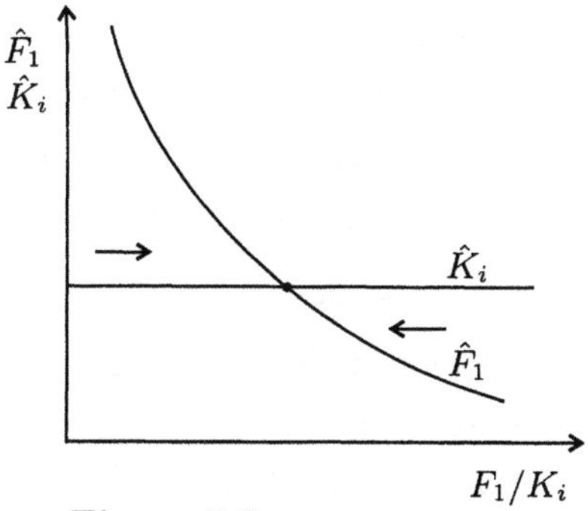

Figure 7.2.
Capital and Foreign Debt

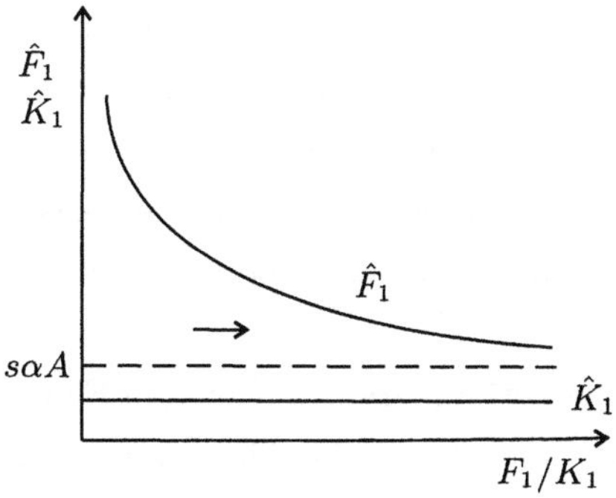

Figure 7.3.
Capital and Foreign Debt
$b > b''$

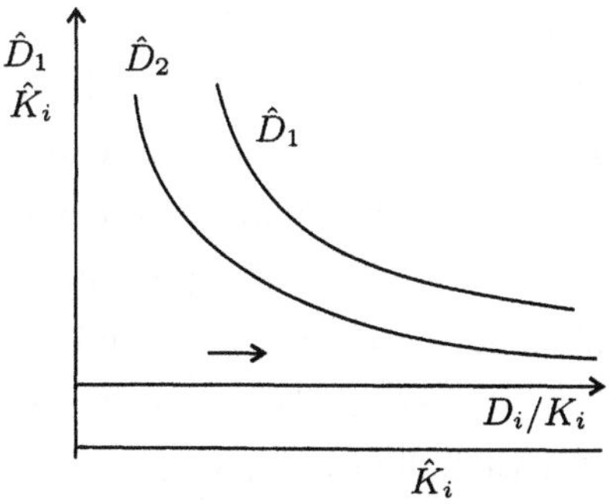

Figure 7.4.
Capital and Public Debt
$b > b'$

7.2.3 Some Shocks

In the following we will examine the processes of adjustment released by three macroeconomic shocks in greater detail:

1) an increase in the deficit ratio in country 1 ($b_1 + b_2 < b''$)
2) an increase in the deficit ratio in country 2 ($b_1 + b_2 < b''$)
3) an increase in the deficit ratio in country 1 ($b_1 + b_2 > b''$).

1) An increase in the deficit ratio of country 1, with $b_1 + b_2 < b''$. Initially, the economy is in the steady state. In both countries, capital grows at the same rate as public debt. It is assumed that the sum of the two deficit ratios is below the critical level b''. Country 1 has a higher deficit ratio than country 2. For that reason, country 1 is an international debtor and country 2 is an international creditor. The foreign debt of country 1 grows at the same rate as capital. And the same applies to the foreign assets of country 2. In this situation the government of country 1 lifts the deficit ratio.

First, consider the dynamics of public debt and capital. In the $\hat{D}_i\hat{K}_i$ growth diagram the original steady states are in the points 1, see Figure 7.5. Due to the increase in the deficit ratio of country 1, the $\hat{D}_1$ line shifts to the right and the $\hat{K}_i$ line moves downwards. The short-run effect is that public debt growth in country 1 increases (point 2) while it remains constant in country 2. Capital growth declines in both countries (point 3). Then, in the medium run, public debt growth declines in both countries and finally converges to capital growth. In the new steady states (points 4), the debt-capital ratios stay constant in both countries. In country 1, the debt-capital ratio has increased due to both, the increase in the deficit ratio and the decline of capital growth. In country 2 the deficit ratio remained constant. Still, the debt-capital ratio has increased due to the decline of capital growth. The time paths of capital growth and public debt growth are shown in Figure 7.6.

Next consider foreign debt. The $\hat{F}_1\hat{K}_1$ growth diagram is shown in Figure 7.7. Originally the economy is in the steady state (point 1). Then, due to the increase in the deficit ratio of country 1, the $\hat{F}_1$ line moves to the right and $\hat{K}_1$ glides downwards.

In the short run, foreign debt growth accelerates, while capital growth declines (points 2). Due to higher foreign debt growth, the ratio of foreign debt to capital increases. This reduces foreign debt growth in the medium

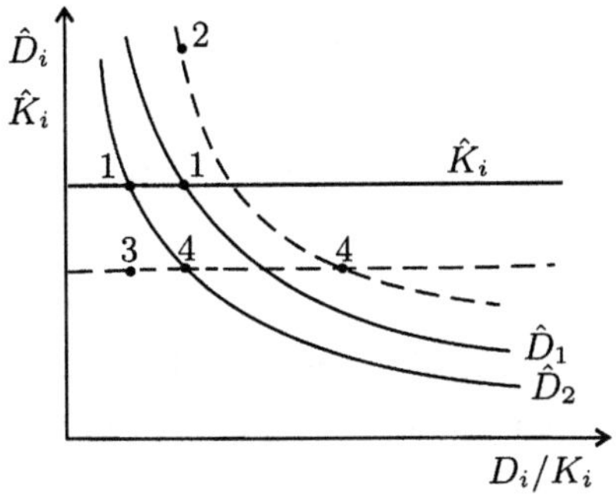

Figure 7.5.
Growth Diagram
Capital and Public Debt

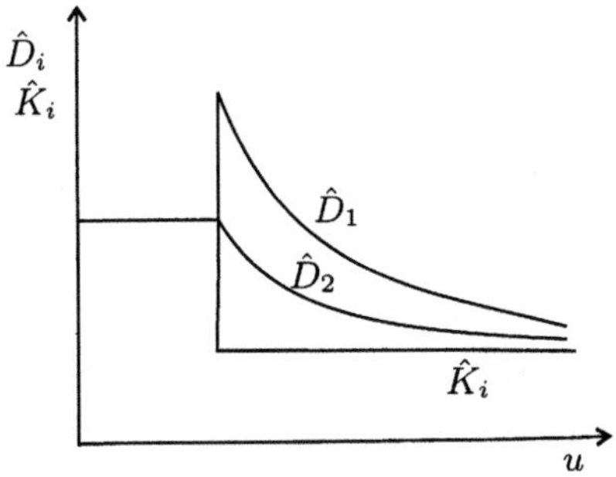

Figure 7.6.
Capital Growth and
Public Debt Growth

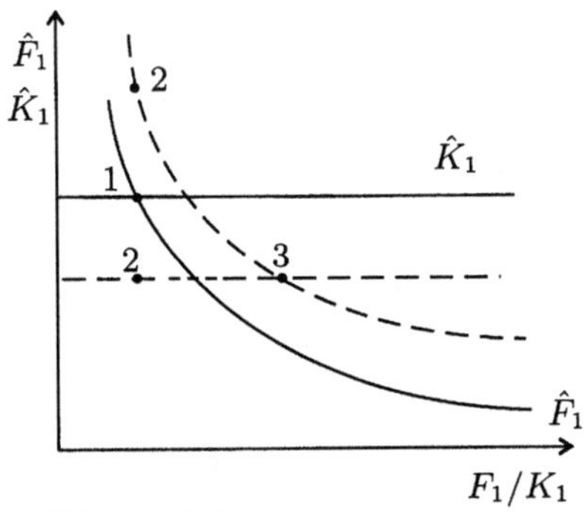

Figure 7.7.
Growth Diagram
Capital and Foreign Debt

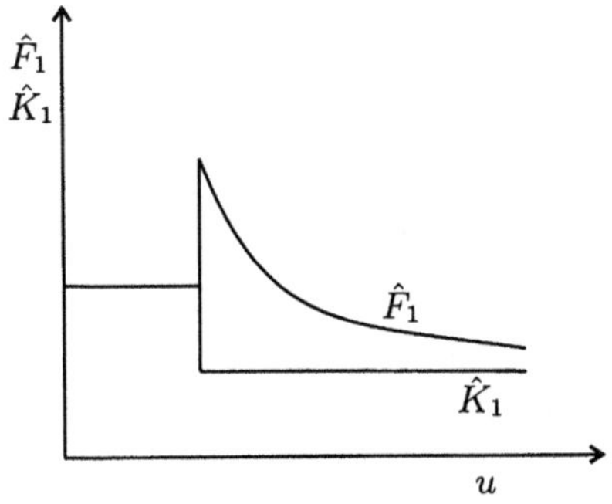

Figure 7.8.
Capital Growth and
Foreign Debt Growth

run. Finally, foreign debt grows at the same rate as capital, so the ratio of foreign debt to capital stays constant (point 3). In the new steady state, the growth rates of foreign debt in country 1 and foreign assets in country 2 are lower than in the original steady state. The ratio of foreign debt to capital in country 1 and the ratio of foreign assets to capital in country 2 are higher than in the original steady state. Figure 7.8 shows the time paths of the growth rates.

Now look at a numerical example. At the beginning, the world economy is in the steady state. The deficit ratio in country 1 is 1% and the budget in country 2 is balanced. In both countries, capital and output as well at the budget deficit and public debt grow at the same constant rate of 1.9%. The foreign debt of country 1 and the foreign assets of country 2 equally grow at 1.9%. The public debt-capital ratio in country 1 is 0.13 and the foreign debt-capital ratio is 0.1. Then country 1 increases the deficit ratio to 2%. In the short run, public debt growth in country 1 increases to 3.8%. Capital growth, output growth and deficit growth decline to 1.8% in both countries. In the medium run, lower deficit growth reduces public debt growth. In the long run, public debt growth converges to capital growth. In the new steady state, public debt, capital and output grow at the rate of 1.8% in both countries. Finally, consider the dynamics of foreign debt and foreign assets. In the short run, foreign debt growth in country 1 and foreign asset growth in country 2 increase from 1.9% to 3%. In the medium run, foreign debt growth and foreign asset growth decline. In the long run, foreign debt growth in country 1 and foreign asset growth in country 2 converge to capital growth. In the new steady state, foreign debt and foreign assets grow at the rate of 1.8%.

2) An increase in the deficit ratio of country 2, with $b_1 + b_2 < b''$. In the $\hat{D}_i\hat{K}_i$ growth diagram, the $\hat{D}_2$ line shifts to the right and the $\hat{K}_i$ line moves downwards, see Figure 7.9. Directly after the shock, capital growth in both countries declines (point 2). Public debt growth in country 2 increases (point 3) whereas public debt growth in country 1 remains constant. Output growth and deficit growth correspond to capital growth, and therefore they are reduced. Reduced deficit growth leads to a decline in public debt growth in both countries. In the long run, public debt growth converges to capital

growth in both countries. In the new steady state, public debt and capital grow at the same rate, so the debt-capital ratios stay constant (points 4).

Now consider foreign debt. The $\hat{F}_1 \hat{K}_1$ growth diagram is presented in Figure 7.10. Due to the increase in the deficit ratio of country 2, the $\hat{F}_1$ line shifts to the left and the $\hat{K}_1$ line slides downwards. In the short run, there is a decline in capital growth and a sharp decline in foreign debt growth. Due to lower foreign debt growth, the ratio of foreign debt to capital increases. Therefore, foreign debt growth accelerates in the medium run. Finally, foreign debt grows at the same rate as capital. Hence, the ratio of foreign debt to capital stays constant. Figure 7.11 shows the time paths of the growth rates.

3) An increase in the deficit ratio of country 1 that leads to a sum of the deficit ratios above the critical level b''. Originally, there is steady-state growth in the world economy. Capital, public debt, the foreign debt of country 1 and the foreign assets of country 2 grow at the same constant rate. Then the government of country 1 increases the deficit ratio. As a consequence, the sum of the two deficit ratios surpasses the critical level b''. The growth diagram with capital and public debt looks structurally identical to Figure 7.5. In the growth diagram with foreign debt and capital, there is no longer a steady state.

Capital grows in both countries. However, foreign debt in country 1 grows at a higher rate and so do foreign assets in country 2. Therefore, the ratio of foreign debt to capital in country 1 and the ratio of foreign assets to capital in country 2 both explode. At each point of time, foreign debt growth in country 1 exceeds capital growth and output growth. Therefore, at some point of time, country 2 finances all the capital in the world. And at some later point of time, country 2 finances all the capital as well as all the public debt. Finally, country 1 has to borrow to pay the interest on its foreign debt. Clearly this process is not sustainable. Figure 7.12 presents the time path of the ratio of foreign debt to capital in country 1.

7.2.4 Summary

As a result, capital and output, in both countries, grow (or decline) at the same constant rate. Capital growth and output growth depend on both deficit ratios. An increase in the deficit ratio of either country reduces capital growth

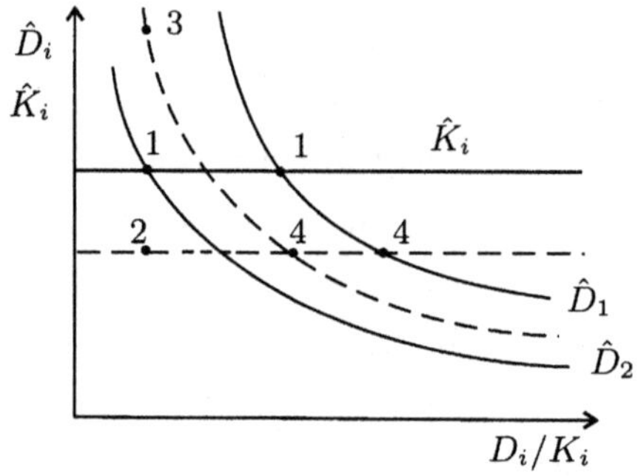

Figure 7.9.
Capital and Public Debt
Increase in b_2

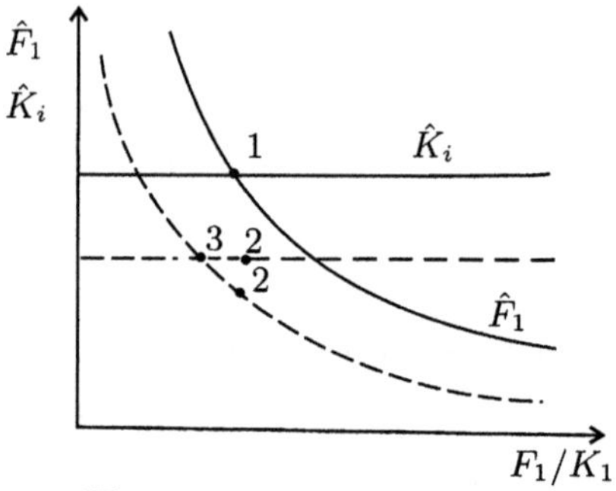

Figure 7.10.
Capital and Foreign Assets
Increase in b_2

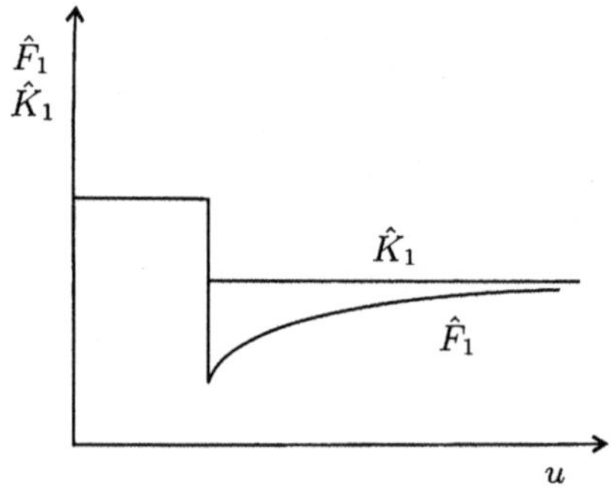

Figure 7.11.
Time Paths of Growth Rates
Increase in b_2

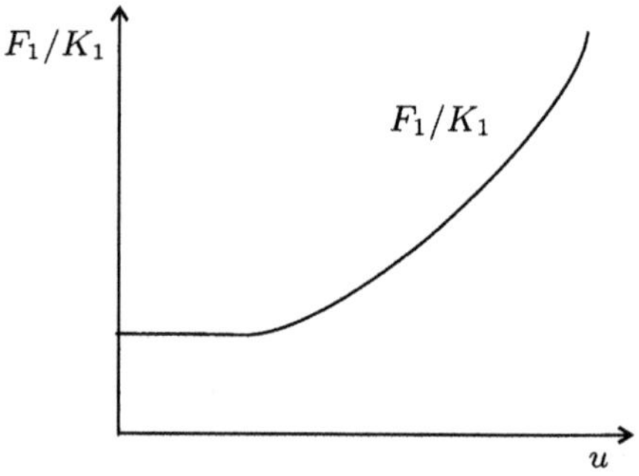

Figure 7.12.
Time Path of F_1/K_1
Increase in b_2, where $b_2 > b''$

and output growth in both countries. The country with the higher deficit ratio is an international debtor, and the country with the lower deficit ratio is an international creditor. Foreign debt growth in the high deficit country depends on the difference in the deficit ratios and on the ratio of foreign debt to capital. Symmetrically, foreign asset growth in the low deficit country depends on the difference in the deficit ratios an on the ratio of foreign assets to capital. In the steady state, public debt, capital, foreign debt and foreign assets grow at the same rate. There are two critical levels for the sum of the two deficit ratios. If the sum of the deficit ratios stays below both of these critical levels, there will be a steady state that proves to be stable.

If the sum of the deficit ratios exceeds the first critical level, then foreign debt in the high-deficit country and foreign assets in the low-deficit country grow faster than capital. The ratio of foreign debt to capital of the high-deficit country explodes, as does the ratio of foreign assets to capital in the low-deficit country. Hence, a steady state is not reached. If the sum of the deficit ratios exceeds the second critical level, then capital growth is negative in both countries. Public debt growth is positive, and so are foreign debt growth in the high deficit country and foreign asset growth in the low deficit country.

7.3 Fixing the Tax Rate

7.3.1 The Model

In each country the government fixes the tax rate and the purchase ratio. Expenditure on goods and services is $G_i = g_i Y_i$ with the purchase ratio $g_i = const$. The tax is levied on the income of domestic residents at the flat rate t_i. Tax revenue is $T_i = t_i(Y_i + rD_i + rF_i)$. Both governments pay the interest rate r on public debt D_i, so public interest amounts to rD_i. The government budget constraints can be written as $B_i = G_i + rD_i - T_i$. Budget deficits augment public debt $\dot{D}_i = B_i$. By using the behavioural functions we obtain: $\dot{D}_i = B_i = gY_i + rD_i - t_i(Y_i + rD_i + rF_i) = (g_i - t_i)Y_i + (1 - t_i)rD_i - t_i rF_i$. Disposable income is made up of factor income, public interest and the interest inflow, net of tax respectively $Y_{d,i} = (1 - t_i)(Y_i + rD_i + rF_i)$. Households save a constant fraction of their disposable income $S_i = sY_{d,i}$ with the saving ratio $s = const$ and of the same size in both countries. Private savings serve to finance public borrowing, and the accumulation of capital and of foreign assets $\dot{D}_i + \dot{F}_i + \dot{K}_i = S_i = s_i(1-t)(Y_i + rD_i + rF_i)$.

The rest of the model is the same as in the previous section and can be represented by a system of nine equations:

$$Y_i = AK_i \tag{1}$$

$$r = \alpha A \tag{2}$$

$$\dot{D}_i + \dot{F}_i + \dot{K}_i = s(1-t_i)(Y_i + rD_i + rF_i) \tag{3}$$

$$\dot{D}_i = (g_i - t_i)Y_i + (1-t_i)rD_i - t_i rF_i \tag{4}$$

$$K_1 = K_2 \tag{5}$$

$$F_1 = -F_2 \tag{6}$$

Here $\alpha, t_i, g_i, s, A, F_i, D_i, K_i$ are exogenous, while $r, \dot{D}_i, \dot{F}_i, \dot{K}_i, Y_i$ are endogenous.

The dynamics of the model can be condensed to a system of three differential equations:

$$\begin{aligned} 2\dot{K}_1 = {} & [s(2-t_1-t_2) - (g_1 - t_1 + g_2 - t_2)]AK_1 - \\ & (1-s)r[(1-t_1)D_1 + (1-t_2)D_2 - (t_1 - t_2)F_1] \end{aligned} \tag{7}$$

$$\dot{F}_1 = s(1-t_1)(Y_1 + rD_1 + rF_1) - \dot{D}_1 - \dot{K}_1 \tag{8}$$

$$\dot{D}_i = (g_i - t_i)Y_i + (1-t_i)rD_i - t_i rF_i \tag{9}$$

To simplify the analysis, we assume that both countries have equal tax rates. However, they may differ with respect to government purchase ratios and therefore have different primary deficit ratios. Given $t = t_1 = t_2$, the dynamics of capital are given by $2\dot{K}_i = [2s(1-t) - (g_1 + g_2 - 2t)]AK_i - (1-s)(1-t)r(D_1 + D_2)$. Therefore, capital growth is:

$$\hat{K}_i = s(1-t)A - \frac{g_1 + g_2 - 2t}{2}A - \frac{(1-s)(1-t)r(D_1 + D_2)}{2K_i} \tag{10}$$

Capital growth depends on the saving ratio, on the primary deficit ratios in both countries and on the ratio of world-wide public debt to capital. Define world-wide public debt as $D = D_1 + D_2$. The dynamics of D are obtained by taking the sum over equations (4) $\dot{D} = \dot{D}_1 + \dot{D}_2 = (g_1 + g_2 - 2t)AK_1 + (1 - t)\alpha AD$. World-wide public debt growth is:

$$\hat{D} = (g_1 + g_2 - 2t)\frac{AK_i}{D} + (1 - t)\alpha A \tag{11}$$

Equations (10) and (11) describe a closed system for capital growth and world-wide public debt growth. Structurally, these equations are identical to the equations obtained in the closed economy, see Part I, Chapter 2, Section 3. The difference is that capital growth in each country and world-wide public debt growth depend on the primary deficit ratios in both countries. We therefore conclude:

Proposition 1. *A steady state only exists if the sum of the primary deficit ratios stays below a critical level and if the saving ratio is large $s > \alpha$.*

As in the closed economy, these conditions are unlikely to be met. Therefore, we conclude that a fixed tax rate is not sustainable.

7.3.2 A Tax Cut

Now we look at the process set in motion by the existence of a primary deficit. At the start there are no deficits. In both countries the budget is balanced and there is no public debt $t_1 = g_1 = t_2 = g_2$ and $D = D_1 = D_2 = 0$. Since both countries have the same saving ratio, and there is no public debt, the foreign position is balanced in both countries. Capital in both countries is of the same size and grows at the same constant rate. In this situation the government of country 1 increases the purchase ratio g_1 and there is a primary deficit $g_1 > t_1$. Owing to the deficit, public debt emerges and starts to grow. Now the government in country 1 has additional expenditures for the servicing of public debt. To finance these interest payments and the primary deficit the government has to borrow again. Therefore public debt grows and interest payment grow as well. Hence, the government enters the vicious circle in which its borrowing has to increase continuously over time. Even if the purchase ratio is reduced back to its original level, interest payments still grow, so that this does not break the circle.

Public debt in country 1 is financed by the savings of country 1 and country 2. Hence, country 1 is an international borrower and country 2 is an international creditor. Due to public debt growth, foreign debt in country 1 and foreign assets in country 2 both grow. Moreover, public debt growth reduces capital growth in both countries. While public debt growth converges to a constant level, capital growth declines continuously. At some point of time, capital growth becomes negative. In the long run, capital declines to zero. Hence there is fatal crowding out.

7.3.3 Summary

Starting from a balanced budget in both countries, a tax cut in country 1 leads to a budget deficit. In country 1, public debt comes into existence and begins to grow. Public debt growth converges to a constant level. In both countries, capital growth and output growth decline continuously, become negative at some point of time, and deteriorate further. Capital and output are driven to zero in finite time. An exception occurs if the saving ratio is very high and if the deficits in both countries are very low. As a main result, a fixed tax rate normally cannot be sustained.

8

Conclusion

8.1 The Closed Economy with AK Production

Endogenous growth comes from learning by doing. Labour efficiency depends on the amount of knowledge accumulated, which in turn is assumed to be proportional to the stock of capital. Therefore the production function is of the AK type. As a result, output is proportional to capital, and output growth is determined by capital growth.

First let us have a look at the Solow model (Chapter 2). Section 2 examines a fixed deficit ratio. As a result, capital and output grow (or decline) at the same constant rate. Capital growth and output growth are determined by the saving ratio, the deficit ratio and the government purchase ratio. An increase in the saving ratio leads to a rise in capital growth and output growth. An increase in the deficit ratio leads to a fall in capital growth and output growth. And an increase in the government purchase ratio has the same effect. In the steady state, public debt grows at the same rate as capital. There is a critical deficit ratio. If the deficit ratio is below the critical level, there will be a steady state that proves to be stable. If the deficit ratio is above the critical level, there will be no steady state. Public debt growth is positive while capital growth and output growth are negative.

Now consider the dynamics in the case where the deficit ratio stays below the critical level. At the start, the economy is in the steady state. Capital and output as well as the budget deficit and public debt grow at the same constant rate of 1.8%. In this situation, the government increases the deficit ratio from 1% to 2%. In the short run, this increases public debt growth to 3.6%. At the same time, capital growth and output growth decline to 1.6%. The budget deficit is proportional to output, therefore the budget deficit grows at the rate of 1.6% as well. In the medium run, lower deficit growth reduces debt growth. In the new steady state, capital, output and debt grow at the same constant rate of 1.6%.

Next have a look at the dynamics of consumption. In the original steady state, consumption grows at the rate of 1.8%. Then the government increases the deficit ratio. In the short run, this allows the government to cut the tax rate. Therefore, consumption improves. However, henceforth consumption grows at the rate of 1.6% only.

Section 3 considers a fixed tax rate. Starting from a balanced budget, a tax cut leads to a budget deficit. Public debt emerges and begins to grow. In general, public debt growth converges to a constant level, while capital growth and output growth decline continuously, become negative at some point of time, and then deteriorate further. Capital and output decline to zero in finite time. An exception occurs if the saving ratio is very high and if the deficit is extremely low. In this case there are two steady states. In these steady states, public debt and capital grow at the same constant rate. One of the steady states is stable, and the other is not. However, the fundamental result is that a fixed tax rate generally cannot be sustained.

Section 4 refers to the optimal deficit ratio. The government optimizes the deficit ratio so as to maximize welfare over an infinite horizon. As a result, there is an optimal deficit ratio which is constant. It depends on the saving ratio and on the rate of time preference. An increase in the saving ratio or the rate of time preference leads to a rise in the optimal deficit ratio. If the saving ratio (rate of time preference) is high, then the optimal deficit ratio is positive. In this situation, the government should borrow from the private sector. And if the saving ratio (rate of time preference) is low, then the optimal deficit ratio is negative. In this situation, the government should lend to the private sector.

Since the optimal deficit ratio is constant, capital, output and consumption grow at the same constant rate. In the steady state, public debt grows at the same rate as capital. There is a steady state that proves to be stable. Now suppose that households increase the saving ratio. To counteract this, the government immediately increases the deficit ratio. As a consequence, capital growth, output growth and consumption growth remain unchanged. In the short run, the increase in the deficit ratio leads to an increase in debt growth. However, the budget deficit grows at the same rate as output. Therefore, in the medium run, debt growth declines. In the long run, it converges to output growth.

Chapter 3 analyses the overlapping generations model. The saving decision of households is derived from individual utility maximization over a finite life cycle. Section 2 assumes that the government fixes the deficit ratio. Capital growth and public debt growth depend on the deficit ratio and on the debt-capital ratio. In the steady state, public debt and capital grow at the same constant rate, so the debt-capital ratio is constant. There is a critical deficit ratio. First assume that the deficit ratio is below the critical level. In this case there are two steady states. One of them is locally stable, and the other is unstable. Second assume that the deficit ratio is above the critical level. In this case there is no steady state. Capital growth declines continuously, becomes negative at some point of time, and deteriorates further. Therefore, capital is driven to zero in finite time.

Now we take a closer look at the case where the deficit ratio is below the critical level. There is a critical level for the initial debt-capital ratio. If the initial debt-capital ratio is below the critical level, then the stable steady state will be reached. However, if the initial debt-capital ratio is above the critical level, then capital is driven to zero in finite time.

Next let us have a look at the dynamics. At the start, the economy is in the steady state. The deficit ratio is given with 1%. Capital and output as well as the budget deficit and public debt grow at the same constant rate of 4.8%. Then the government increases the deficit ratio. In the short run, this increases debt growth to 6%. At the same time, it reduces capital growth, output growth and budget deficit growth to 4.6%. In the medium run, capital growth, output growth and budget deficit growth decline further. Due to the reduction in budget deficit growth, debt growth declines. In the long run, the growth rates converge. In the new steady state, capital, output, the budget deficit and public debt grow at the same constant rate of 4.5%.

Section 3 considers a fixed tax rate. Starting from a balanced budget, a tax cut leads to a budget deficit. Public debt emerges and begins to grow. Normally, public debt growth converges to a constant level, while capital growth and output growth decline continuously, becomes negative at some point of time, and deteriorates further. Capital is driven to zero in finite time. Only in the special case where the elasticity of future consumption is very high and the primary deficit ratio is extremely low, there is an exception. In this case there are two steady states. In these steady states, debt and capital grow at the same constant rate. One of the steady states is stable, and the other is unstable. Still, the essential result is that a fixed tax rate generally cannot be sustained.

8.2 Human Capital and Innovations in the Closed Economy

Chapter 4 presents a model with endogenous growth trough human capital formation. Households fix the saving ratio and the educational spending ratio. In Section 2 the government fixes the fixed deficit ratio. As a result, physical capital growth, human capital growth and output growth depend on the deficit ratio and on the physical-human capital ratio. Public debt growth depends on the deficit ratio and on the debt-output ratio. In the steady state all growth rates are constant and equal, so the physical-human capital ratio and the debt-output ratio are also constant. There is a critical deficit ratio. First assume that the deficit ratio is below the critical level. In this case, there is a stable steady state. An increase in the deficit ratio reduces the steady state growth rate. Now assume that the deficit ratio is increased above the critical level. In this case there is no steady state. In the short run, physical capital growth becomes negative. After some time, output growth becomes negative. Both physical capital growth and output growth decline continuously and therefore physical capital and output are driven down to zero in finite time.

Now have a look at the dynamics. At the beginning there is a deficit ratio of 1%. The budget deficit and public debt, as well as physical and human capital and output, grow at a rate of 1.95%. The government then increases the deficit ratio to 2%. In the short run, physical capital growth declines to 1.70%. Human capital growth increases to 1.97%. Output growth, which depends on physical and human capital growth, declines to 1.89%. Public debt growth increases to 3.85%. The budget deficit grows at the same rate as output. In the medium run, this leads to a decline in debt growth. In the long run, public debt growth, physical capital growth, human capital growth and output growth converge. In the new steady state, they all grow at the rate of 1.88%.

Section 3 considers the fixed tax rate. Starting from a balanced budget, a tax cut leads to a budget deficit. Public debt comes into existence and begins to grow. Public debt growth converges to a constant level. Physical capital growth and output growth decline continuously, become negative at some point of time and decline further. Physical capital and output decline to zero in finite time. There is an exception. If the saving ratio is very large a very small primary deficit can be sustained. In this case there is a steady state, in which physical capital, human capital, output, and public debt grow at the same rate. However the fundamental result is that a fixed tax rate generally cannot be sustained.

Chapter 5 analyses a model in which economic growth is driven by endogenous technical progress. Technological progress comes from the development of new intermediate products. Intermediate products are developed in a research sector. Incentives for research are given by patents which guaranty profits for the development of new intermediate products. Households are assumed to have a constant saving ratio. It is shown how public debt affects research activity and economic growth. Section 2 considers a fixed deficit ratio. As a result, capital growth depends on the deficit ratio. Capital growth and intermediate product number growth depend on the capital-output ratio. Public debt growth depends on the deficit ratio, on the debt-output ratio and on the debt-capital ratio. In the steady state, all growth rates are constant and the same, so the debt-capital ratio, the debt-output ratio and the capital-output ratio are constant. There is a critical deficit ratio. First assume that the deficit ratio is below the critical level. In this case, there is a stable steady state. An increase in the deficit ratio reduces the steady state growth rate. Now assume that the deficit ratio is increased above the critical level. In this case, there is no steady state. In the short run, capital growth becomes negative. After some time, the intermediate product number stops to grow. Capital growth and output growth are negative and decline continuously. As a consequence, capital and output are driven to zero in finite time.

Starting from a balanced budget, a tax cut leads to a budget deficit. Public debt comes into existence and begins to grow. Public debt reduces research activity and capital accumulation. Therefore, at first, intermediate product number growth, capital growth and output growth decline. At some point of time, the intermediate product number stops to grow and capital growth becomes negative. Then capital growth declines further. As a result, capital and output decline to zero in finite time.

8.3 The Open Economy with *AK* Production

In open economy models we assume throughout that households fix the saving ratio. First consider a small open economy with a fixed deficit ratio (Chapter 6, Section 2). Here two cases have to be distinguished. In the first case, the country has a high productivity, and the marginal product of domestic capital exceeds the world interest rate. As a consequence, there is a capital inflow, and the country is an international debtor. It is assumed that the rest of the world limits international credit. Therefore, the foreign debt of the country cannot exceed a certain proportion of the stock of capital. In the second case, the country has a low productivity, and the marginal product of domestic capital is below the world interest rate. Therefore, there is a capital outflow, and the country is an international creditor. Domestic residents regard wealth held in the form of domestic bonds as more secure than wealth in the form of foreign bonds. For that reason, they limit the amount of foreign assets in relation to domestic assets, which consist of private and government bonds.

Now consider the high-productivity country in more detail. The country is an international debtor, and foreign debt is proportional to capital. Then, as a result, capital, foreign debt and output grow (or decline) at the same constant rate. The growth rate is determined by the saving ratio, the deficit ratio, the government purchase ratio and the maximum ratio of foreign debt to capital. An increase in the saving ratio or the maximum ratio of foreign debt to capital leads to a rise in capital growth, foreign debt growth and output growth. An increase in the deficit ratio or the government purchase ratio leads to a fall in capital growth, foreign debt growth and output growth. In the steady state, public debt and capital grow at the same constant rate. There is a critical deficit ratio. If the deficit ratio is below the critical level, there will be a steady state that proves to be stable. If the deficit ratio is above the critical level, there will be no steady state. Public debt growth is positive while capital growth, foreign debt growth and output growth are negative. The dynamics induced by an increase in the deficit ratio are very similar to those in the closed economy.

Next turn to the low-productivity country, which is an international creditor. Foreign assets are proportional to domestic assets. Capital growth and output growth are determined by the saving ratio, the deficit ratio, the government purchase ratio, the maximum ratio of foreign to domestic assets, and the ratio of public debt to capital. Public debt growth is determined by the deficit ratio and the public debt to capital ratio. Foreign asset growth depends on capital growth and on public debt growth. In the steady state, public debt and capital grow at the same constant rate, so the debt-capital ratio is constant. There is a steady state that proves to be stable. In the steady state, as a result, foreign assets grow at the same rate as capital, output and public debt. An increase in the saving ratio or the maximum ratio of foreign to domestic assets leads to a rise in steady-state growth. An increase in the deficit ratio or in the purchase ratio leads to a fall in steady-state growth.

Now consider the dynamics. At the start, the economy is in the steady state. Let the deficit ratio be given with 1%. Then, public debt, capital and foreign assets grow at the same constant rate of 1.3%. Now the government increases the deficit ratio to 2%. In the short run, this increases debt growth to 2.7%. At the same time, capital growth declines to 1.1%, and foreign-asset growth increases to 1.4%. The budget deficit grows at the rate of 1.1%. In the medium run, debt growth declines and capital growth increases. Domestic asset growth and foreign asset growth both decline. In the long run, the growth rates converge. In the new steady state, public debt, capital and foreign assets and grow at the same constant rate of 1.2%.

Section 3 turns to the fixed tax rate. Again the low-productivity country and the high-productivity country are analysed. Starting from a balanced budget, a tax cut leads to a budget deficit. Public debt arises and begins to grow. Public debt growth converges to a constant level, while capital growth and output growth decline continuously, become negative at some point of time, and deteriorate further. Capital and output are driven to zero in finite time. Only if the saving ratio is very high and the deficit ratio is very low, there will be two steady states. In these steady states, public debt and capital grow at the same rate. One of the steady states is stable, the other is not. As a result, in general a fixed tax rate is not sustainable.

Finally, the two-country model is examined (Chapter 7). It is assumed that labour efficiency depends on knowledge created all over the world. This knowledge depends on the amount of capital used worldwide. Section 2 probes into the fixed deficit ratio. As a result, capital and output, in both countries, grow (or decline) at the same constant rate. Capital growth and output growth depend on both deficit ratios. An increase in the deficit ratio of either country reduces capital growth and output growth in both countries. The country with the higher deficit ratio is an international debtor, and the country with the lower deficit ratio is an international creditor. Foreign debt growth in the high deficit country depends on the difference in the deficit ratios and on the ratio of foreign debt to capital. Symmetrically, foreign asset growth in the low deficit country depends on the difference in the deficit ratios and on the ratio of foreign assets to capital. In the steady state, public debt, capital, foreign debt, and foreign assets grow at the same rate. There are two critical levels for the sum of the two deficit ratios. If the sum of the deficit ratios stays below both of these critical levels, there will be a steady state that proves to be stable.

If the sum of the deficit ratios exceeds the first critical level, then foreign debt in the high-deficit country and foreign assets in the low-deficit country will grow faster than capital. The ratio of foreign debt to capital in the high-deficit country explodes, as does the ratio of foreign assets to capital in the low-deficit country. Let country 1 be the high-deficit country that is an international debtor, and let country 2 be the low-deficit country that is an international creditor. At each point of time, foreign debt growth in country 1 exceeds capital growth and output growth. Therefore, at some point of time, country 2 finances all the capital in the world. And at some later point of time, country 2 finances all the capital as well as all the public debt. Finally country 1 has to borrow to pay the interest on its foreign debt. Clearly this process is not sustainable.

If the sum of the deficit ratios exceeds the second critical level, then capital growth will be negative in both countries. Public debt growth is positive, and so are foreign debt growth in the high deficit country and foreign asset growth in the low deficit country. Again, this process is not sustainable.

Now look at the dynamics in the case where the sum of the deficit ratios stays below both critical levels. At the beginning, the world economy is in the steady state. In both countries, capital and output as well at the budget deficit and public debt grow at the same constant rate of 1.9%. The foreign debt of country 1 and the foreign assets of country 2 grow at the same rate as capital. Then country 1 increases the deficit ratio. In the short run, public debt growth in country 1 increases to 3.8%. Capital growth and output growth decline to 1.8% in both countries. Deficit growth corresponds to output growth. In the medium run, lower deficit growth reduces public debt growth. In the long run, public debt growth converges to capital growth. In the new steady state, capital, output and public debt grow at the rate of 1.8% in both countries. Now look at the dynamics of foreign debt and foreign assets. In the short run, the increase in the deficit ratio of country 1 increases foreign debt growth in country 1 and foreign asset growth in country 2 from 1.9% to 3%. In the medium run, foreign debt growth and foreign asset growth decline. In the long run, foreign debt growth in country 1 and foreign asset growth in country 2 converge to capital growth. In the new steady state, foreign debt and foreign assets grow at the rate of 1.8%.

Finally assume a fixed tax rate (Section 3). Starting from a balanced budget in both countries, a tax cut in country 1 leads to a budget deficit. In country 1, public debt comes into existence and begins to grow. Public debt growth converges to a constant level. In both countries, capital growth and output growth decline continuously, become negative at some point of time, and deteriorate further. Capital and output are driven to zero in finite time. So far we have looked at the normal case. However, there is an exception. If the saving ratio is high and the sum of the two deficit ratios stays below a critical level, there will be two steady states. In these steady states, capital, output, public debt, foreign debt in country 1, and foreign assets in country 2 grow at the same constant rate. One of these steady states is stable, the other is unstable. As the fundamental result, a fixed tax rate generally cannot be sustained.

9

Result

The present book deals with the dynamics of public debt and economic growth. The analysis is conducted within the framework of endogenous growth theory. The government is in control of three instruments: the government purchase ratio, the deficit ratio and the tax rate. We assume that the purchase ratio is given exogenously. Then the government can follow either of two strategies, it fixes the deficit ratio or the tax rate. If the government fixes the deficit ratio, then according to the government budget constraint the tax rate will be endogenous. On the other hand, if the government fixes the tax rate, the deficit ratio will be endogenous.

First assume a fixed deficit ratio. Then capital growth and output growth are determined by the deficit ratio. In the steady state, public debt grows at the same rate as capital. There is a critical deficit ratio. If the deficit ratio is below the critical level, there will be a steady state that proves to be stable. If the deficit ratio is above the critical level, there will be no steady state. In this case, capital and output are driven down to zero. Now assume that the deficit ratio stays below the critical level. Then an increase in the deficit ratio leads to a decline in capital growth and output growth. There is an optimal deficit ratio that maximizes welfare over an infinite horizon. If the saving ratio is sufficiently large, the optimal deficit ratio will be positive. In this situation, the government should borrow from the private sector. Conversely, if the saving ratio is rather small, the optimal deficit ratio will be negative. In this situation, the government should lend to the private sector. As a result, a fixed deficit ratio generally can be sustained.

Second assume a fixed tax rate. Then, as a rule, there is no steady state. Starting from a balanced budget, a reduction of the tax rate leads to a budget deficit. Public debt emerges and begins to grow. Public debt growth converges to a constant level, while capital growth and output growth decline continuously, become negative at some point of time, and deteriorate further. Capital and output decline to zero in finite time. As an exception, if the saving ratio is very high and if the primary deficit ratio is extremely low, there will be two steady states, one of them being stable, the other unstable. In these steady states, capital, output, and public debt grow at the same constant rate. As an implication, a fixed tax rate generally cannot be sustained.

Symbols

A	scale parameter, intermediate product number
B	budget deficit
C	consumption
D	public debt
E	labour efficiency
F	foreign debt
G	government purchases
H	human capital
I	investment
K	capital (physical)
L	labour
M	intermediate product output
N	labour
P	price, function
Q	function
R	function
S	savings
T	tax revenue
U	discriminant
W	welfare
Y	output
Z	educational expenditures

b budget deficit ratio
g government purchase ratio
h primary deficit ratio
m maximum foreign debt ratio
foreign asset ratio
n rate of labour growth
r interest rate
s saving ratio
t tax rate
u utility, time
w wage rate
x debt-capital ratio
z education spending ratio

α parameter of production function
β parameter of production function
γ parameter of utility function
δ parameter of utility function
λ research productivity
μ parameter
θ parameter
ρ discount rate
Π profits

References

ABEL, A. B., N. G. MANKIW, L. H. SUMMERS, AND R. J. ZECKHAUSER (1987): "Assessing Dynamic Efficiency: Theory and Evidence," *Review of Economic Studies*, 56, 1 – 20.

AGHION, P., AND P. HOWITT (1998): *Endogenous Growth Theory.* Cambridge Massachusetts, London, England.

ALESINA, A., AND G. TABELLINI (1990): "A Positive Theory of Fiscal Deficits and Government Debt," *Review of Economic Studies*, 57, 403 – 414.

ALOGOSKOUFIS, G. S., AND F. VAN DER PLOEG (1991): "On Budgetary Policies, Growth, and External Deficits in an Interdependent World," *Journal of the Japanese and International Economies*, 5, 305 – 324.

——— (1993): "Endogenous Growth, Convergence and Fiscal Policies in an Interdependent World," in *Open-Economy Macroeconomics: Proceedings of a Conference held in Vienna by the International Economic Association*, ed. by H. Frisch, and A. Wörgötter. Houndmills.

ARNOLD, L. (1999): "Does Policy Affect Growth?," *Finanzarchiv*, 56, 141 – 164.

——— (2000): "Stability of the Market Equilibrium in Romer's Model of Endogenous Technological Change: A Complete Characterization," *Journal of Macroeconomics*, 22, 69 – 84.

ARROW, K. J., AND M. J. BOSKIN (eds.) (1988): *The Economcis of Public Debt.* New York.

ARROW, K. J., AND M. KURZ (1970): *Public Investment, the Rate of Return, and Optimal Fiscal Policy.* Baltimore.

ASCHAUER, D. A. (1990): "Finite Horizons, Intertemporal Substitution, and Fiscal Policy," *Public Finance Quarterly*, 18, 77 – 91.

AUERBACH, A. J., AND E. FELDSTEIN, M. (1987): *Handbook of Public Economics.* Amsterdam.

AUERBACH, A. J., AND L. J. KOTLIKOFF (1987): *Dynamic Fiscal Policy.* Cambridge.

AZARIADIS, C. (1993): *Intertemporal Macroeconomics.* Oxford.

AZARIADIS, C., AND P. REICHLIN (1996): "Increasing Returns and Crowding Out," *Journal of Economic Dynamics and Control*, 20, 847 – 877.

BARRO, R. J. (1974): "Are Government Bonds Net Wealth?," *Journal of Political Economy*, 82, 1095 – 1117.

——— (1976): "Reply to Feldstein and Buchanan," *Journal of Political Economy*, 84, 343 – 350.

——— (1989a): "The Neoclassical Approach to Fiscal Policy," in *Modern Business Cycle Theory*, ed. by R. J. Barro. Cambridge.

——— (1989b): "The Ricardian Approach to Budget Deficits," *Journal of Economic Perspectives*, 3, 37 – 54.

BARRO, R. J., AND X. SALA-I MARTIN (1992): "Public Finance in Models of Economic Growth," *Review of Economic Studies*, 59, 645 – 661.

——— (1995): *Economic Growth.* New York.

BERNHEIM, B. D. (1989): "A Neoclassical Perspective on Budget Deficits," *Journal of Economic Perspectives*, 3, 55 – 72.

BLANCHARD, O., AND P. WEIL (2001): "Dynamic Efficiency, the Riskless Rate, and Debt Ponzi Games under Uncertainty," *Advances in Macroeconomics (http://www.bepress.com/bejm/advances/vol1/iss2/art3)*, 1(2), Article 3.

BLANCHARD, O. J. (1985): "Debt, Deficits, and Finite Horizons," *Journal of Political Economy*, 93, 223 – 247.

BLANCHARD, O. J., AND S. FISCHER (1989): *Lectures on Macroeconomics.* Cambridge.

BOSKIN, M. J., J. S. FLEMMING, AND S. GORINI (eds.) (1987): *Private Saving and Public Debt.* Oxford.

BRÄUNINGER, M. (1996): "Dynamics of Optimal Social Security Finance," *Public Finance*, 51, 507 – 521.

——— (1998): *Rentenversicherung und Kapitalbildung.* Heidelberg.

——— (1999a): "Generalised Social Security Finance in a Two Country World," *Scottish Journal of Political Economy*, 46, 287 – 302.

——— (1999b): "Human Capital and Growth in Small Open Economies," *Jahrbuch für Wirtschaftswissenschaften*, 50, 23 – 38.

——— (2001): "Ersparnis und Kapitalakkumulation im Romer Modell," *Jahrbuch für Wirtschaftswissenschaften*, 52, 177 – 189.

BUITER, W. H. (1979): *Temporary Equilibrium and Long-Run Equilibrium.* New York.

——— (1981): "Time Preference and International Lending and Borrowing in an Overlapping Generations Model," *Journal of Political Economy*, 89, 769 – 797.

——— (1985): "A Guide to Public Sector Debt and Deficits," *Economic Policy*, 1, 13 – 79.

——— (1989): *Budgetary Policy, International and Intertemporal Trade in the Global Economy.* Amsterdam.

——— (1990): *Principles of Budgetary and Financial Policy.* Cambridge.

——— (1992): "Fiscal Policy Coordination as Fiscal Federalism: Economic Integration, Public Goods and Efficiency in Growing Economies," *European Economic Review*, 36, 647 – 653.

——— (1993): "Permanent International Productivity Growth Differentials in an Integrated Global Economy," *Scandinavian Journal of Economics*, 95, 467 – 493.

BUITER, W. H., AND K. M. KLETZER (1991): "Persistent Differences in National Productivity Growth Rates with a Common Technology and Free Capital Mobility: The Role of Private Thrift, Public Debt, Capital Taxation, and Policy toward Human Capital Formation," *Journal of the Japanese and International Economies*, 5, 325 – 353.

——— (1992): "Who's Afraid of the Public Debt," *American Economic Review, Papers and Proceedings*, 82, 290 – 294.

BUITER, W. H., AND J. TOBIN (1979): "Debt Neutrality: A Brief Review of Doctrine and Evidence," in *Social Security versus Private Saving*, ed. by G. M. von Furstenberg. Cambridge.

BURBIDGE, J. B. (1983): "Government Debt in an Overlapping Generations Model with Bequests and Gifts," *American Economic Review*, 73, 222 – 227.

CALVO, G., AND M. KING (eds.) (1998): *The Debt Burden and its Consequences for Monetary Policy.* Houndsmills.

CARLBERG, M. (1983): "Is Deficit Spending Feasible in the Long Run?," *Zeitschrift für Wirtschafts- und Sozialwissenschaften*, 103, 409 – 418.

——— (1984): "Kreditfinanzierung versus Steuerfinanzierung der Staatsausgaben - ein langfristiger Vergleich," *Kredit und Kapital*, 17, 84 – 101.

——— (1985a): "External versus Internal Public Debt - A Theoretical Analysis of the Long-Run Burden," *Zeitschrift für Nationalökonomie*, 45, 141 – 154.

——— (1985b): "Langfristige Grenzen der Staatsverschuldung - Ein Beitrag zur Theorie der optimalen Finanzpolitik," *Jahrbuch für Sozialwissenschaft*, 36, 262 – 273.

——— (1988): *Public Debt, Taxation and Government Expenditures in a Growing Economy.* Berlin.

——— (1993): *Open Economy Dynamics.* Heidelberg.

——— (1995): *Sustainability and Optimality of Public Debt.* Heidelberg.

——— (1997): *International Economic Growth.* Heidelberg.

——— (1998): *Intertemporal Macroeconomics: Deficits, Unemployment, and Growth.* Heidelberg New York.

CASS, D. (1965): "Optimum Growth in an Aggregative Model of Capital Accumulation," *Review of Economic Studies*, 32, 233 – 240.

——— (1972): "On Capital Overaccumulation in the Aggregative, Neoclassical Model of Economic Growth," *Journal of Economic Theory*, 4, 200 – 223.

CHIANG, A. C. (1984): *Fundamental Methods of Mathematical Economics.* New York.

——— (1992): *Elements of Dynamic Optimization.* New York.

DE LA CROIX, D., AND P. MICHEL (2002): *A Theory of Economic Growth: Dynamics and Policy in Overlapping Generations.* Cambridge.

DIAMOND, P. A. (1965): "National Debt in a Neoclassical Growth Model," *American Economic Review*, 55, 1126 – 1150.

DORNBUSCH, R. (1985): "Intergenerational and International Trade," *Journal of International Economics*, 18, 123 – 139.

——— (1986): *Dollars, Debts and Deficits.* Cambridge.

DORNBUSCH, R., AND M. DRAGHI (eds.) (1990): *Public Debt Management.* Cambridge.

EISNER, R. (1992): "Deficits: Which, How Much, So What?," *American Economic Review, Papers and Proceedings*, 82, 295 – 298.

ELMENDORF, D., AND N. G. MANKIW (1999): "Government Debt," in *Handbook of Macroeconomics 1C*, ed. by J. B. Taylor, and M. Woodford. Amsterdam,.

ETHIER, W. J. (1982): "National and International Returns to Scale in the Modern Theory of International Trade," *American Economic Review*, 72, 389 – 405.

FEHR, H., AND P. GOTTFRIED (1993): "Optimale Verschuldungspolitik und öffentliche Investitionen," *Finanzarchiv*, 50, 324 – 343.

FELDERER, B. (ed.) (1993): *Public Pension Economics.* Wien.

FELDSTEIN, M. (1976): "Perceived Wealth in Bonds and Social Security: A Comment," *Journal of Political Economy*, 84, 331 – 336.

——— (1985): "Debt and Taxes in the Theory of Public Finance," *Journal of Public Economics*, 28, 233 – 245.

FLEMMING, J. S. (1987): "Debt and Taxes in War and Peace: The Case of a Small Open Economy," in *Private Saving and Public Debt*, ed. by M. J. B. et al. Oxford.

——— (1988): "Debt and Taxes in War and Peace: The Closed Economy Case," in *The Economics of Public Debt*, ed. by K. J. Arrow, and M. J. Boskin. New York.

FRENKEL, J., AND A. RAZIN (1987): *Fiscal Policy and the World Economy.* Cambridge MA.

FRIED, J., AND P. HOWITT (1988): "Fiscal Deficits, International Trade and Welfare," *Journal of International Economics*, 24, 1 – 22.

FRIEDMAN, B. J. (1992): "Learning from the Reagan Deficits," *American Economic Review, Papers and Proceedings*, 82, 299 – 303.

FRIEDMAN, B. M. (1988): *Day of Reckoning.* New York.

FRIEDMAN, B. M., AND E. HAHN, F. H. (1990): *Handbook of Monetary Economics.* Amsterdam.

GALE, D. (1973): "Pure Exchange Equilibrium of Dynamic Economic Models," *Journal of Economic Theory*, 6, 12 – 36.

——— (1983): *Money: In Disequilibrium.* Cambridge.

GANDOLFO, G. (1980): *Economic Dynamics.* Amsterdam.

——— (1986): *International Economics.* Berlin.

GREINER, A. (1996a): *Fiscal Policy and Economic Growth.* Aldershot.

——— (1996b): "Fiscal Policy in a Model of Endogenous Growth," *Public Finance Quarterly*, 24, 371 – 390.

GRILL, R. (1989): *Der Staat im Modell optimalen Wachstums.* Frankfurt.

GROSSMAN, G., AND E. HELPMAN (1991): *Innovation and Growth in the Global Economy.* Cambridge, MA.

GROSSMANN, G., AND N. YANAGAWA (1993): "Asset Bubbles and Endogenous Growth," *Journal of Monetary Economics*, 31, 3 – 20.

GROSSMANN, H. (1990): *Auslandsverschuldung, Terms of Trade und überlappende Generationen.* Frankfurt.

HALIASSOS, M., AND J. TOBIN (1990): "The Macroeconomics of Government Finance," in *Handbook of Monetary Economics, Amsterdam*, ed. by B. M. Friedman, and F. H. Hahn.

HAMADA, K. (1966): "Economic Growth and Long-Run Capital Movements," *Yale Economic Essays*, 6, 49 – 96.

——— (1969): "Optimal Capital Accumulation by an Economy Facing an International Capital Market," *Journal of Political Economy*, 77, 684 – 697.

——— (1986): "Strategic Aspects of International Fiscal Interdependence," *Economic Studies Quarterly*, 37, 165 – 180.

HELPMAN, E., A. RAZIN, AND E. SADKA (eds.) (1988): *Economic Effects of the Government Budget.* Cambridge.

HOMBURG, S., AND W. F. RICHTER (1993): "Harmonizing Public Debt and Public Pension Schemes in the European Community," in *Public Pension Economics*, ed. by B. Felderer. Wien.

HONKAPOHJA, S. (ed.) (1990): *The State of Macroeconomics.* Oxford.

HUBER, B. (1990a): *Staatsverschuldung und Allokationseffizienz.* Baden-Baden.

——— (1990b): "Zur Theorie optimaler Staatsverschuldung," *Finanzarchiv*, 48, 434 – 450.

IHORI, T. (1978): "The Golden Rule and the Role of Government in a Life Cycle Growth Model," *American Economic Review*, 68, 389 – 396.

——— (1988a): "Debt Burden and Intergeneration Equity," in *The Economics of Public Debt*, ed. by K. J. Arrow, and M. J. Boskin. New York.

——— (1988b): "Optimal Deficits in a Growing Economy," *Journal of the Japanese and International Economies*, 2, 526 – 542.

——— (1996): *Public Finance in an Overlapping Generations Economy*. Houndmills.

JÄGER, A., AND C. KEUSCHNIGG (1992): "The Burden of Public Debt in Open Economies," *Finanzarchiv*, 49, 181 – 201.

JOSTEN, S. D. (2000a): "Public Debt Policy in an Endogenous Growth Model of Perpetual Youth," *Finanzarchiv*, 57, 197 – 215.

——— (2000b): *Staatsverschuldung, intertemporale Allokation und Wirtschaftswachstum*. Frankfurt.

——— (2000c): "Staatsverschuldung und Wirtschaftswachstum in einem Diamond-OLG-Modell mit AK-Technologie," *Jahrbuch für Wirtschaftswissenschaften*, 51, 237 – 254.

JOSTEN, S. D. (2001): "National Debt, Borrowing Constraints, and Human Capital Accumulation in an Endogenous Growth Model," *Finanzarchiv*, 58(3), 317 – 228.

JUDD, K. L. (1987): "Debt and Distortionary Taxation in a Simple Perfect Foresight Model," *Journal of Monetary Economics*, 20, 51 – 72.

KEUSCHNIGG, C. (2000): "Public Debt and Generational Balance in Austria," *Empirica*, 27, 225 – 252.

KING, I., AND D. FERGUSON (1993): "Dynamic Inefficieny, Endogenous Growth, and Ponzi Games," *Journal of Monetary Economics*, 32, 79 – 104.

KITTERER, W. (1986): "Sind Steuern und Staatsverschuldung äquivalente Instrumente zur Finanzierung der Staatsausgaben?," *Kredit und Kapital*, 19, 271 – 291.

——— (1988): "Staatsverschuldung und intertemporale Allokation," *Jahrbücher für Nationalökonomie und Statistik*, 204, 346 – 363.

KOTLIKOFF, L. J. (1993): "From Deficit Delusion to the Fiscal Balance Rule," in *Public Pension Economics*, ed. by B. Felderer. Wien.

KRAUSE-JUNK, G., E. (1990): *Public Finance and Steady Economic Growth*. The Hague.

LAITNER, J. (1984): "Transition Time Paths for Overlapping Generations Models," *Journal of Economic Dynamics and Control*, 7, 111 – 129.

LICHTENAUER, P. (1997): *Konsolidierung des Budgets, Abbau der Staatschulden und Kapitalbildung*. Frankfurt.

LINDBECK, A., AND J. W. WEIBULL (1986): "Intergenerational Aspects of Public Transfers, Borrowing and Debt," *Scandinavian Journal of Economics*, 88, 239 – 267.

LUCAS, R. E. (1988): "On the Mechanics of Economic Development," *Journal of Monetary Economics*, 22, 2 – 42.

LUCAS, R. E. (1993): "Making a Miracle," *Econometrica*, 61, 251 – 273.

MANKIW, N., D. ROMER, AND D. WEIL (1992): "A Contribution to the Empirics of Economic Growth.," *Quarterly Journal of Economics*, 100, 225 – 251.

MASSON, P. R. (1985): "The Sustainability of Fiscal Deficits," *IMF Staff Papers*, 32, 577 – 605.

MAUSSNER, A., AND R. KLUMP (1996): *Wachstumstheorie*. Berlin.

MCCANDLESS, G. T., AND N. WALLACE (1991): *Introduction to Dynamic Macroeconomic Theory*. Cambridge.

MICHAELIS, J. (1989a): *Optimale Finanzpolitik im Modell überlappender Generationen*. Frankfurt.

——— (1989b): "Staatsverschuldung als Quelle der Nicht- Neutralität - Ein Beitrag zum Ricardianischen Äquivalenztheorem," *Kredit und Kapital*, 22, 453 – 469.

MITCHELL, D. W. (1988): "The Feasibility of Perpetual Deficits," *Journal of Macroeconomics*, 10, 407 – 419.

MODIGLIANI, F. (1961): "Long-Run Implications of Alternative Fiscal Policies and the Burden of the National Debt," *Economic Journal*, 71, 730 – 755.

MODIGLIANI, F., AND R. HEMMING (1983): *The Determinants of National Saving and Wealth*. New York.

PERSSON, T. (1985): "Deficits and Intergenerational Welfare in Open Economies," *Journal of International Economics*, 19, 67 – 84.

PHELPS, E. S. (1961): "The Golden Rule of Accumulation: A Fable for Growthmen," *Amercian Economic Review*, 51, 638 – 643.

——— (1967): *Golden Rules of Economic Growth*. Amsterdam.

——— (1994): *Structural Slumps*. Harvard.

PHELPS, E. S., AND K. SHELL (1969): "Public Debt, Taxation and Capital Intensiveness," *Journal of Economic Theory*, 1, 330 – 346.

RAMSEY, F. P. (1928): "A Mathematical Theory of Saving," *Economic Journal*, 38, 543 – 559.

RANKIN, N., AND B. ROFFIA (2002): "Maximum Sustainable Government Debt in the Overlapping Generations Model," *The Manchester School*, forthcoming.

RAZIN, A., AND L. SVENSSON (1983): "The Current Account and the Optimal Government Debt," *Journal of International Money and Fincance*, 2, 215 – 224.

REITHER, F. (1988): *Kapitalstock, Staatsverschuldung und rationale Erwartungen*. Hamburg.

RICHTER, W. F., AND W. WIEGARD (1993): "Zwanzig Jahre Neue Finanzwissenschaft," *Zeitschrift für Wirtschafts- und Sozialwissenschaften*, 113, 337 – 400.

ROMER, D. (1996): *Advanced Macroeconomics.* New York.

ROMER, P. (1986): "Increasing Returns and Long-Run Growth," *Journal of the Political Economy*, 94, 1002 – 1035.

——— (1987): "Growth Based on Increasing Returns due to Specialization," *American Economic Review: Papers and Proceedings*, 77, 56 – 62.

——— (1990): "Endogenous Technical Change," *Journal of Political Economy*, 98, 71 – 102.

RUFFIN, R. J. (1979): "Growth and the Long-Run Theory of International Capital Movements," *American Economic Review*, 69, 832 – 842.

——— (1985): "International Factor Movements," in *Handbook of International Economics*, ed. by R. W. Jones, and P. B. Kenen. Amsterdam.

SAINT-PAUL, G. (1992): "Fiscal Policy in an Endogenous Growth Model," *Quarterly Journal of Economics*, 107, 1243 – 1259.

SAMUELSON, P. A. (1958): "An Exact Consumption-Loan Model of Interest With or Without the Social Contrivance of Money," *Journal of Political Economy*, 66, 467 – 482.

——— (1975): "Optimum Social Security in a Life-Cycle Growth Model," *International Economic Review*, 16, 539 – 544.

SARGENT, T. J. (1987): *Dynamic Macroeconomic Theory.* Cambridge.

SCHLIEPER, U. (1984): "Staatsverschuldung im langfristigen Gleichgewicht," in *Intertemporale Allokation*, ed. by H. Siebert. Frankfurt.

SCHMID, M. (1988): "Fiscal Strategies, Foreign Indebtedness and Overlapping Generations," *Empirica - Austrian Economic Papers*, 15, 95 – 115.

——— (1990): "Fiscal Ponzi Games in a World Economy," in *Real Adjustment Processes under Floating Exchange Rates*, ed. by F. Gehrels et. al. Berlin.

SEATER, J. J. (1993): "Ricardian Equivalence," *Journal of Economic Literature*, 31, 142 – 190.

SEIDAMAN, L. S. (1987): "The Government Deficit in a Growth Model," *Journal of Macroeconomics*, 9, 593 – 611.

SIEBERT, H. (1984): *Intertemporale Allokation.* Frankfurt.

——— (1988): "Foreign Debt and Capital Accumulation," *Weltwirtschaftliches Archiv*, 124, 618 – 630.

SOLOW, R. M. (1956): "A Contribution to the Theory of Economic Growth," *Quarterly Journal of Economics*, 70, 65 – 94.

——— (1988): "Growth Theory and After," *American Economic Review*, 78, 307 – 317.

——— (2000): *Growth Theory: An Exposition.* New York, Oxford.

STIGLITZ, J. E. (1988): "On the Relevance or Irrelevance of Public Financial Policy," in *The Economics of Public Debt*, ed. by K. J. Arrow, and M. J. Boskin. New York.

TOBIN, J. (1980): *Asset Accumulation and Economic Activity.* Oxford.

——— (1986): "The Monetary-Fiscal Mix: Long-Run Implications," *American Economic Association, Papers and Proceedings*, 76, 213 – 218.

TOBIN, J., AND W. BUITER (1976): "Long-Run Effects of Fiscal and Monetary Policy on Aggregate Demand," in *Monetarism*, ed. by J. L. Stein. Amsterdam.

TROSTEL, P. A. (1993): "The Nonequivalence between Deficits and Distortionary Taxation," *Journal of Monetary Economics*, 31, 207 – 227.

TURNOVSKY, S. J., AND P. SEN (1991): "Fiscal Policy, Capital Accumulation and Debt in an Open Economy," *Oxford Economic Paper*, 43, 1 – 24.

VAN DER PLOEG, F. (1992): "The Macroeconomics of Growth: An International Perspective," *Oxford Review of Economic Policy*, 8, 15 – 286.

——— (1994): *Handbook of International Macroeconomics.* Oxford.

——— (1996): "Budgetary Policies, Foreign Indebtedness, the Stock Market, and Economic Growth," *Oxford Economic Papers*, 48, 382 – 396.

VAUSGHN, K. I., AND R. E. WAGNER (1992): "Public Debt Controversies: An Essay in Reconciliation," *Kyklos*, 45, 37 – 49.

VERBEEK, J. (1991): "Growth, Budget Deficits, and Fiscal Policies in an Overlapping Generations Model," *Journal of Economics*, 53, 185 – 203.

VON FURSTENBERG, G. M. (ed.) (1980): *The Government and Capital Formation.* Cambridge, Mass.

WEIL, P. (1985): "Essays on the Valuation of Unbacked Assets," Ph.D. thesis, Harvard.

——— (1987): "Permanent Budget Deficits and Inflation," *Journal of Monetary Economics*, 20, 393 – 410.

WEIZSÄCKER, R. K. (1992): "Staatsverschuldung und Demokratie," *Kyklos*, 45, 51 – 67.

WELLISCH, D. (1991): *Intertemporale und internationale Aspekte staatlicher Budgetdefizite.* Tübingen.

WENZEL, H. D. (1986): "Öffentliche Kreditaufnahme und öffentliche Investitionen im Wachstumgleichgewicht," *Kredit und Kapital*, 19, 496 – 521.

WENZEL, H. D., AND M. WREDE (1993): "Golden Rule Fiscal Policy," *Schweizerische Zeitschrift für Volkswirtschaft und Statistik*, 129, 123 – 149.

WENZEL, H.-D., AND M. WREDE (2000): "Public Debt in a Federation - Growth and Stability," *Jahrbücher für Nationalökonomie und Statistik*, 220, 95 – 107.

WILCOX, D. W. (1989): "The Sustainability of Government Deficits: Implications of the Present-Value Borrowing Constraint, Journal of Money," *Credit and Banking*, 21, 291 – 306.

YAARI, M. (1965): "Uncertain Lifetime, Life Insurance, and the Theory of the Consumer," *Review of Economic Studies*, 32, 137 – 150.

YELLEN, J. L. (1989): "Symposium on the Budget Deficit," *Journal of Economic Perspectives*, 3, 17 – 21.

ZEE, H. H. (1987): "Government Debt, Capital Accumulation, and the Terms of Trade in a Model of Interdependent Economies," *Economic Inquiry*, 25, 599 – 618.

——— (1988): "The Sustainability and Optimality of Government Debt," *IMF Staff Papers*, 35, 658 – 685.

ZHANG, J. (1996): "Optimal Public Investment in Education and Endogenous Growth," *Scandinavian Journal of Economics*, 98, 387 – 404.

——— (1997): "Government Debt, Human Capital and Endogenous Growth," *Southern Economic Journal*, 64, 281 – 292.

GPSR Compliance

The European Union's (EU) General Product Safety Regulation (GPSR) is a set of rules that requires consumer products to be safe and our obligations to ensure this.

If you have any concerns about our products, you can contact us on ProductSafety@springernature.com

In case Publisher is established outside the EU, the EU authorized representative is:

Springer Nature Customer Service Center GmbH
Europaplatz 3
69115 Heidelberg, Germany

Batch number: 10725973

Printed by Printforce, the Netherlands